THE DEFINITIVE

AC/DC

SONGBOOK

UPDATED EDITION

Amsco Publications
New York/London/Paris/Sydney/Copenhagen/Berlin/Tokyo/Madrid

Cover photograph: © Rob Verhorst/Getty Images
Project editor: David Bradley

This book Copyright © 2003, 2011 by Amsco Publications,
A Division of Music Sales Corporation, New York

Order No. AM 1001572
International Standard Book Number: 978.0.8256.3752.0
HL Item Number: 14041344

Exclusive Distributor for the United States, Canada, Mexico and U.S. possessions:
Hal Leonard Corporation
7777 West Bluemound Road, Milwaukee, WI 53213 USA

Exclusive Distributor for the rest of the World:
Music Sales Limited
14-15 Berners Street, London W1T 3LJ England

Contents

Legend of Music Symbols

Left hand fingering   Hand vibrato   Hammeron   Pulloff

Palm mute   Bend   Quick bend   Pre-bend   Release bend   Unison bend

Tremolo picking   Trill   Picked slide   Legato slide

Short slide up or down   Pick slide   Muffled strings   Natural harmonic

Artificial harmonic   Pinch harmonic   Right hand tap   Ghost note (partially implied)

Ain't No Fun
(Waiting 'Round To Be A Millionaire)

By Angus Young, Malcolm Young and Bon Scott

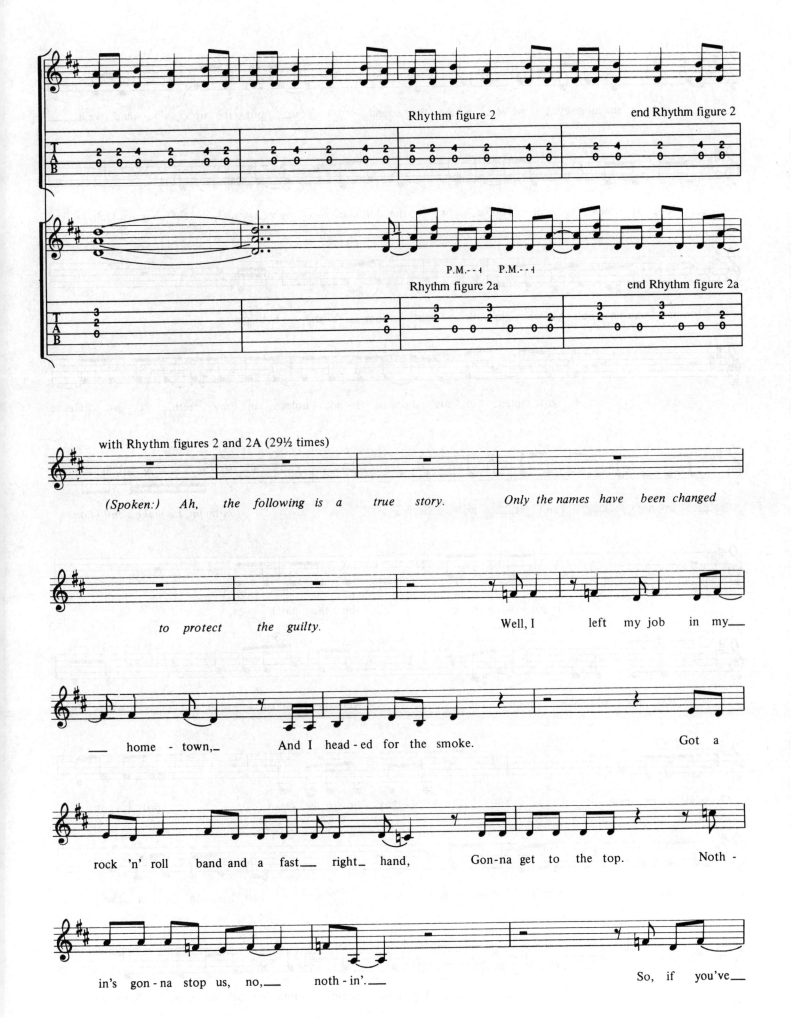

Rhythm figure 2   end Rhythm figure 2

Rhythm figure 2a   end Rhythm figure 2a

with Rhythm figures 2 and 2A (29½ times)

(Spoken:) Ah, the following is a true story. Only the names have been changed

to protect the guilty.   Well, I left my job in my___

___ home - town,___ And I head - ed for the smoke.   Got a

rock 'n' roll band and a fast___ right___ hand, Gon-na get to the top.   Noth -

in's gon - na stop us, no,___ noth - in'.___   So, if you've___

9

in' nine to five._ *She knows her place, that wom - an.* But just you

wait. One of these days see me driv - in' 'round town In my

rock 'n' Rolls Royce with the sun - roof down._ My bot - tle of booze,_ no sum -

mer - time_ blues, Shout - ing loud, "Look at me," in my rock 'n' roll voice. No, it

Chorus
G5

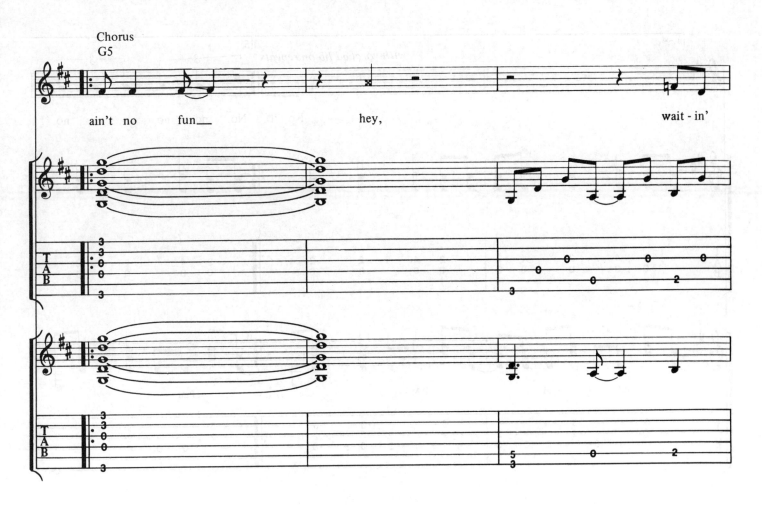

ain't no fun_ hey, wait - in'

10

Additional Lyrics

2. Well it ain't no fun,
   Oh, I want to be rich.
   No it ain't no fun,
   Ain't no fun digging this ditch.

Anything Goes

By Angus Young & Malcolm Young

Intro

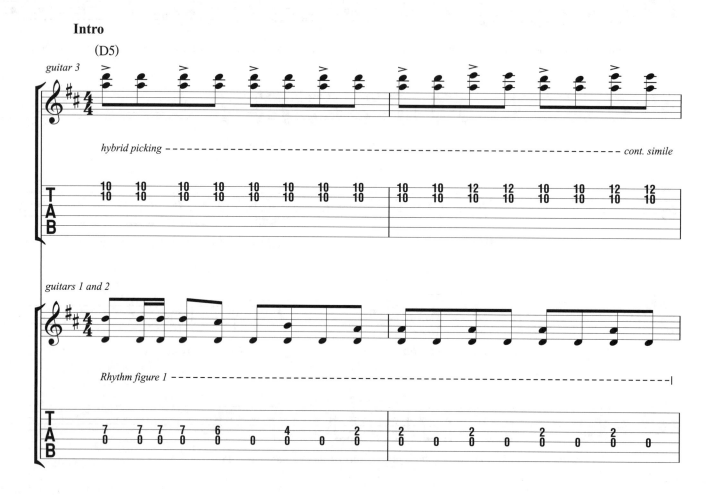

16

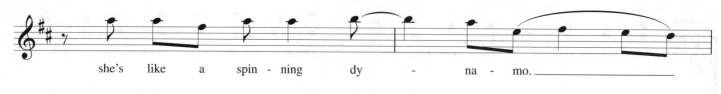

she's like a spin - ning dy - na - mo._____

G5

You're hand - ing out the to - ken prize,_____

guitars 1 and 2

giv - ing you a brand new ___ ride._____

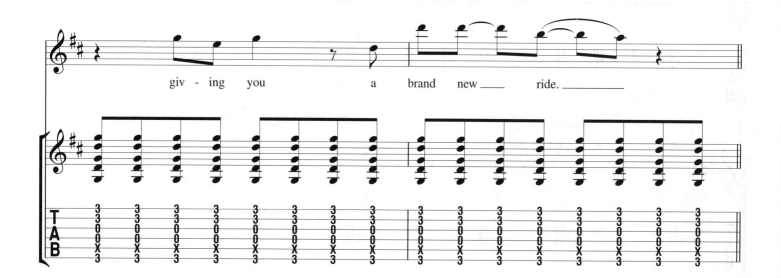

Chorus
w/Rhythm figure 1 (Guitars 1 and 2) 3 times
2nd time play 4 times
(D5)

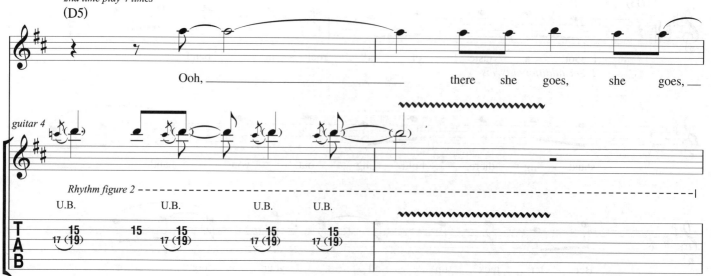

Ooh,_____ there she goes, she goes, ___

guitar 4

18

𝄋 Bridge

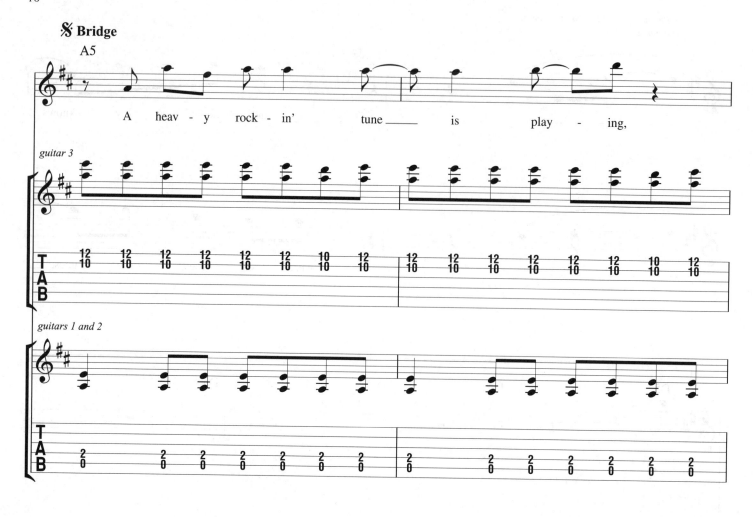

A heav - y rock - in' tune _____ is play - ing,

play - ing as the night rolls _____ on. _____

A5

Sneak - ing off with Ro - me - o,

To Coda ⊕

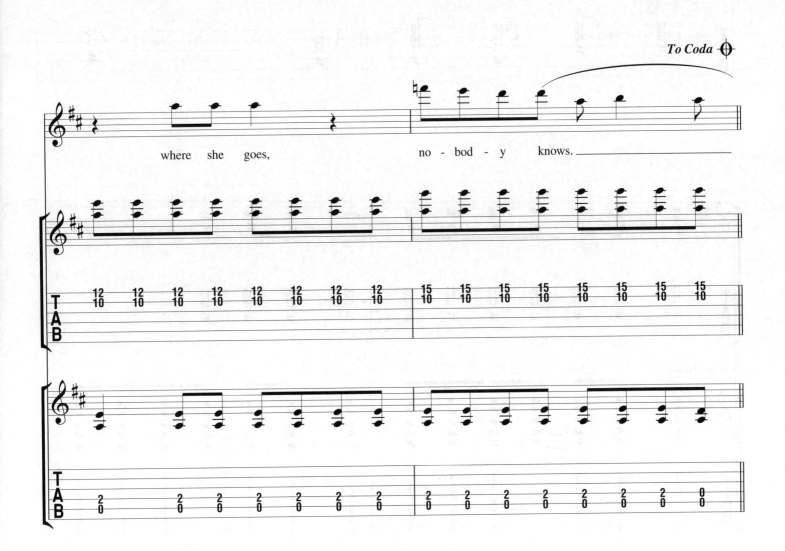

where she goes, no - bod - y knows.

Guitar solo
w/Rhythm figure 1 (Guitars 1 and 2) 2 times

G5

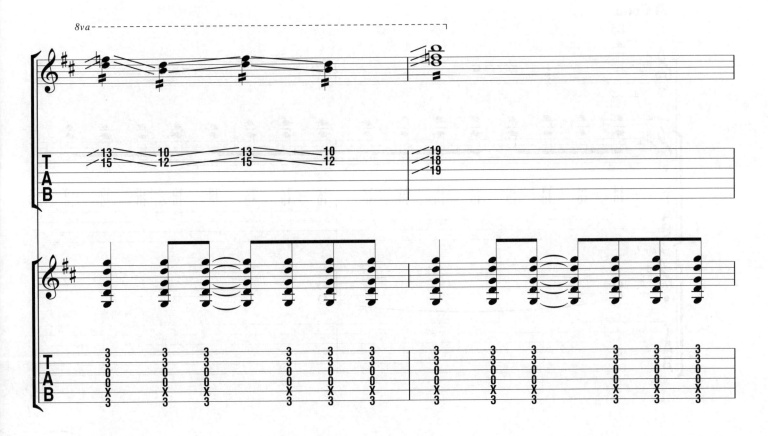

w/Rhythm figure 1 (Guitars 1 and 2) 2 times

D5

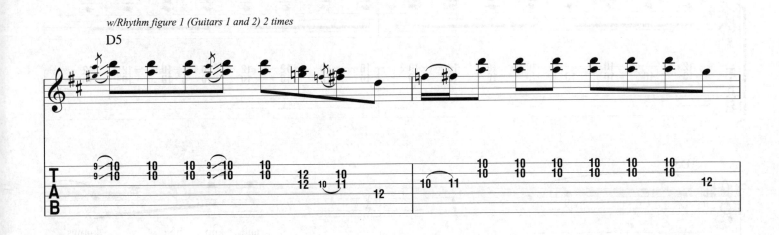

D.S. 𝄋 al Coda ⊕

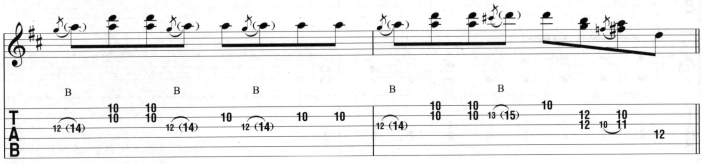

⊕ Coda

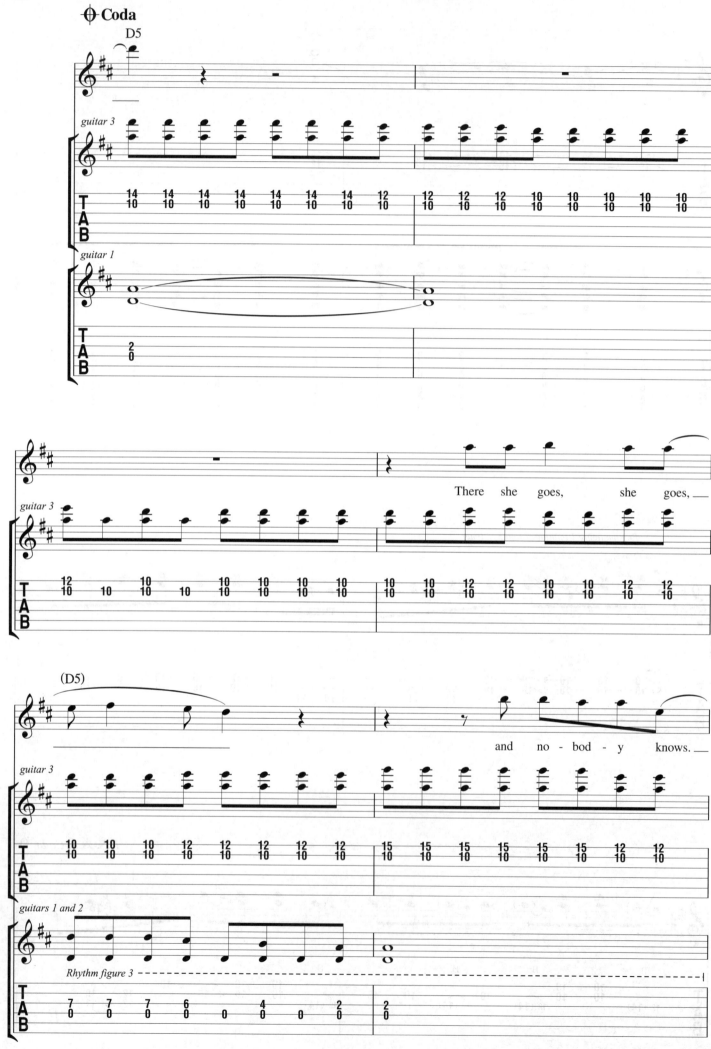

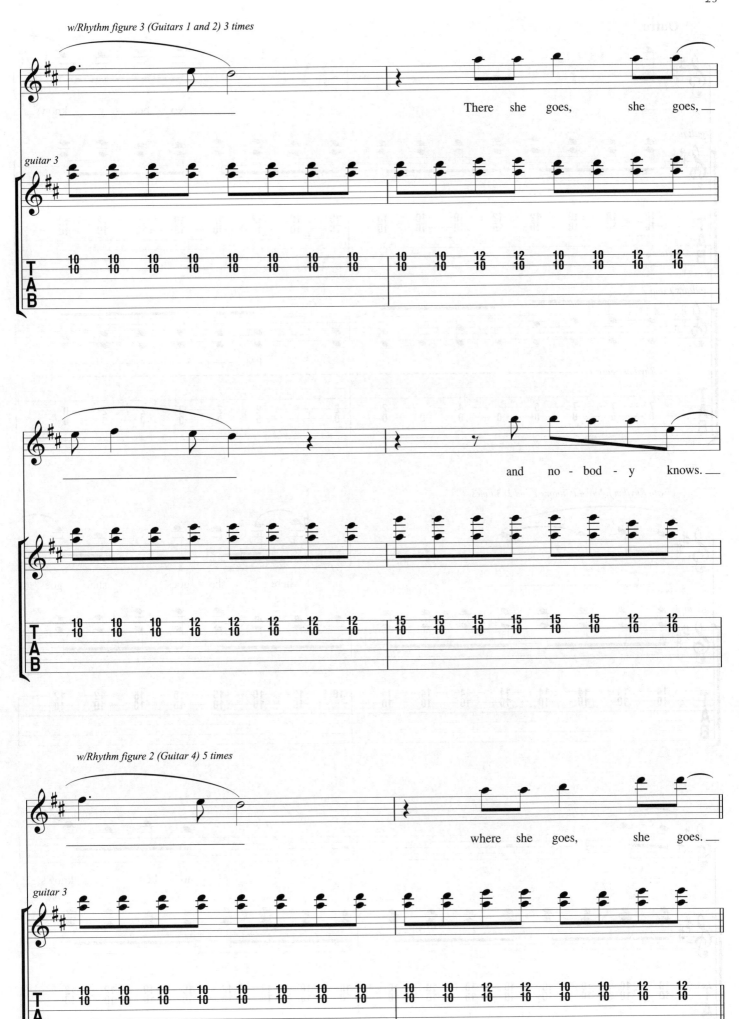

24

Outro

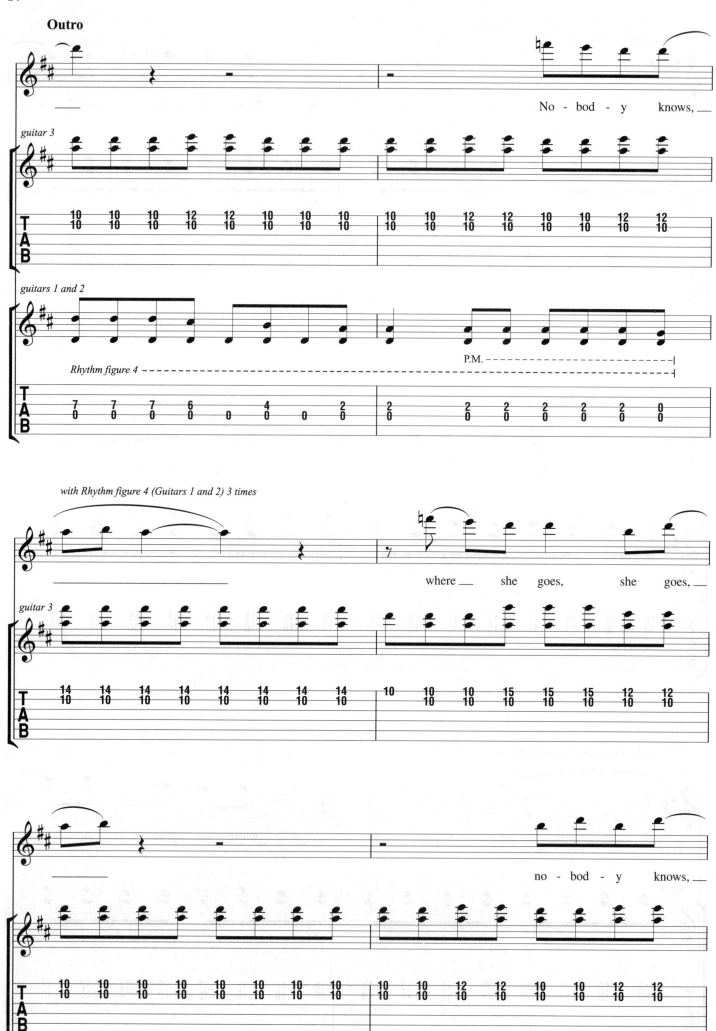

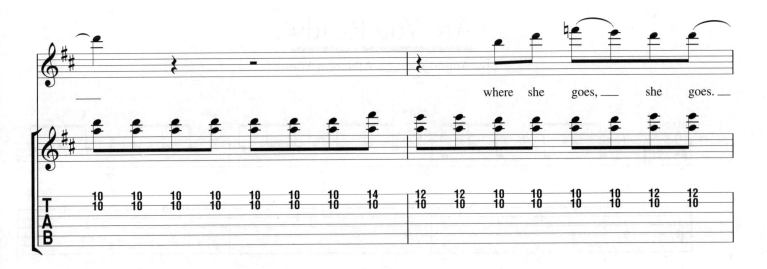

where she goes, ___ she goes. ___

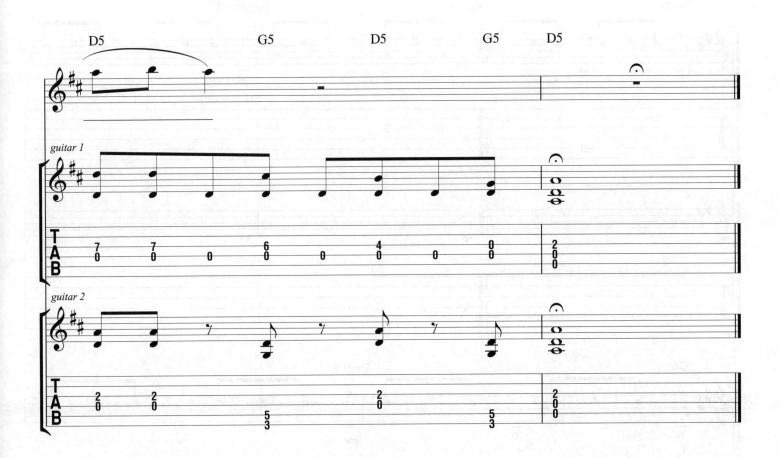

Additional lyrics

2nd Verse:
Bangin' drums, workin' out "all fast"
A heavy tune I can play it loud
You know she's blowing away all the others
You're never man enough to take it on all night
You better razzle-dazzle on that stage
Keep rockin' on all through the night

2nd Bridge:
A heavy rockin' tune is playing
On a flat screen color T.V.
Sneaking over creepy-crawlies
Never give it up
To take it out through the night

Are You Ready

By Angus Young & Malcolm Young

Back Seat Confidential

By Angus Young, Malcolm Young and Bon Scott

*guitar 1 tacet first two times

guitars 1 & 2*

play four times

1. 3. Old man's car it's a Sat- ur- day night,-
2. See additional lyrics

guitars 1 & 2 Rhythm figure 2

end Rhythm figure 2

guitars 1 & 2 with Rhythm figure 2 *seven times*

Got me a wom-an, me I feel al - right.-

Rock and roll-in' at the drive in show,—

Gon- na sit in the back in the pas- sion row.

40

Additional lyrics

2. Said to buy a rubber by the cigarette stand,
Dying to get it off so that I can get in.
Doing my best to make good connection,
She say what you gonna do 'bout my protection.
All right mama gotta listen to me,
Last chance thrill it's half past three.
Huggin' an a kissin' will be real nice,
Every man's got his price.

Back In Black

By Angus Young, Malcolm Young and Brian Johnson

1. Back in black_ I hit the sack, I've been too long, I'm glad to be back, yes, I'm _
2. *See additional lyrics*

_ let loose from the noose,_ That's kept me hang-in' a - bout._ I keep

look-in' at the sky 'cause it's get-tin' me high._ For-get the hearse 'cause I'll nev-er die. I got

nine lives, cat's eyes, A - bus-in' ev-'ry one of them and run-nin' wild. 'Cause I'm

Rhythm figure 3

end Rhythm figure 3

with Rhythm figure 3 (3 times)

Coda

D   E

back   in___   black.___

A   E

A E   B   B/A   B   A E   B   B/A   B

Well I'm   back _____   back _____

with Rhythm figure 2

49

Additional Lyrics

2. Back in the back of a Cadillac
   Number one with a bullet, I'm a power pack.
   Yes, I'm in a bang with the gang,
   They gotta catch me if they want me to hang.
   'Cause I'm back on the track, and I'm beatin' the flack
   Nobody's gonna get me on another rap.
   So, look at me now, I'm just makin' my play
   Don't try to push your luck, just get outta my way.

Ballbreaker

By Angus Young and Malcolm Young

Chorus

You are a ball-break-er.

55

56

58

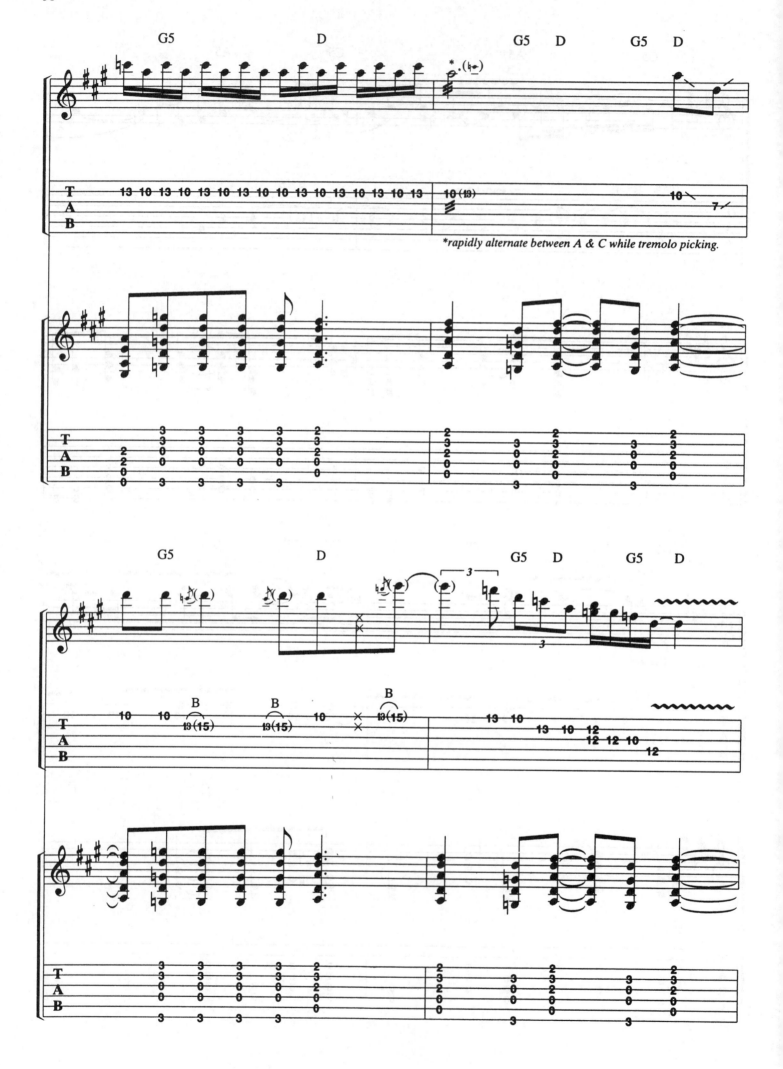

*rapidly alternate between A & C while tremolo picking.

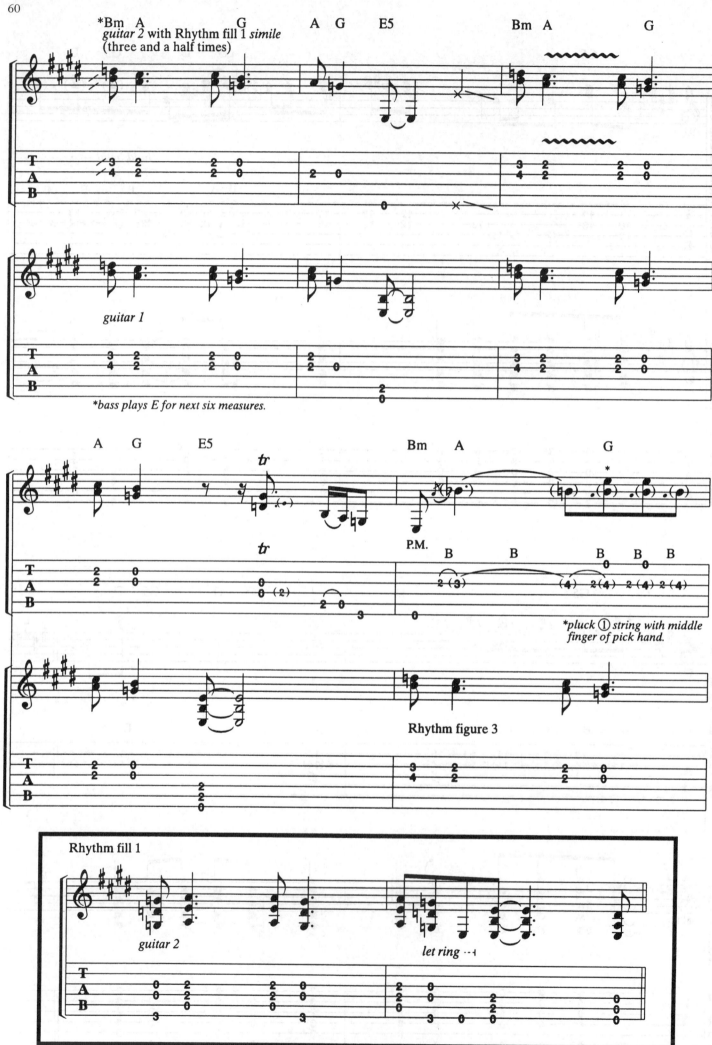

66

*rapidly alternate between fretted note
and open ② string while tremolo picking.

* ⑤ string sounds symphathetically.

Ball - break - er!

70

guitars 1 & 2

Additional lyrics

2. Engine roll, time to go.
   A razorback, a hog attack.
   A-buildin' steam, a-whippin' cream.
   She likes a fat smokin' stack.

Pre-chorus:
Hangin' off her legs,
She threw me on the bed.
Her hand went for my throat.
As I began to choke,
She said, "Honey, shoot your load."

Big Jack

By Angus Young & Malcolm Young

it so hard. ___ A - when it comes ___ to lov - in',

Big Jack is on his way. _____ Wink ___

B5

___ of sat - is - fac - tion, his time is go - in' on. ___

guitars 1 and 2

Pre-Chorus

1. I'm like a bad de - fend -
2. *See additional lyrics*

Rhythm figure 2 -

w/Rhythm figure 2 (Guitars 1 and 2) 2 times

- er, smok - in' ho - ly Joe. ___ He's a big pre - tend -

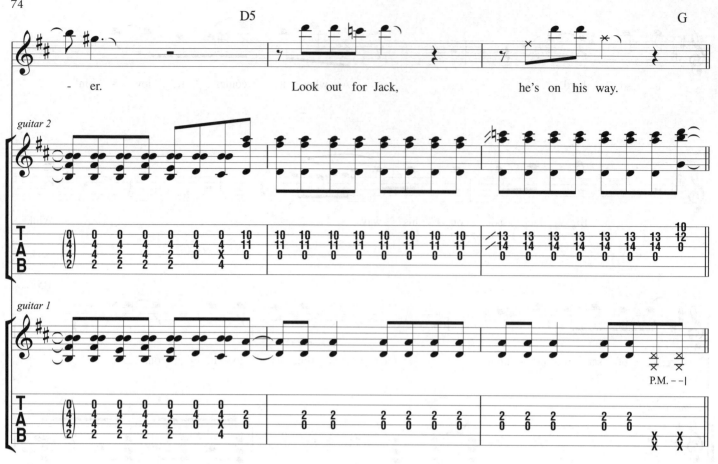

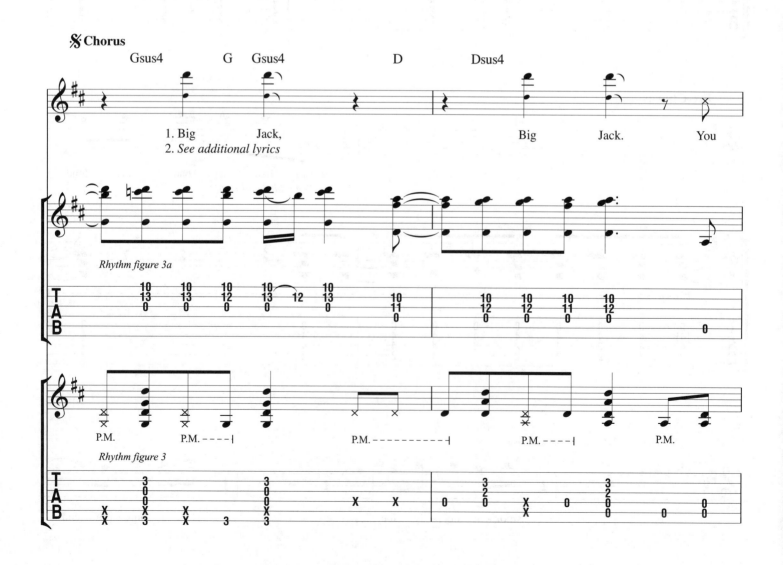

76

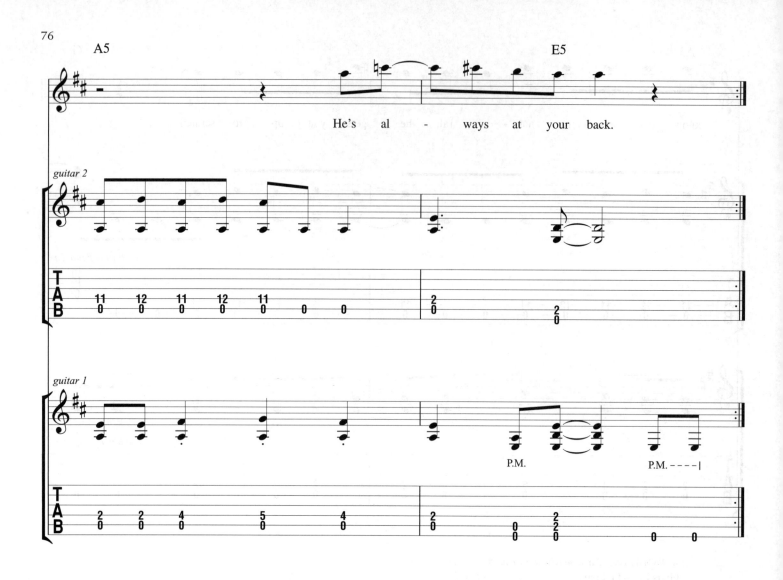

He's al - ways at your back.

Guitar solo

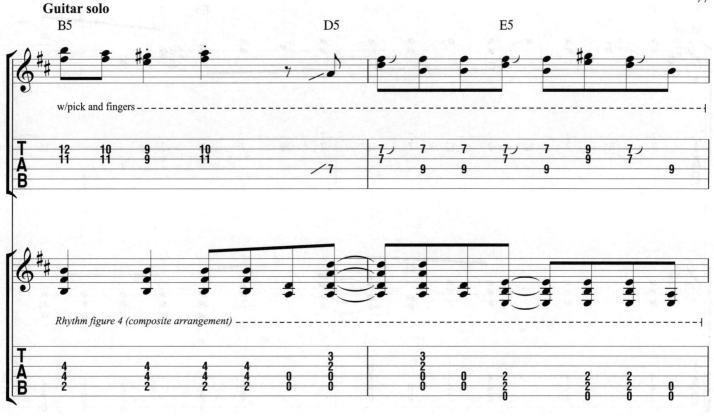

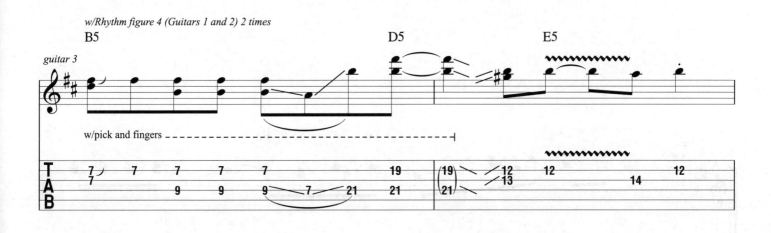

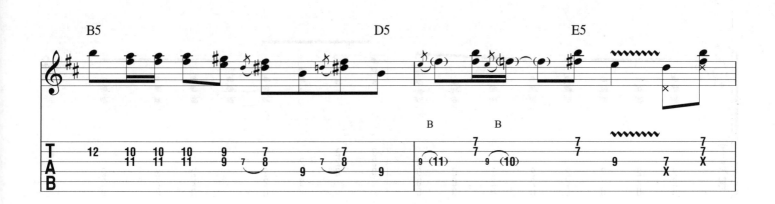

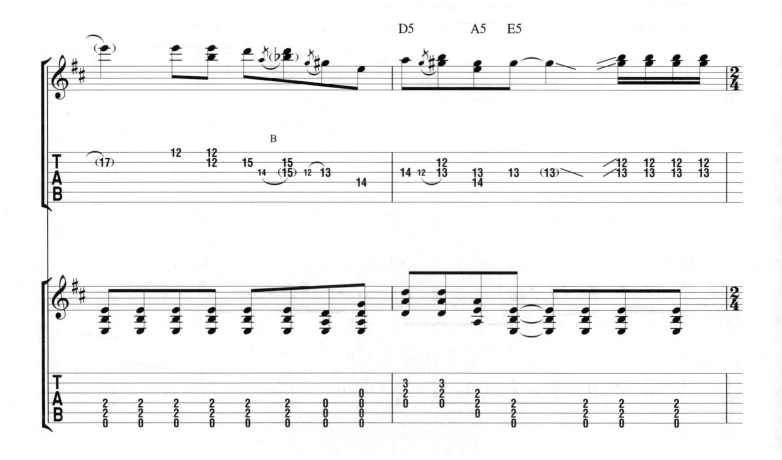

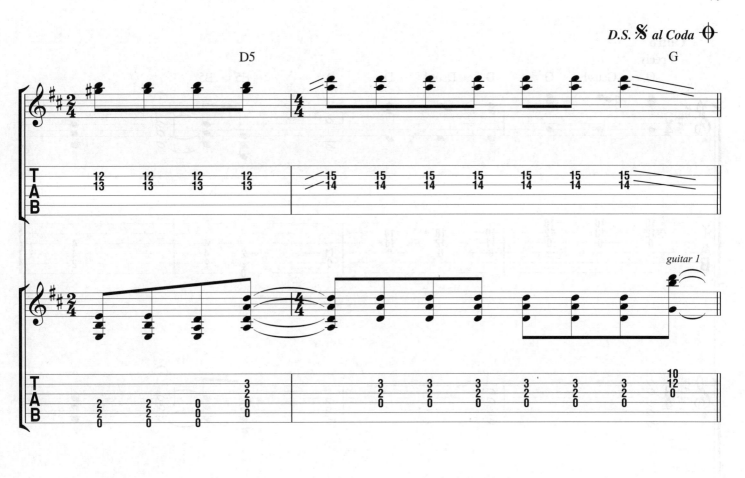

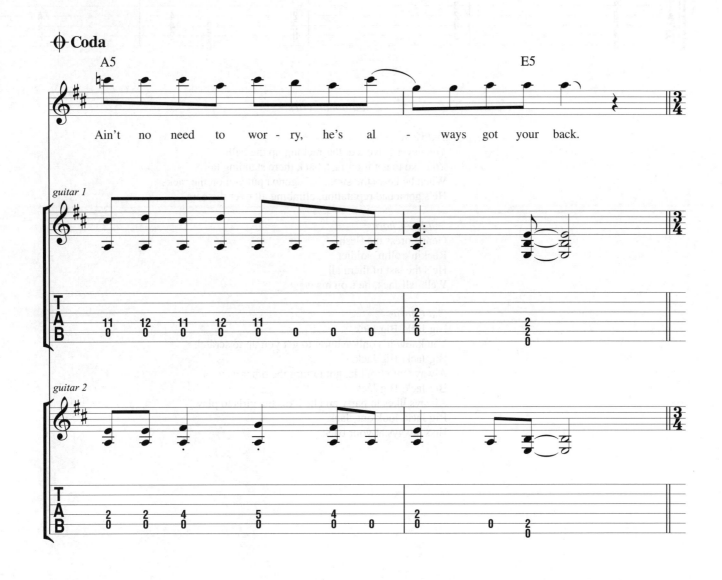

Ain't no need to wor - ry, he's al - ways got your back.

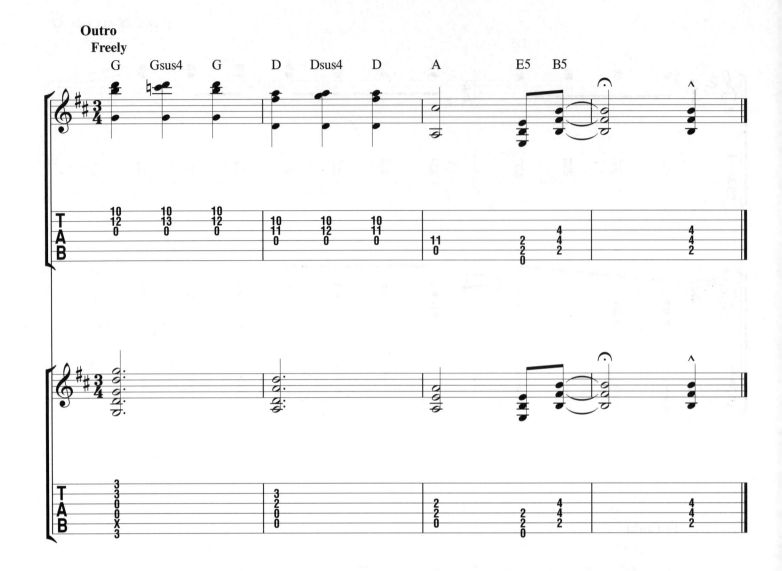

Additional lyrics

2nd Verse:
You never leave a dollar racking up the balls
You like to get it on fast, back there standing tall
When he hears the siren, he's gonna put you on the racks
He's got a bad reputation, climbing all over the bars

2nd Pre-Chorus:
Gonna press the flesh
Rockin' rollin' soldier
He's the last of them all
Well, tell Jack, he's on his way

2nd Chorus:
Big Jack, Big Jack
You know it's only natural to get you up to scratch
Big Jack, Big Jack
Always into trouble, got to turn the other way
Big Jack, Big Jack
Always likes to party and he likes the girls to play
Big Jack, look out, Jack
He's always at your back

Beating Around the Bush

By Angus Young, Malcolm Young and Bon Scott

D5

E5

D.S. al Coda

3. You're

86

Additional Lyrics

2. Wish I knew what's on your mind,
   Why you being so unkind.
   Remember those nights we spent alone,
   Talking on the telephone.
   Thoughts of you go through my brain,
   You told me that you felt the same.
   I also thought you loved me too,
   Tell me who would lie with you.

Chorus: I was talking legs,
   And he was talkin' knees.
   Or was he down upon his knees,
   Beating around the bush.

3. You're the meanest woman I'll ever know,
   And sticks and stones won't break my bones.
   I know what you're looking for,
   Eating your cake you'll want some more.
   I'm gonna give you just one more chance,
   Try to save our romance.
   Jump in the fire I'm goin' down,
   The rest is up to you.

Chorus: You can chew it up,
   You can spit it out.
   Lettin' it all hang out,
   Beating around the bush.

Bedlam In Belgium

By Angus Young, Malcolm Young and Brian Johnson

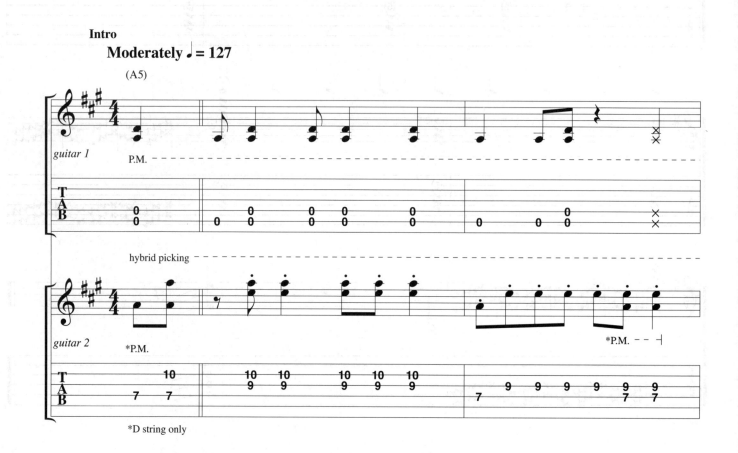

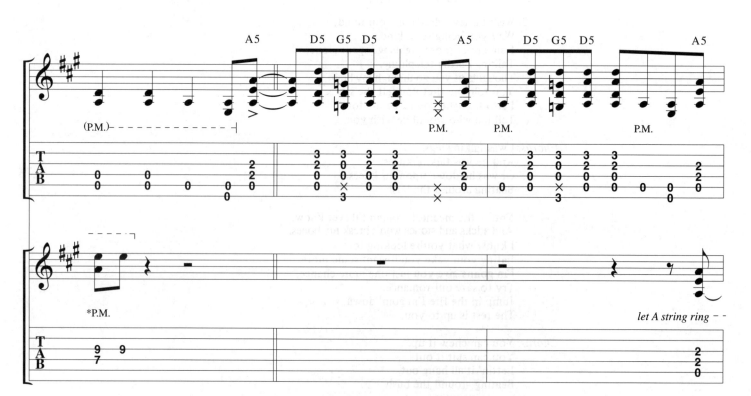

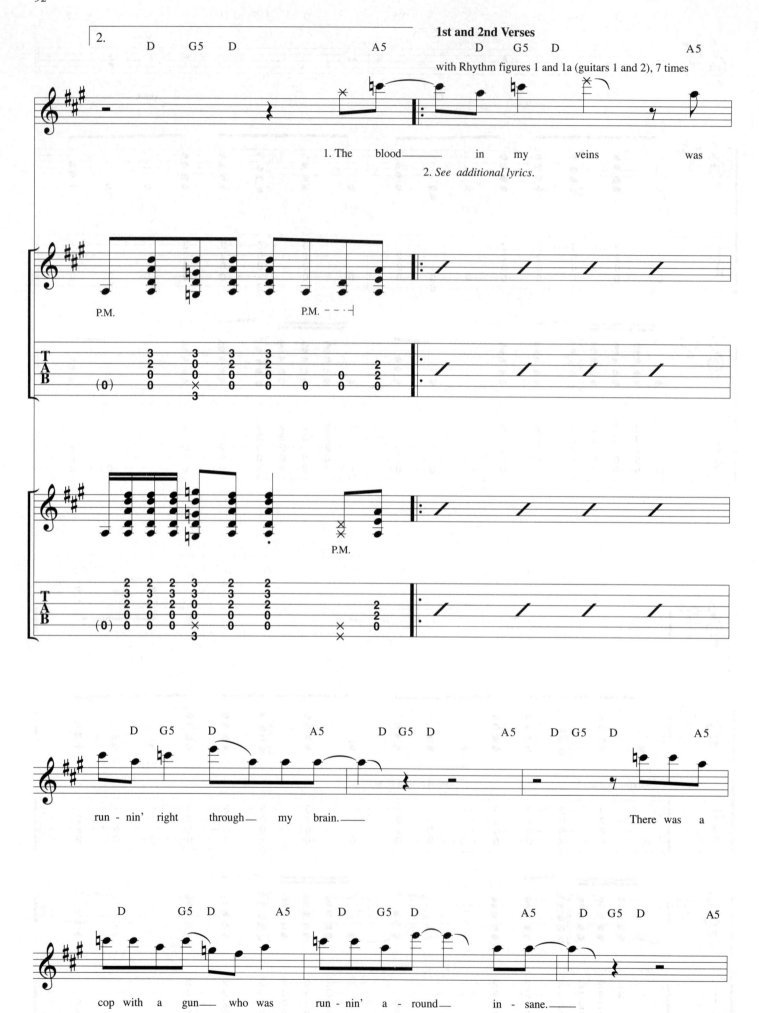

1st and 2nd Verses

with Rhythm figures 1 and 1a (guitars 1 and 2), 7 times

1. The blood_____ in my veins was

2. *See additional lyrics.*

P.M.

P.M. - - - ⌐

P.M.

run - nin' right through___ my brain.___ There was a

cop with a gun___ who was run - nin' a - round___ in - sane.___

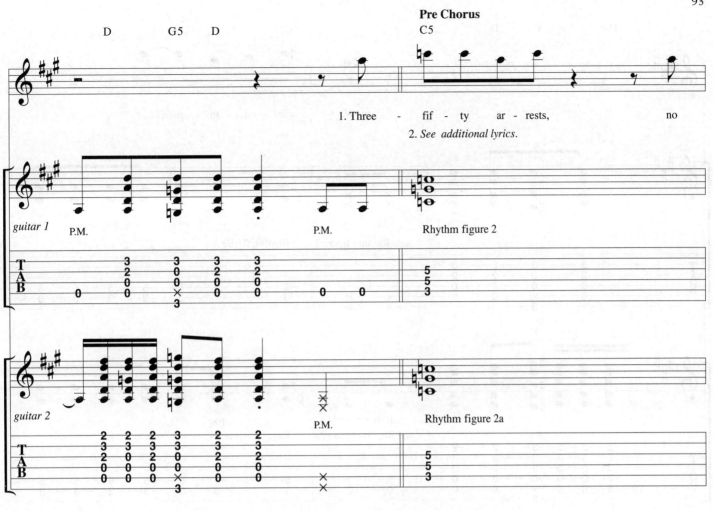

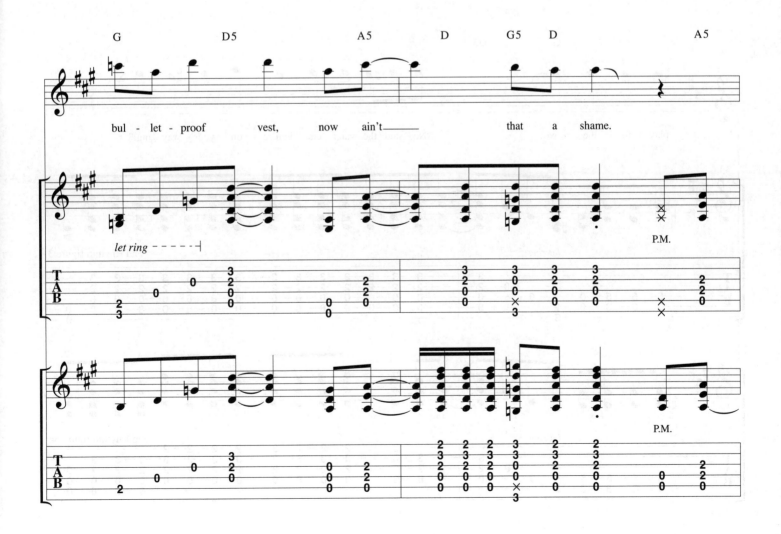

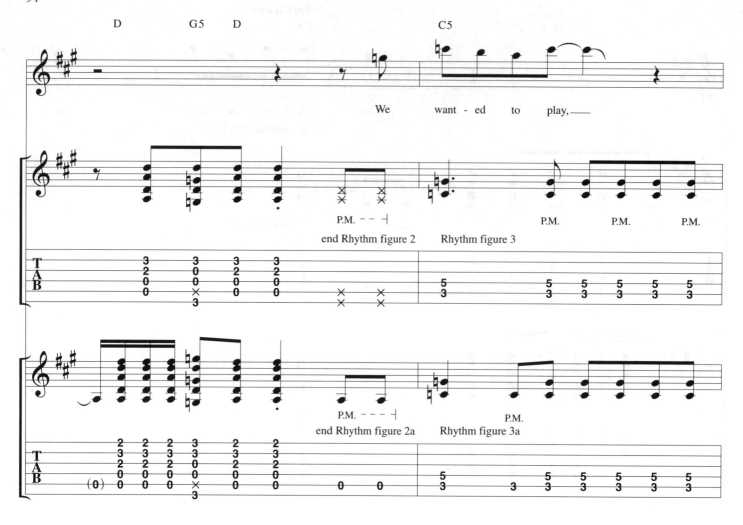

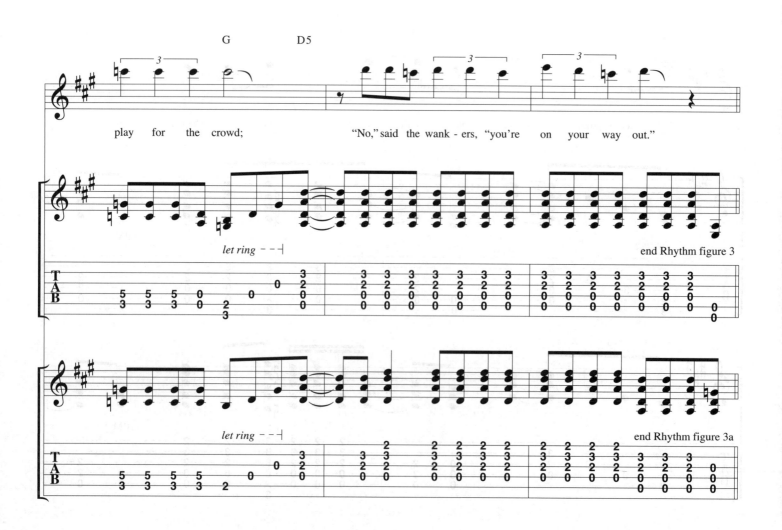

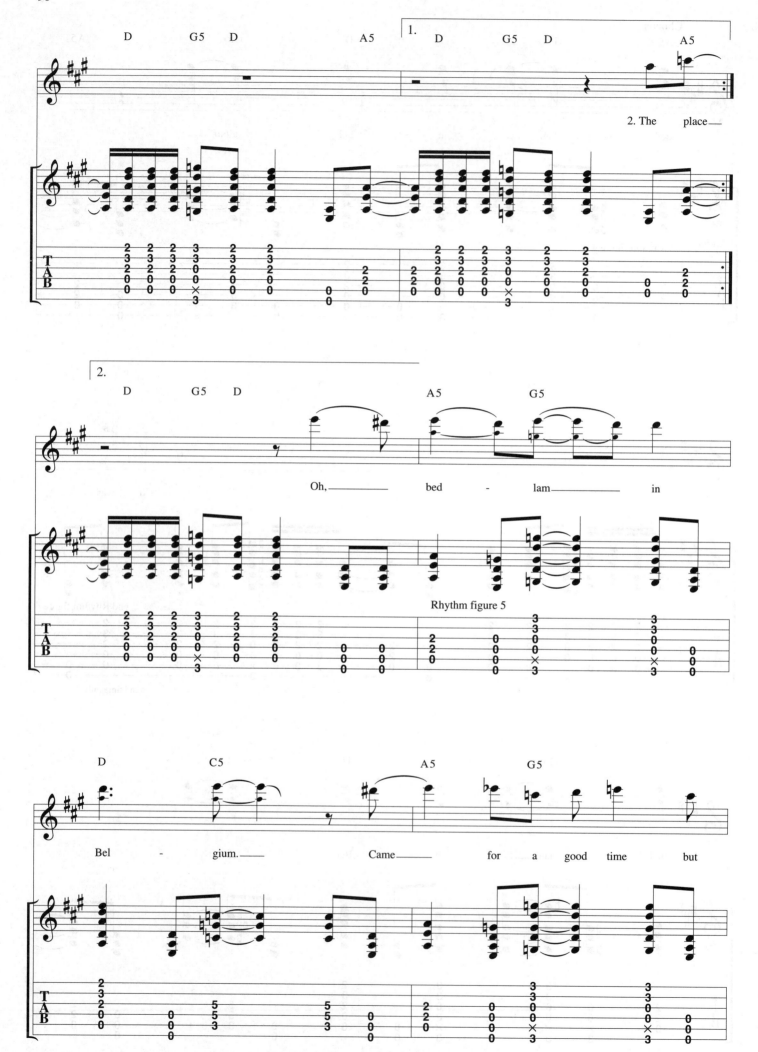

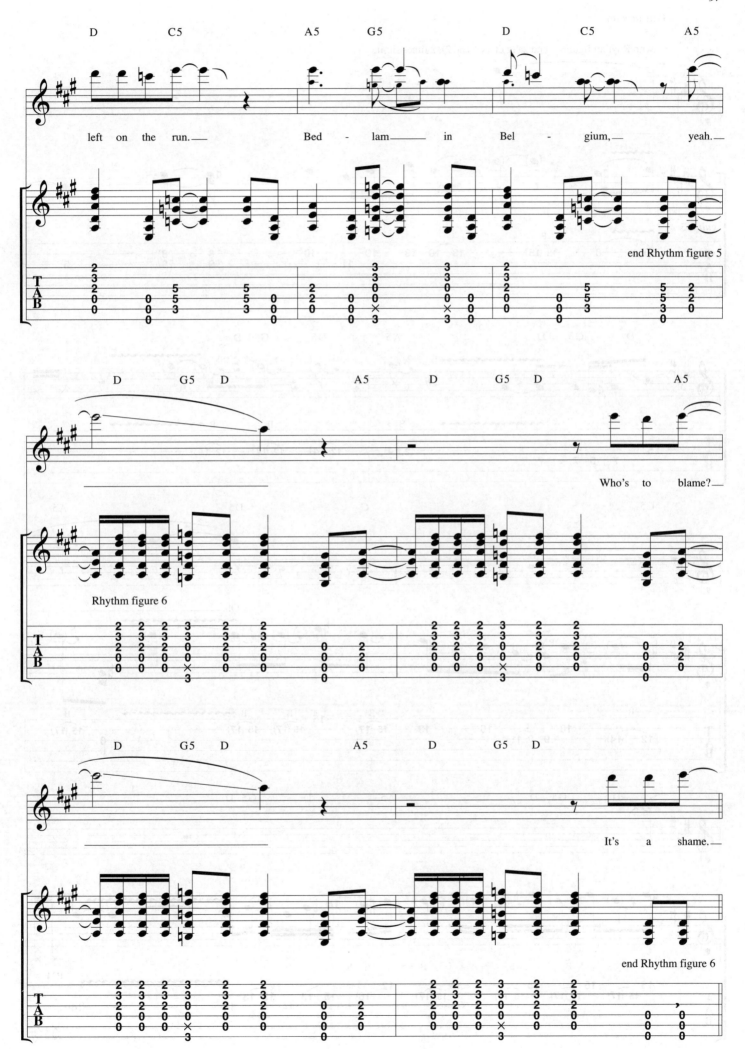

*Open G string
sounds sympathetically
(don't pick).

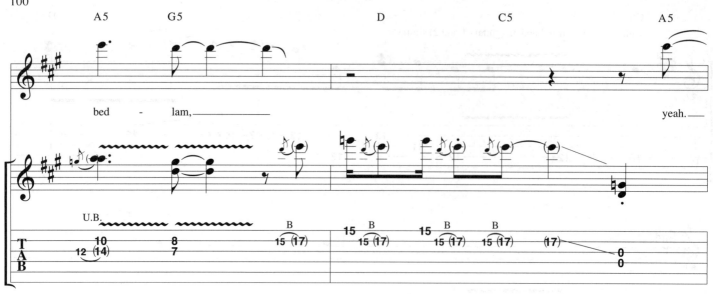

bed - lam,_____

yeah._____

You gon - na run out.

guitar 3

pick scrape - - - - - - - -

guitar 1

guitar 2

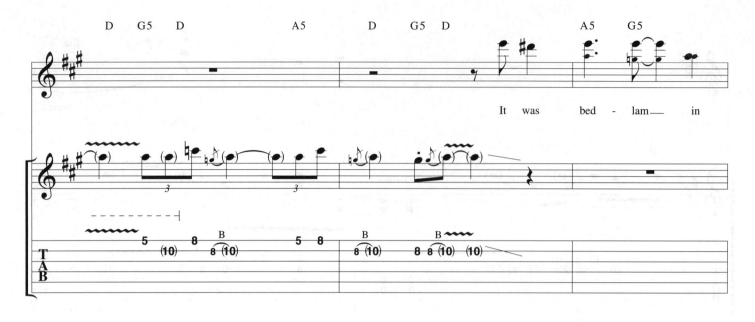

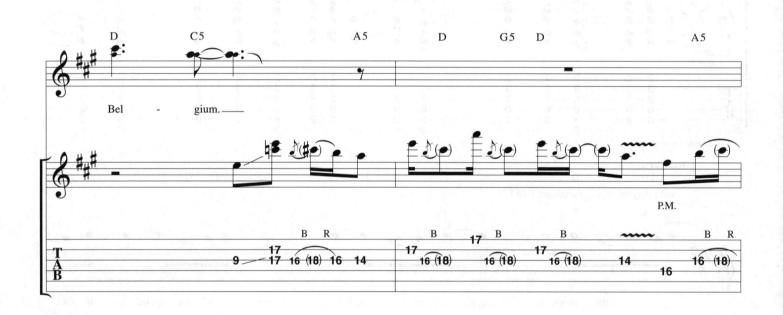

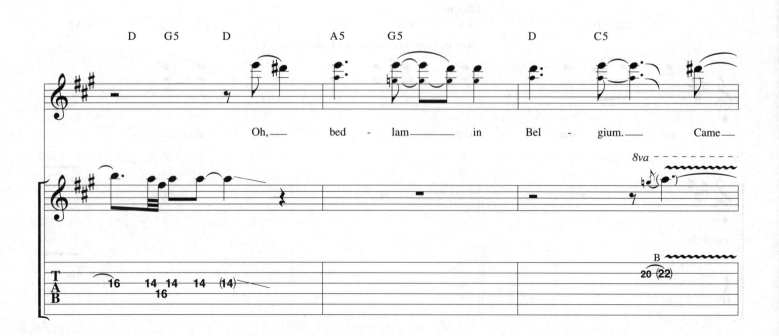

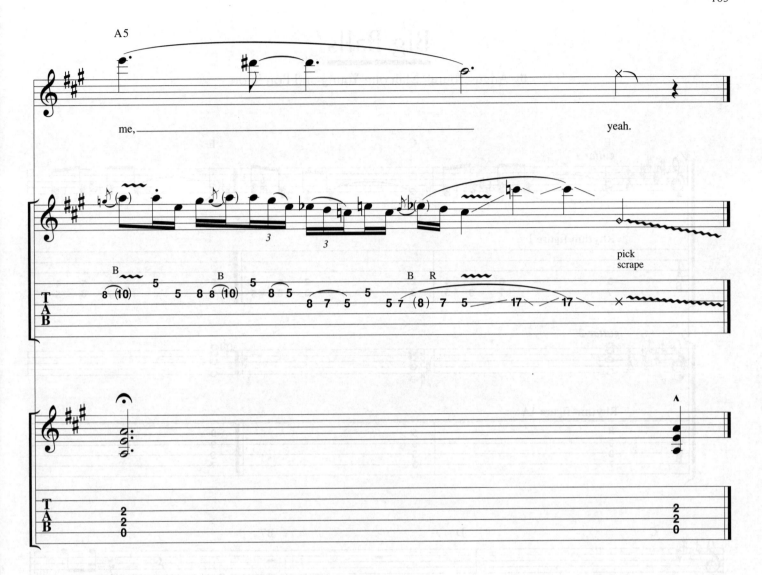

me,   yeah.

Additional Lyrics

(Second Verse)
2. The place was a-jumpin'
   And the booze was going down.
   There's a curfew in town,
   You've been working overtime.

(Second Pre-chorus)
2. We don't play just for pay so we'd like to say,
   Stay just the same.
   He gave me a crack in the back with his gun;
   I bled so bad I could feel the blood run.

Big Balls

By Angus Young, Malcolm Young and Bon Scott

(half-spoken) 1. Well, I'm

Coda

Bol-locks, knack-ers, bol-locks, knack-ers, Bol-locks, knack-ers, bol-locks, knack-ers,

guitars 1 and 2

Additional Lyrics

2. And my balls are always bouncing,
My ballroom always full,
And everybody comes and comes again.
If your name is on the guest list,
No one can take you higher,
Everybody says I've got
Great balls of fire.

3. Some balls are held for charity,
And some for fancy dress,
But when they're held for pleasure,
They're the balls that I like best.
My balls are always bouncing
To the left and to the right,
It's my belief that my big balls
Should be held every night.

Big Gun

By Angus Young and Malcolm Young

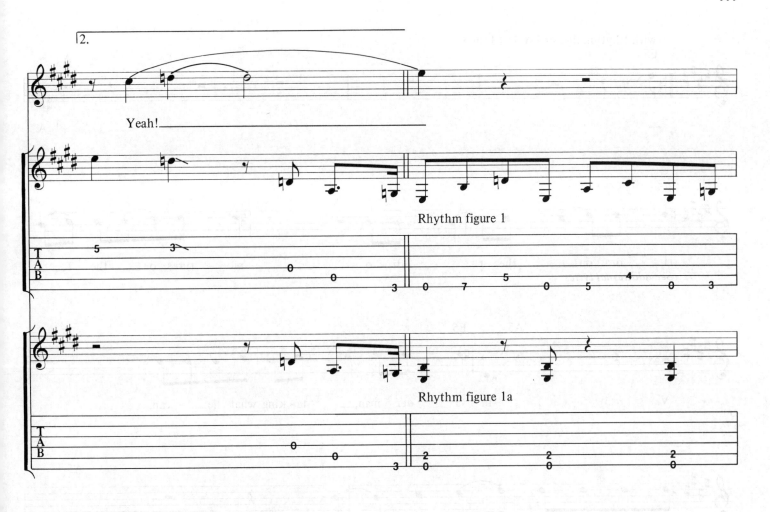

Yeah!

Rhythm figure 1

Rhythm figure 1a

A5

Yeah, yeah! Yeah!

end Rhythm figure 1

end Rhythm figure 1a

112

Chorus

Big gun!   Big   gun!   N - num-ber__ one.__

Big gun!   Big gun kick the hell out-ta you.__

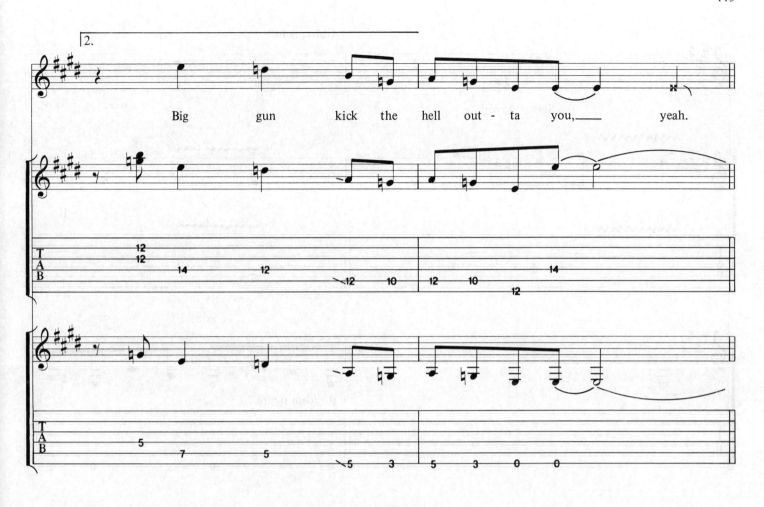

Big gun kick the hell out - ta you,___ yeah.

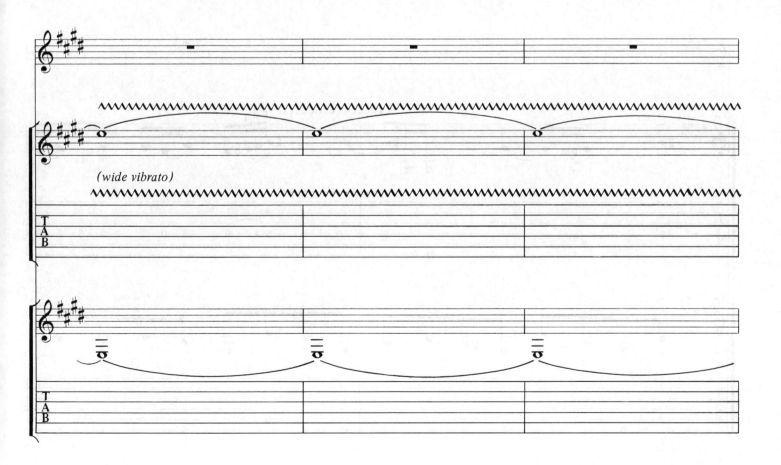

(wide vibrato)

Guitar solo

Show - down!

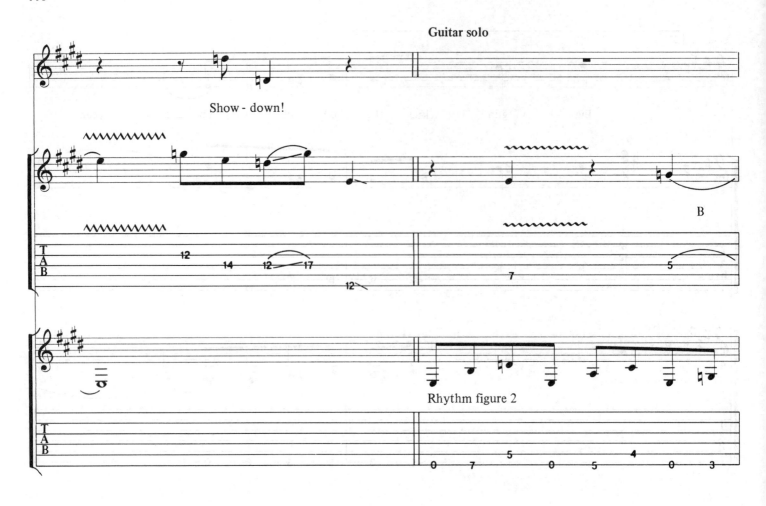

Rhythm figure 2

B

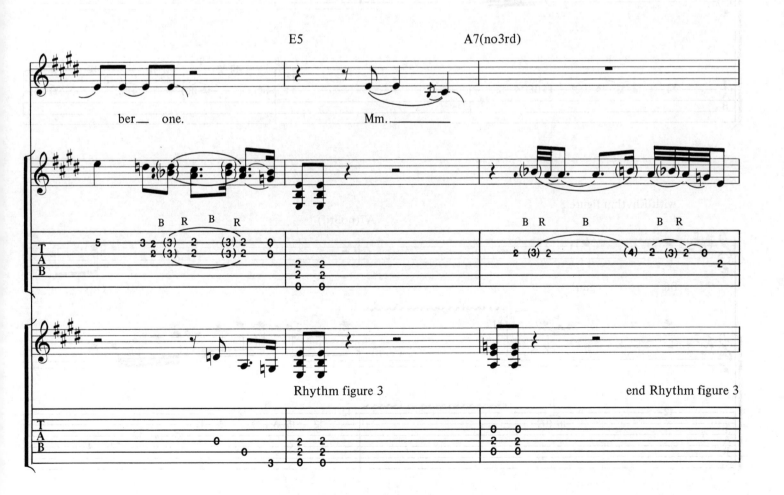

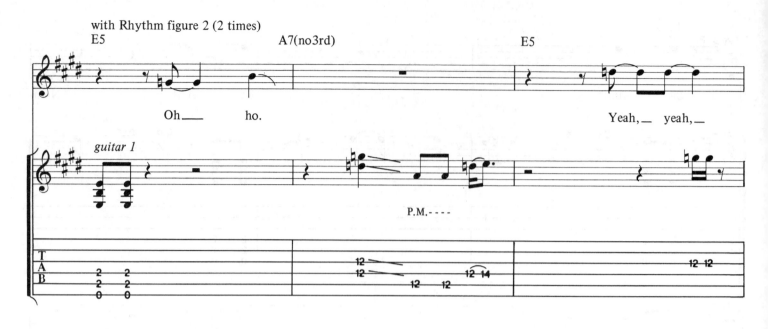

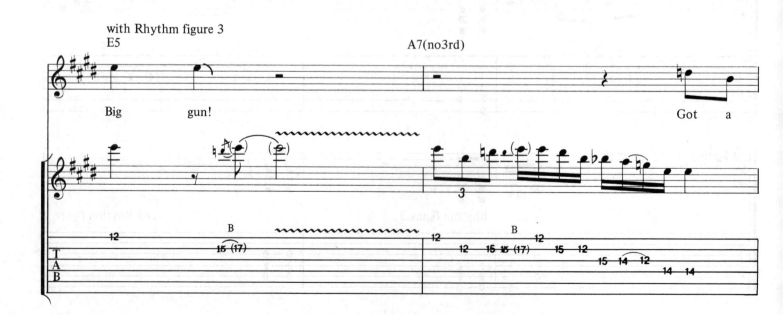

122

Oww!

Additional lyrics

2 Terminators, Uzi makers, shootin' up Hollywood.
Snakes alive with a forty-five, gettin' off and doin' no good.
If you ain't wise they'll cannibalize, tear the flesh off of you.
Classified live lady killers preyin' in a human zoo.
He'd saddle you up and take you to town.
Better look out when he comes around.
(to Chorus)

Boogie Man

By Angus Young and Malcolm Young

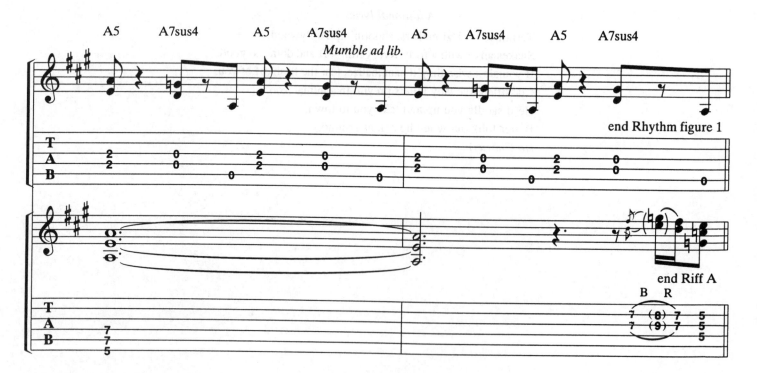

Verse 1

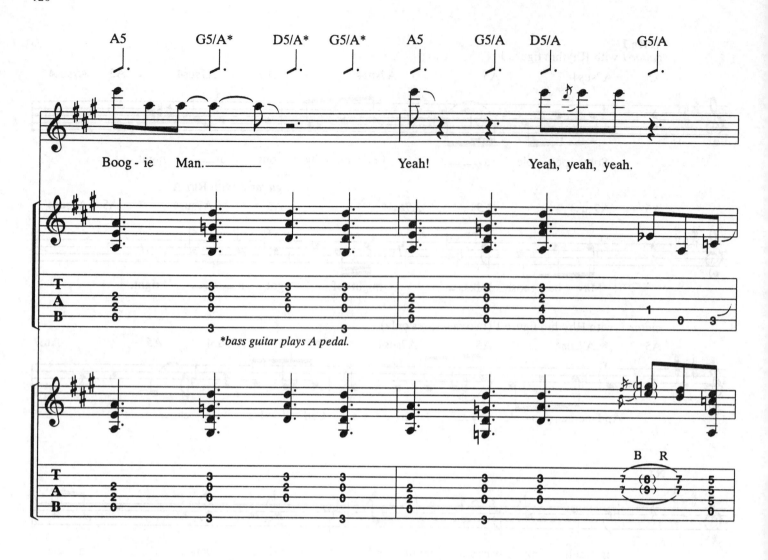

*bass guitar plays A pedal.

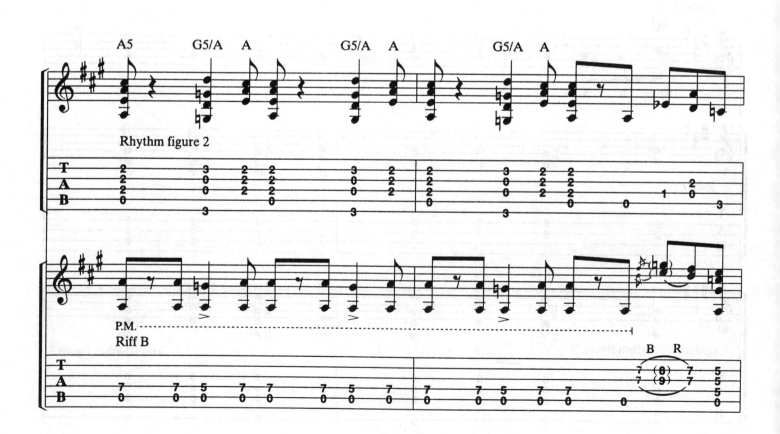

131

132

134

135

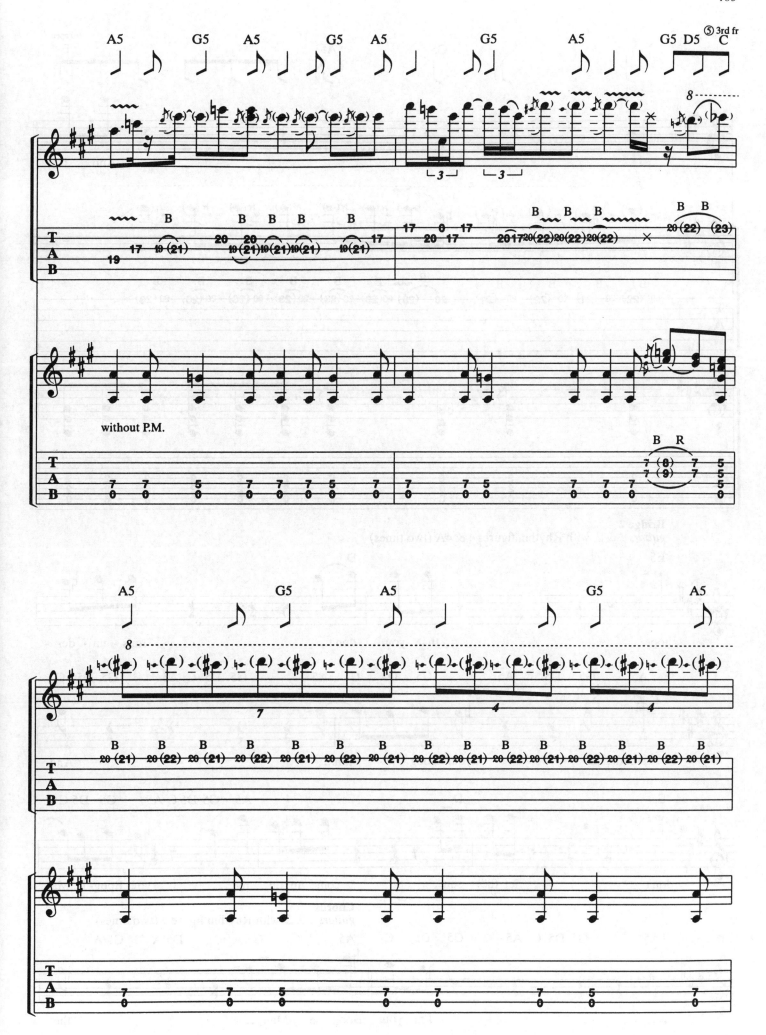

Can I Sit Next To You Girl

By Angus Young and Malcolm Young

Tune down 1/2 step:
⑥ = Eb ③ = Gb
⑤ = Ab ② = Bb
④ = Db ① = Eb

Moderately fast rock ♩ = 136

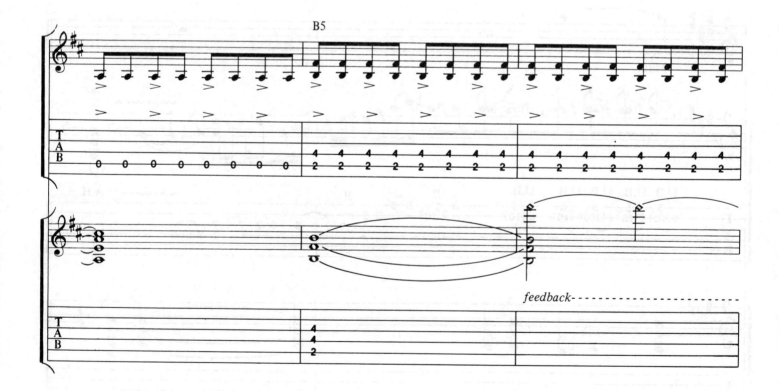

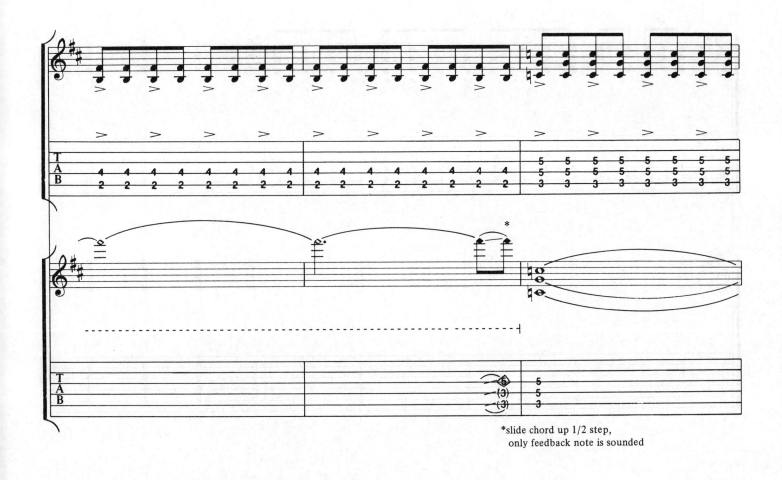

*slide chord up 1/2 step,
only feedback note is sounded

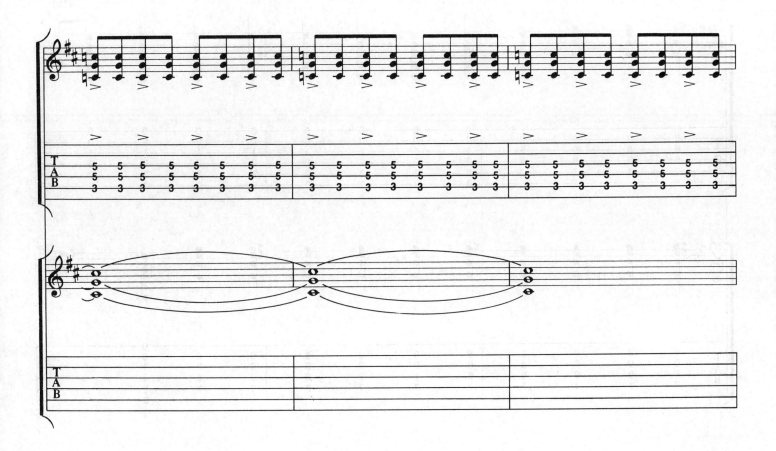

142

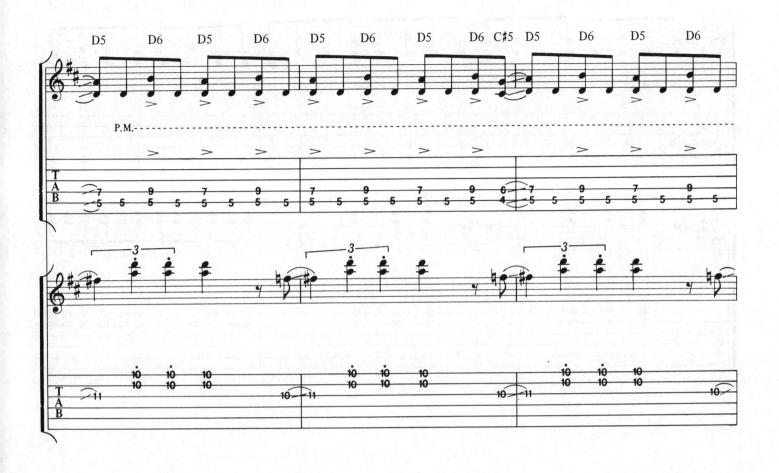

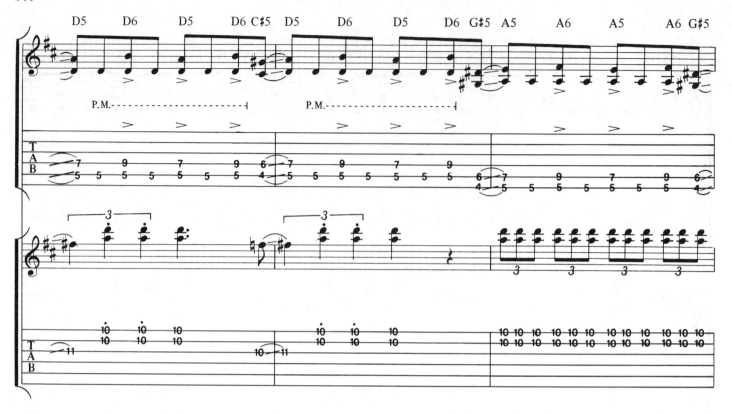

149

150

152

153

Additional Lyrics

2. Intermission, we were doin' alright,
   'Til this guy came up and stood by her side.
   I took him by surprise,
   When I gave him one of my lies.
   She started smilin' and bein' real fine,
   And that's when I said,

Can't Stop Rock 'N' Roll

By Angus Young & Malcolm Young

1. Don't ya give me no line
2. Don't ya play me no jive

155

158

Can't Stand Still

By Angus Young & Malcolm Young

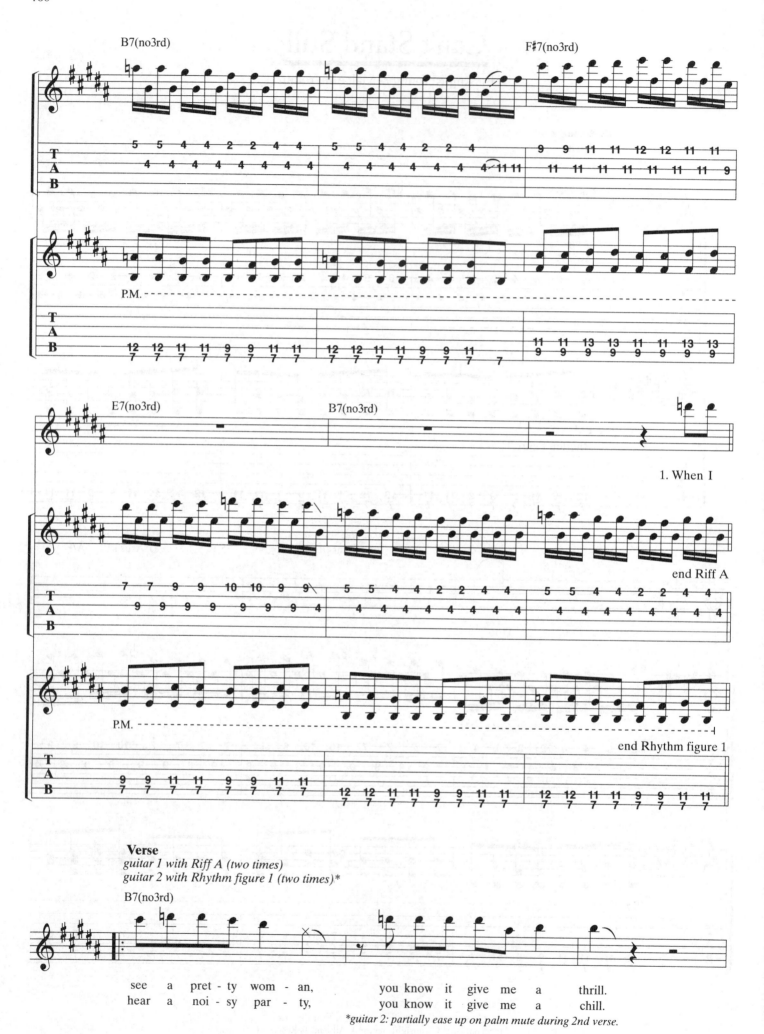

Verse
guitar 1 with Riff A (two times)
guitar 2 with Rhythm figure 1 (two times)*

see   a   pret - ty wom - an,   you know it give me   a   thrill.
hear   a   noi - sy par - ty,   you know it give me   a   chill.

*guitar 2: partially ease up on palm mute during 2nd verse.

162

Guitar solo
guitar 1 with Riff A
guitar 2 with Rhythm figure 2
B7(no3rd)

164

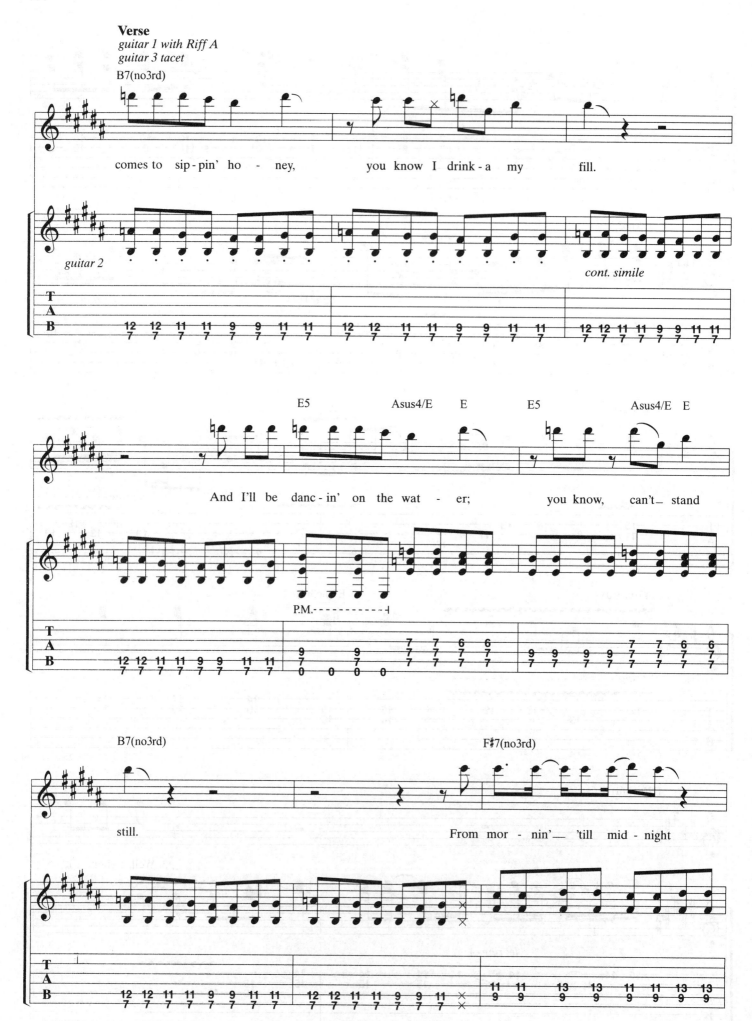

Outro Chorus
guitar 1 with Riff A (first nine measures)
guitar 2 with Rhythm figure 2 (first nine measures)

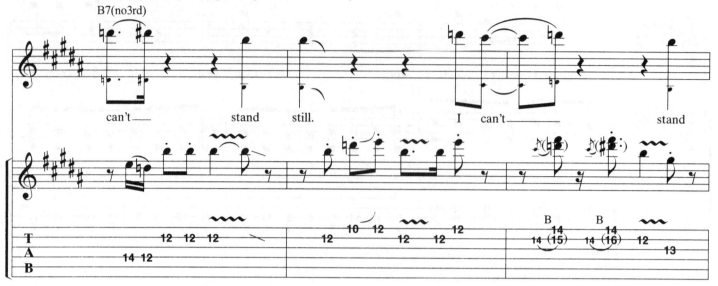

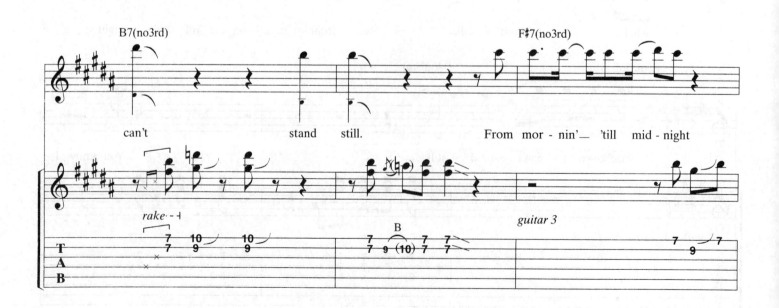

*two guitars arranged for one.

Carry Me Home

By Angus Young, Malcolm Young and Bon Scott

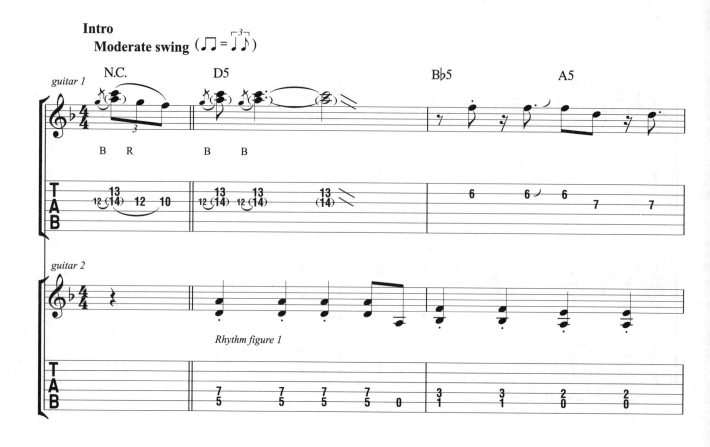

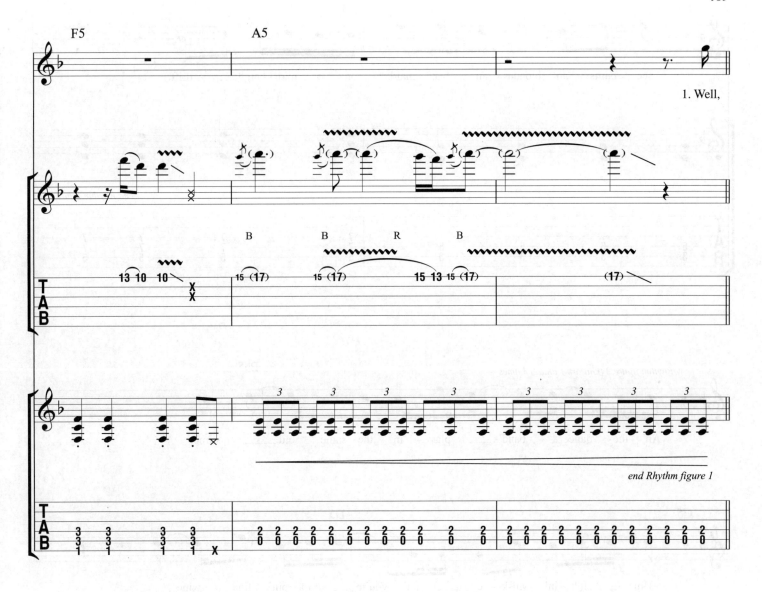

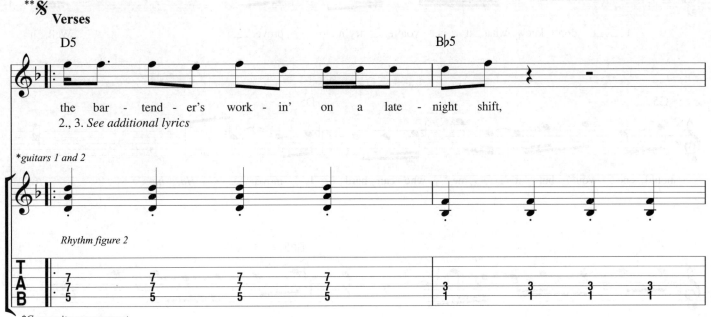

*Composite arrangement
**Guitar 1 strum whole-note chords on D.S.

see bums an' blondes an' bar - maids on a mid - night __ drift.

end Rhythm figure 2

w/Rhythm figure 2 (Guitars 1 and 2) 3 times

An' the dance __ band's __ play - in' the same old __ slime.

I'm __ sink - in' whisk - ey __ an' you're __ sip - pin' fine wine. __

I __ don't know what it is you're __ try'n to prove. __ Well, it

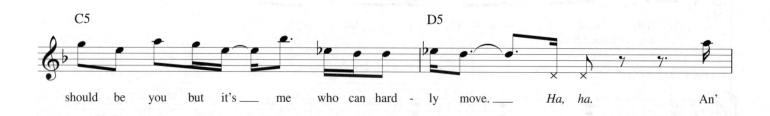

should be you but it's __ me who can hard - ly move. __ *Ha, ha.* An'

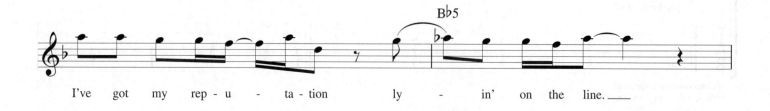

I've got my rep - u - ta - tion ly - in' on the line. __

Come on, ba - by, be a good dog an', an' help the blind.__ Oh__ won't you

guitars 1 and 2 on D.S.

Chorus

car - ry me home,__ won't you car - ry me home.__

guitar 1 on D.S.

guitars 1 and 2

Rhythm figure 3

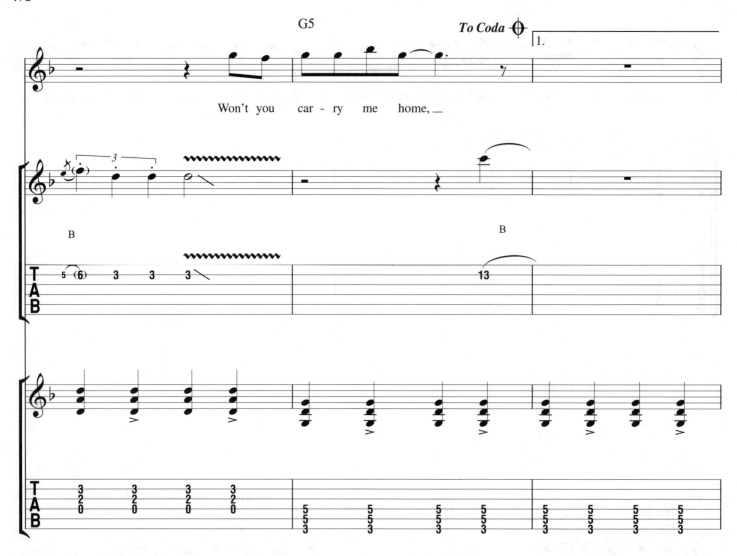

Won't you car-ry me home, __

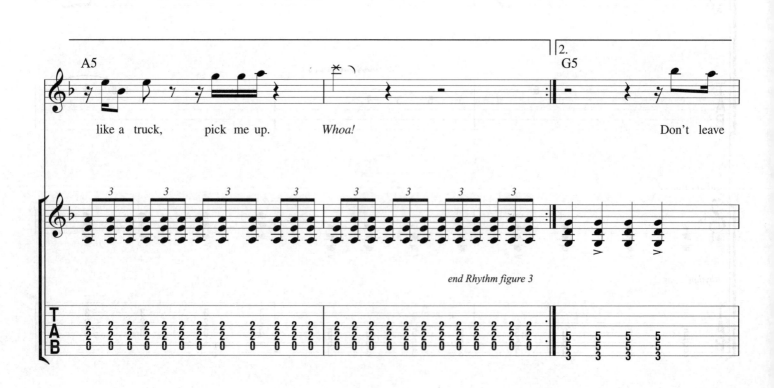

like a truck, pick me up. *Whoa!*

Don't leave

end Rhythm figure 3

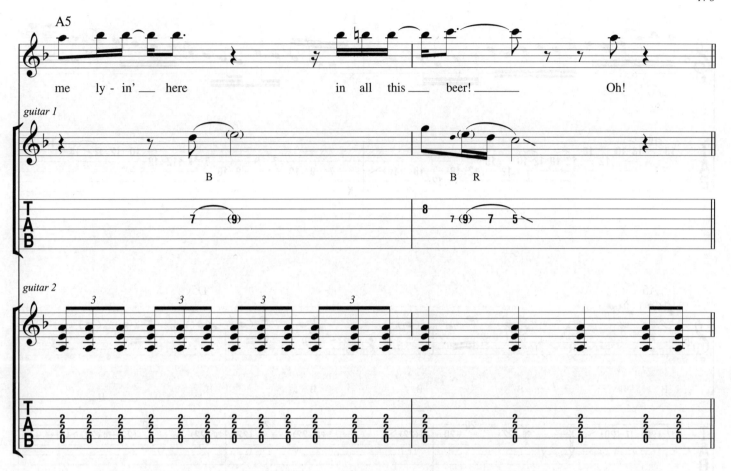

me ly - in' ___ here   in all this ___ beer! _____ Oh!

Guitar solo

w/Rhythm figure 1 (Guitar 2) 2 times

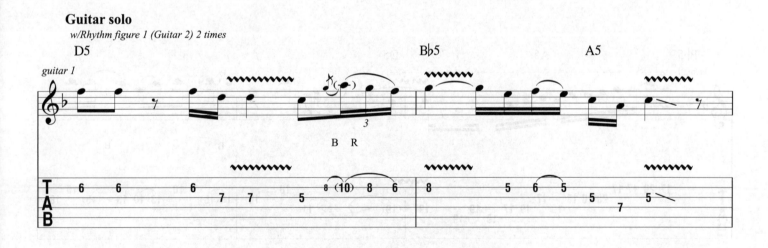

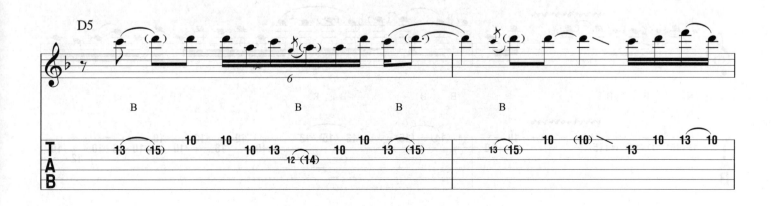

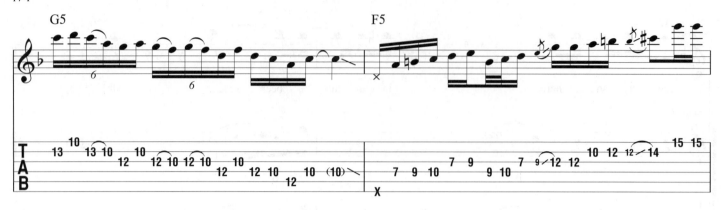

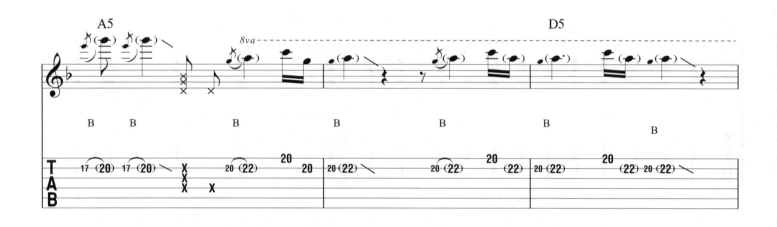

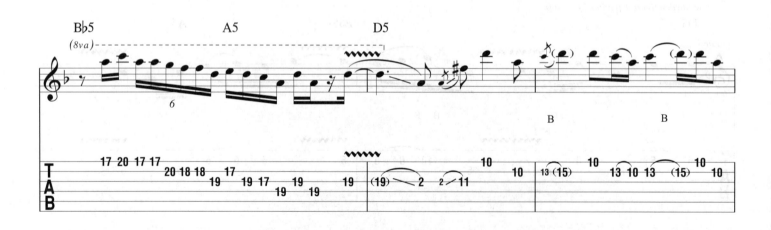

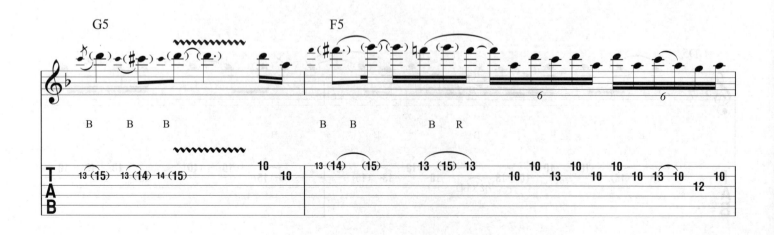

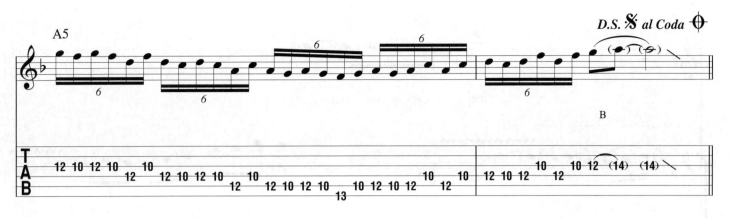

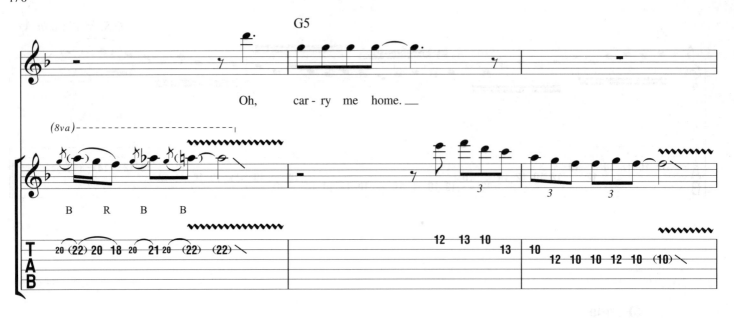

Oh, car-ry me home. ____

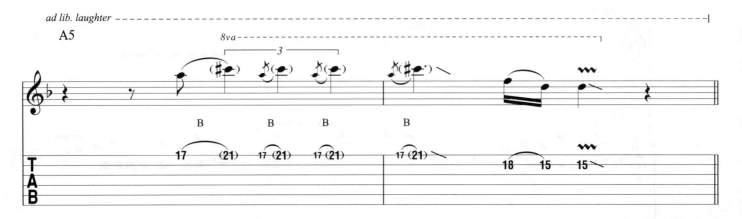

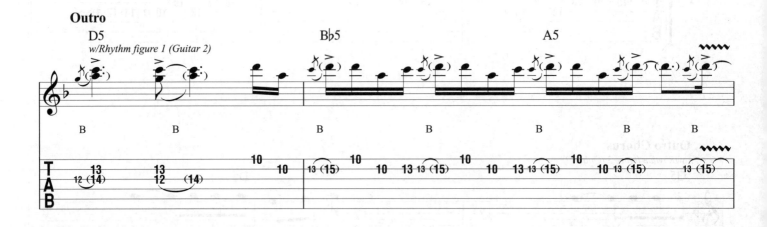

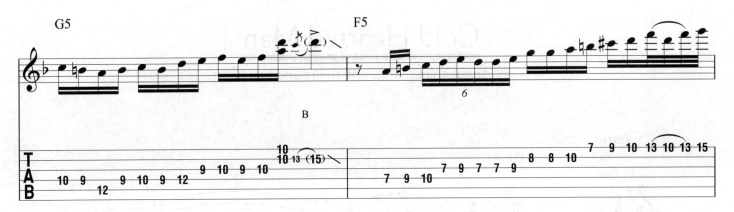

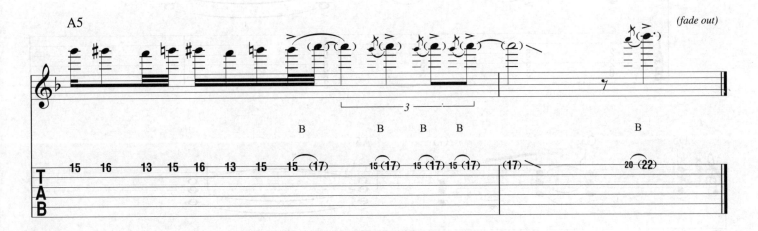

Additional lyrics

2. You ain't no lady but you sure got taste in men
   That head of yours has got you by, time and time again
   My arms and legs are aching and my head's about to blow
   And your back's needin' breakin' and I'd hate to spoil the show
   But I just spent next week's wages, I'm right outta coin
   But you want more and it's half past four, and they wanna close the joint
   And we can't afford a taxi, and it's too late for the bus
   But I've been told by friends of mine you're someone I can trust

3. You drank all your booze and half of mine
   I'm bleary-eyed and your waitin' for the sunshine to come 'n' kill me
   Just like the man who through me on the floor
   Don't matter, while I'm down here might just as well try 'n' find the fuckin' door
   'Scuse me, have you seen it? It's about this big
   And have ya got a plastic bag 'cause I'm gonna be sick
   I'm dead drunk and heavin', hangin' upside down
   And you're getting' up and leavin', do you think I'm gonna drown

Cold Hearted Man

By Angus Young, Malcolm Young and Bon Scott

1. No one knew __ where he came from, __ he nev - er knew him - self. __
2. See additional lyrics

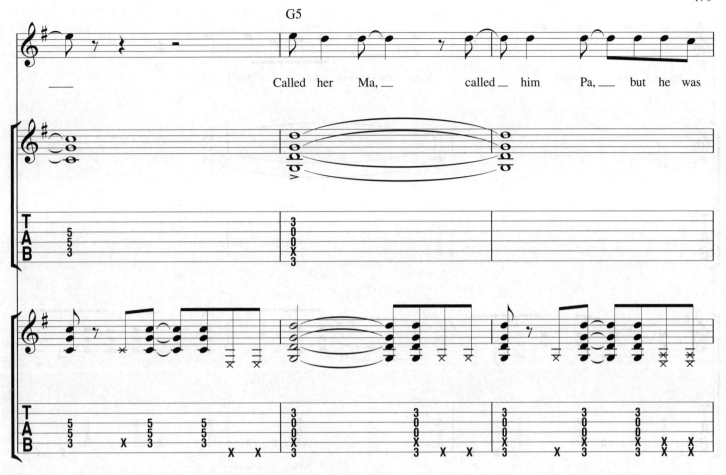

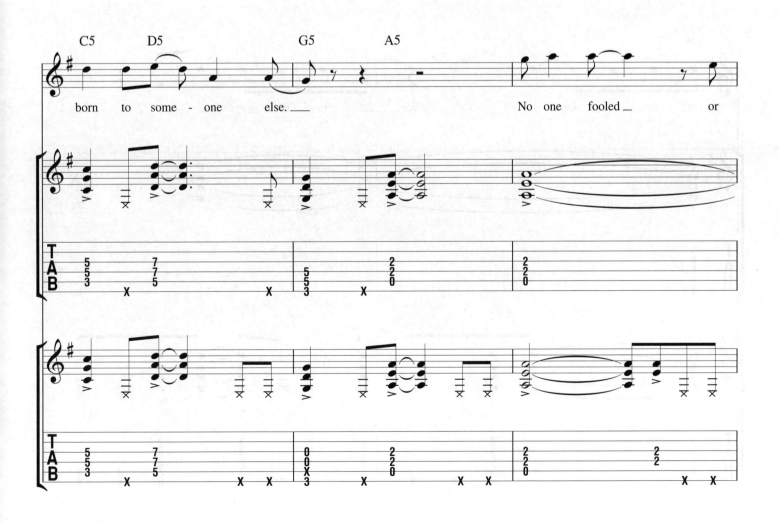

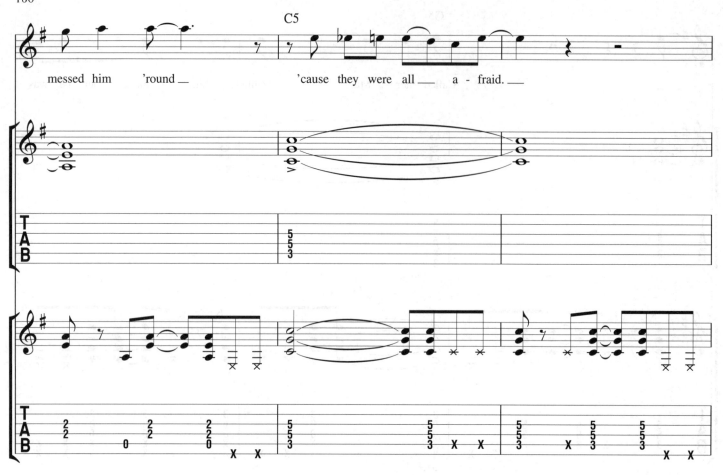

messed him 'round ___ 'cause they were all ___ a - fraid. ___

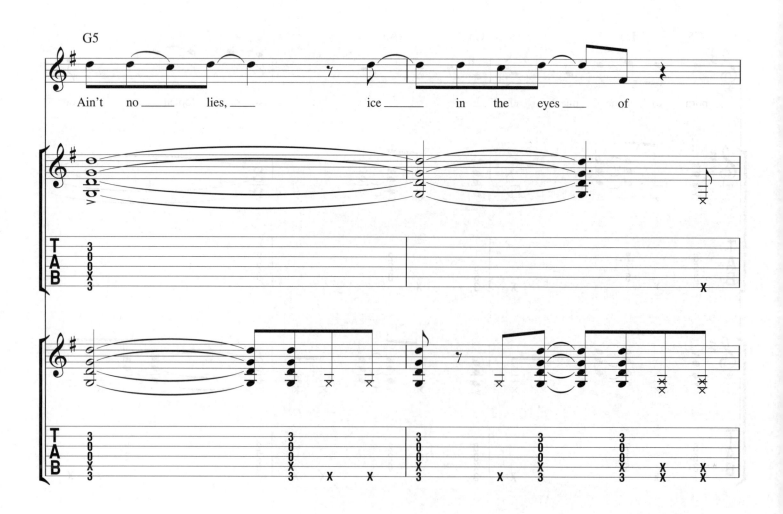

Ain't no ___ lies, ___ ice ___ in the eyes ___ of

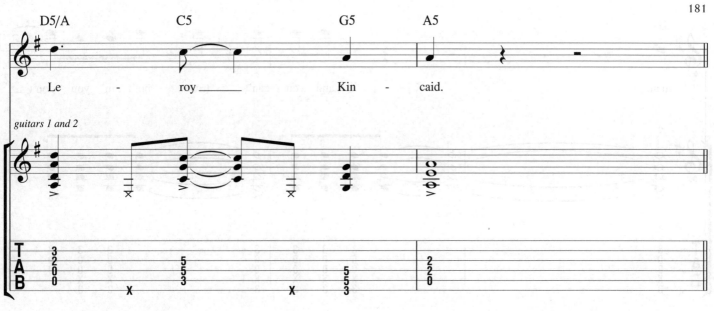

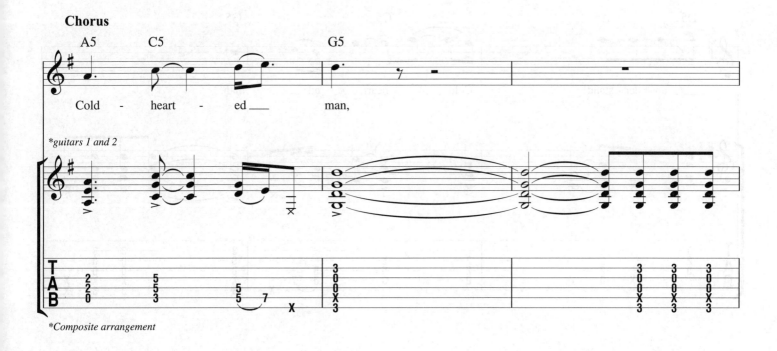

*Composite arrangement

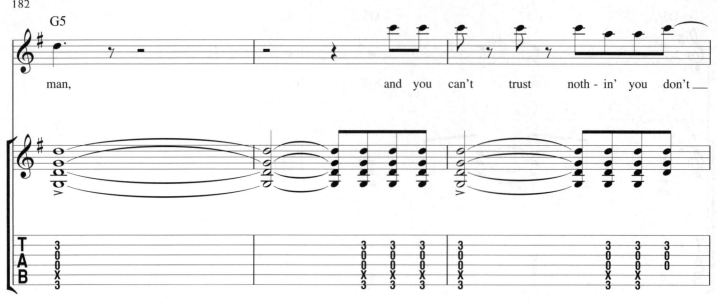

and you can't trust noth-in' you don't___

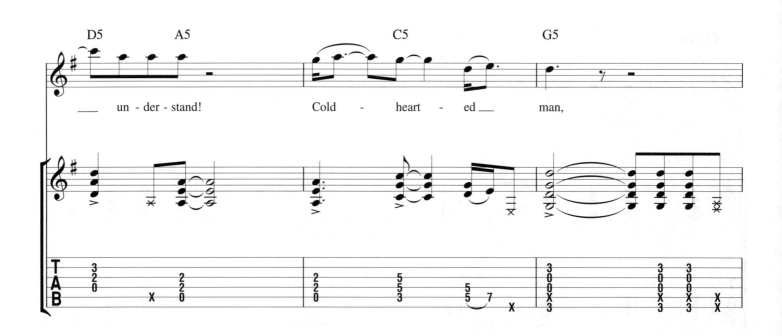

___ un-der-stand! Cold - heart - ed ___ man,

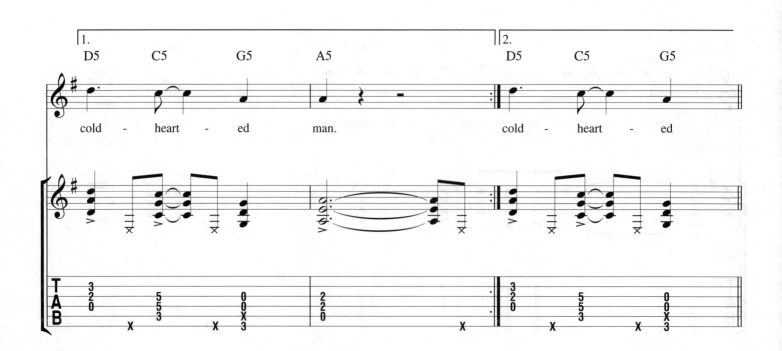

cold - heart - ed man. cold - heart - ed

Bridge

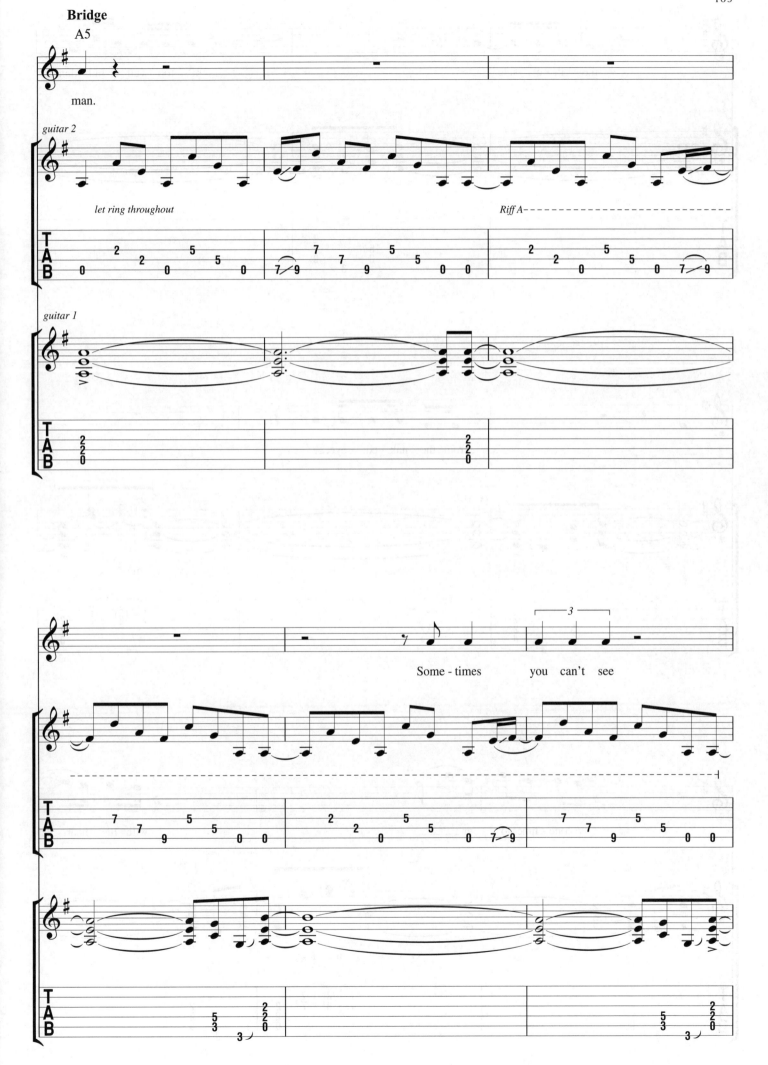

184

w/Riff A (Guitar 2) 3 times

the oth - er side, ___   it's too well ___ hid - den ___

guitar 1

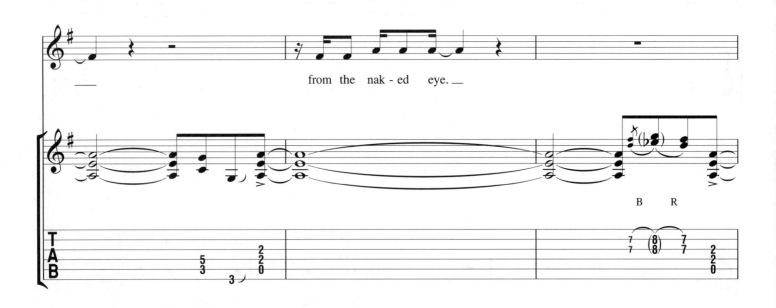

___   from the nak - ed eye. ___

B   R

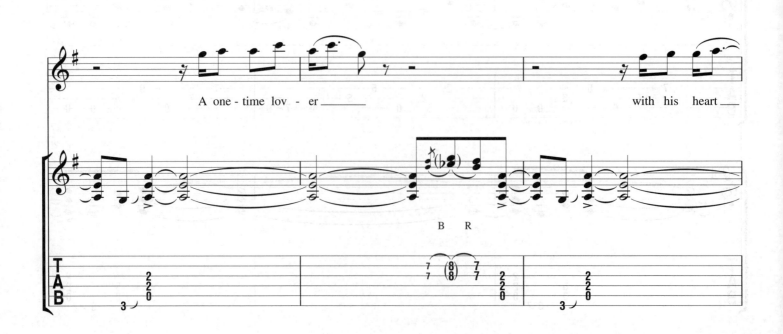

A one - time lov - er ___   with his heart ___

B   R

185

in his hand.

Two - time los - er,

C5   D5

a   brok - en   man.

guitar 2

guitar 1

Outro Chorus

A5 C5   G5

Cold - heart - ed   man,   he was a

*guitars 1 and 2

*Composite arrangement

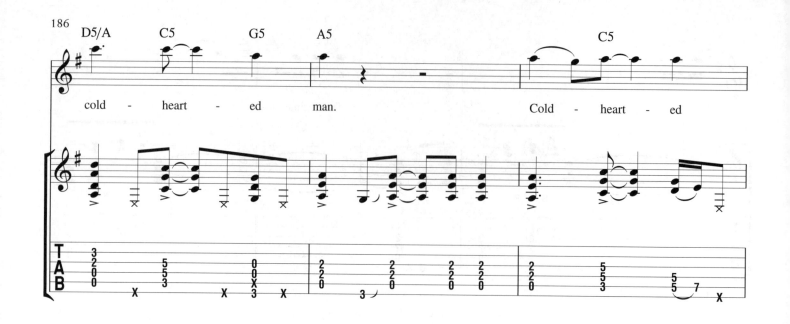

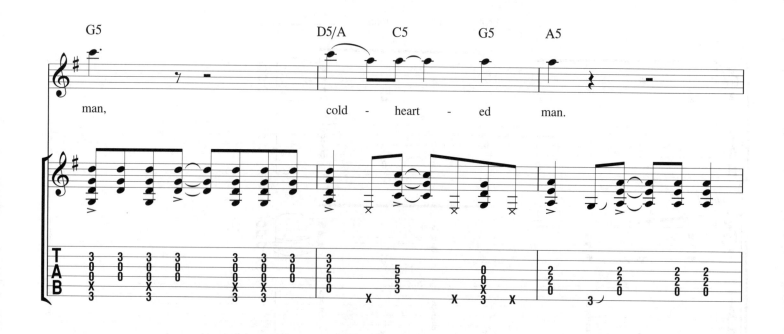

man.   Cold - heart - ed ___ man,

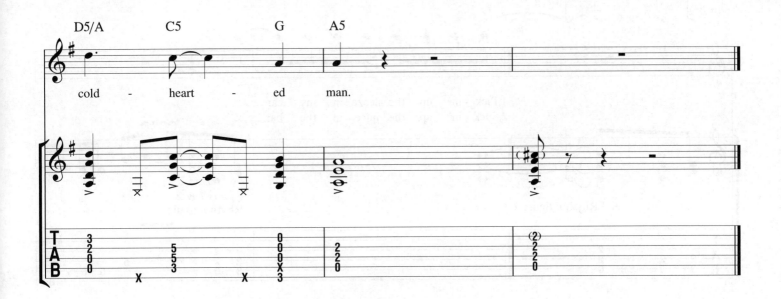

cold - heart - ed man.

Additional lyrics

2. Like a snake, he had no friends
   He didn't need no one
   Hurt his pride deep inside
   He was another mother's son
   Reputation, broken glass
   Everybody prayed
   For their lives on the street
       where they happened to meet
   Leroy Kincaid

Come And Get It

By Angus Young & Malcolm Young

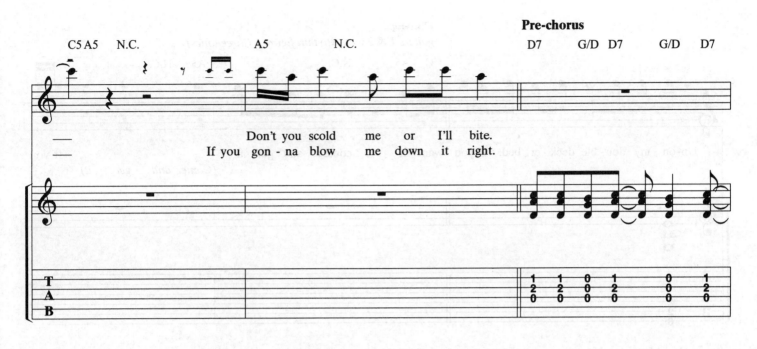

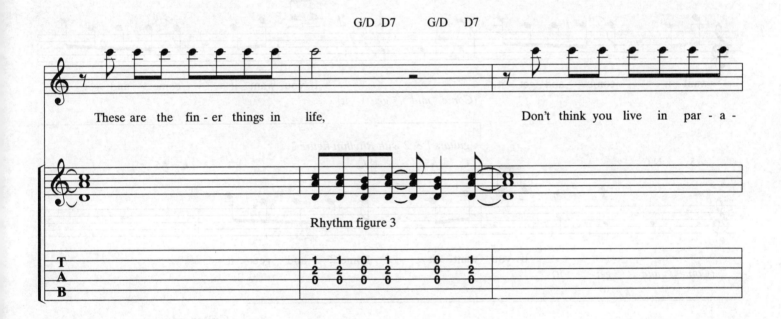

Come and get me!

193

Crabsody In Blue

By Angus Young, Malcolm Young and Bon Scott

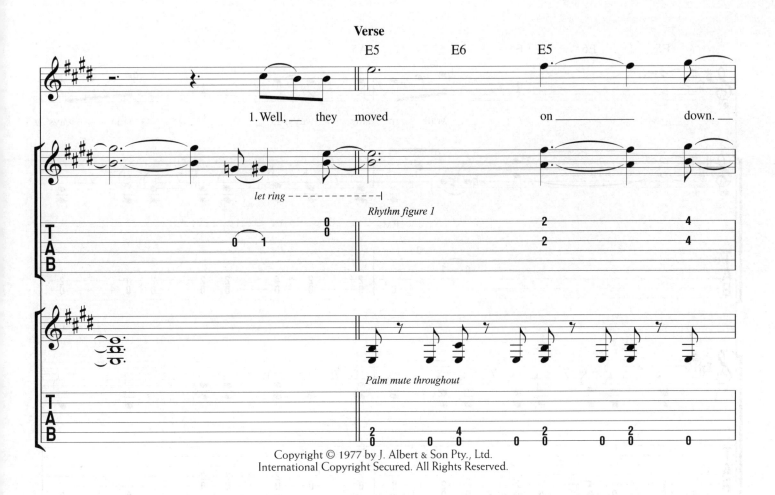

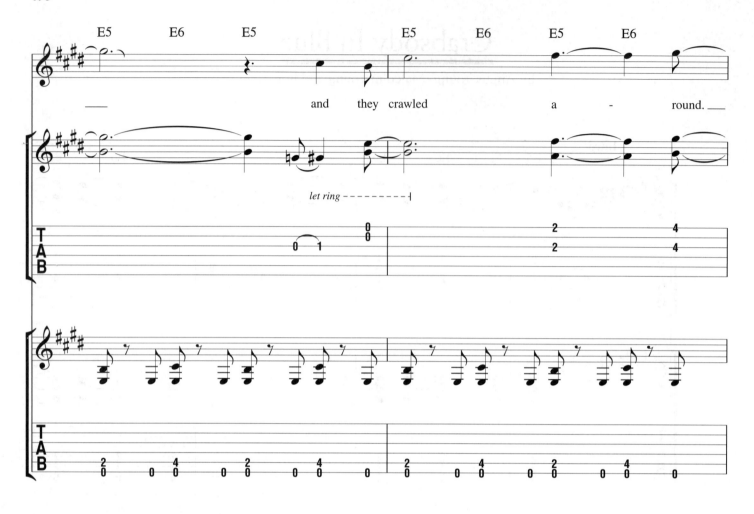

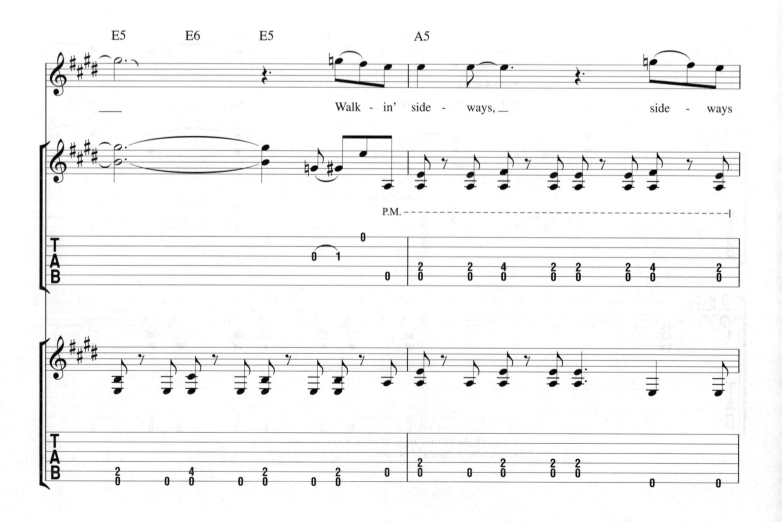

walk - in', _   give me the blues. _____   2. And you

Verse
w/Rhythm figure 1 (Guitar 1)

start   to _____ scratch _   when they start   to _____ hatch. _

guitar 2

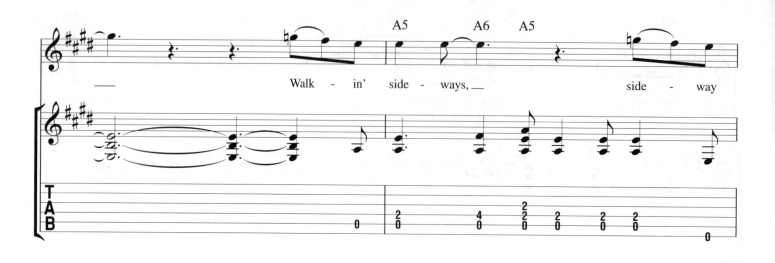

Chorus

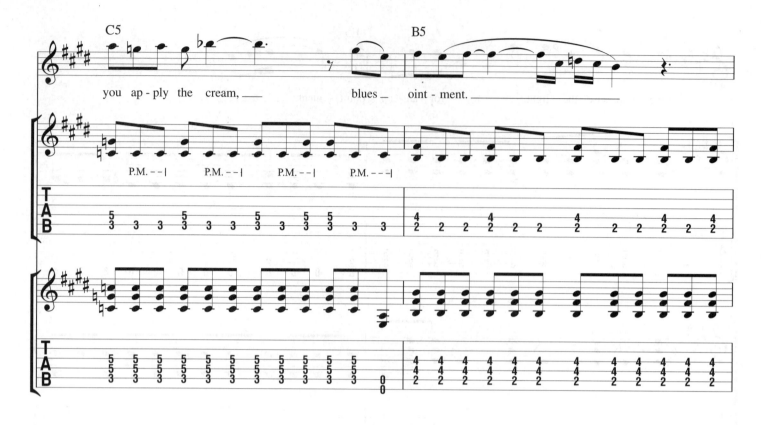

you ap-ply the cream, ____ blues ____ oint - ment. ____

Guitar solo

w/Rhythm figure 1 (Guitar 1) first 7 bars

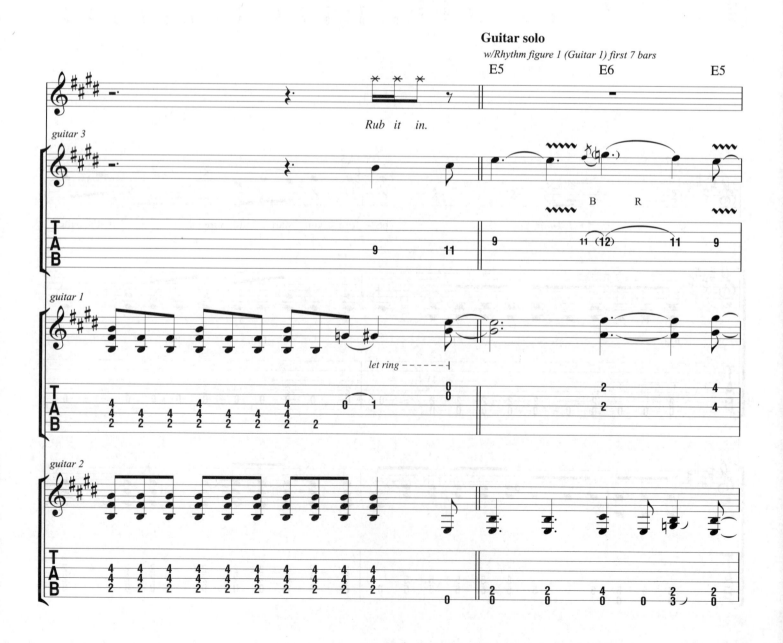

Rub it in.

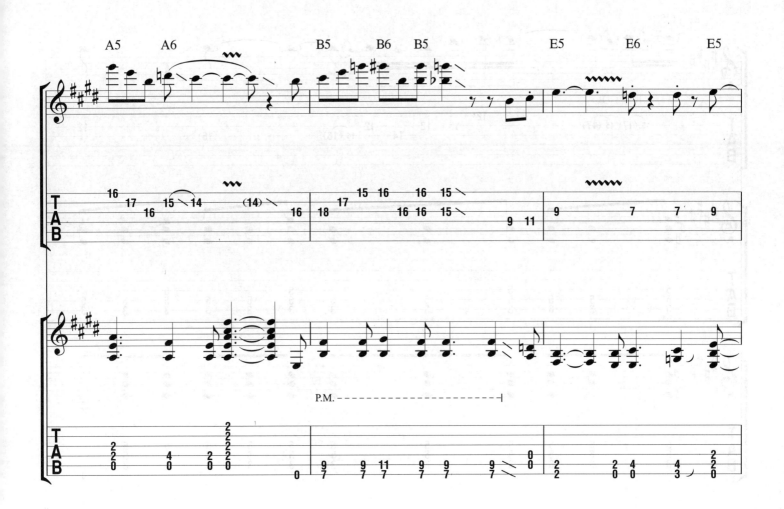

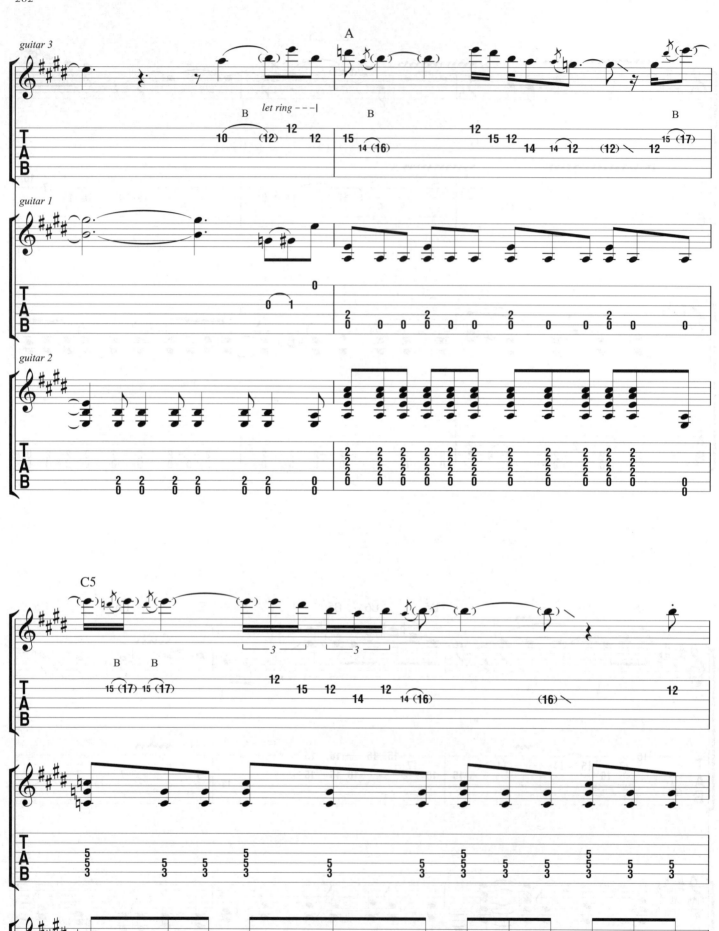

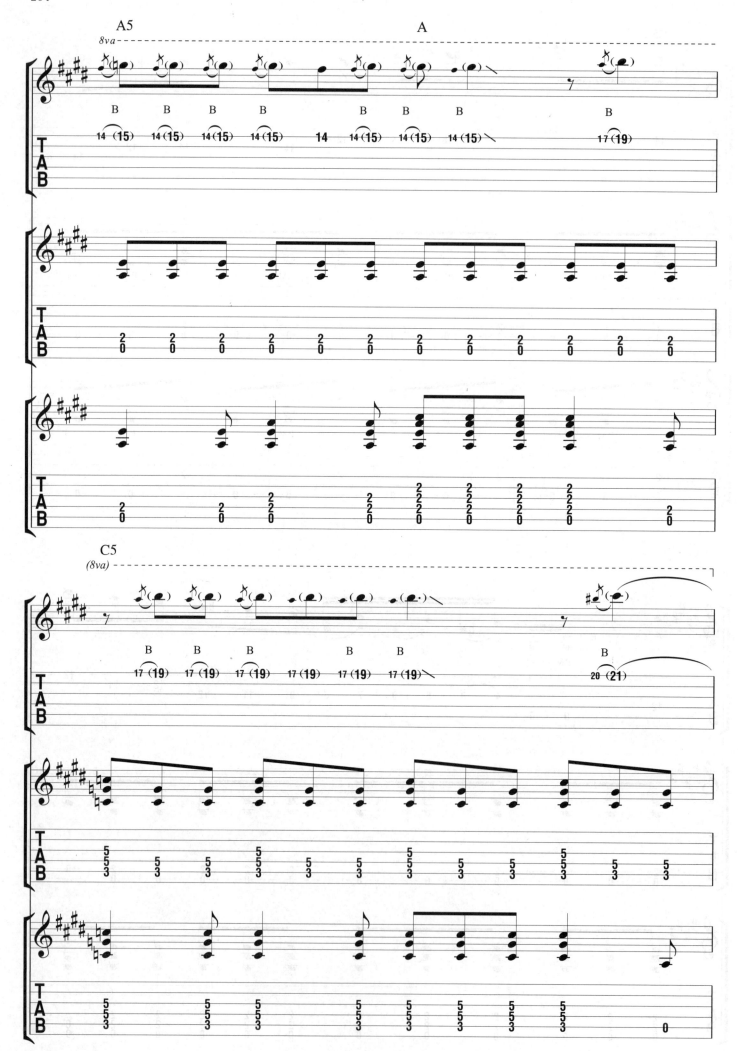

Verse
w/Rhythm figure 1 (Guitar 1)

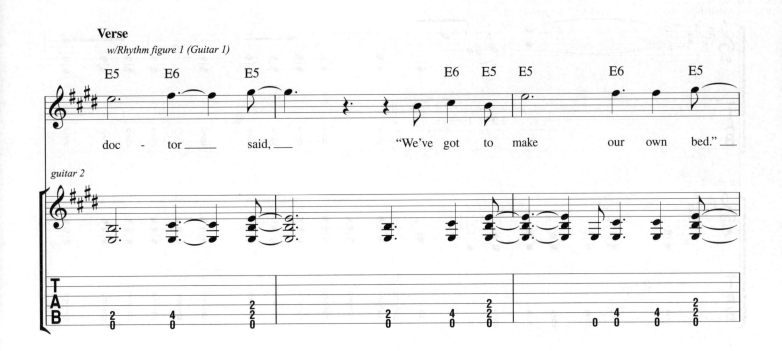

doc - tor ___ said, ___ "We've got to make our own bed." ___

206

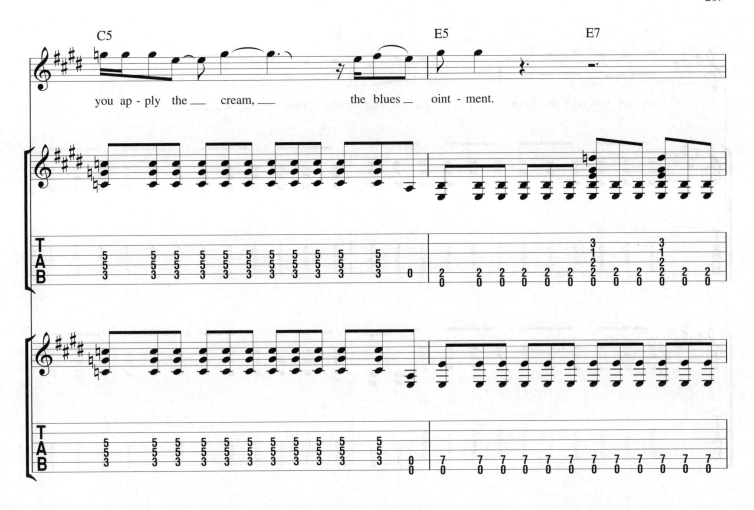

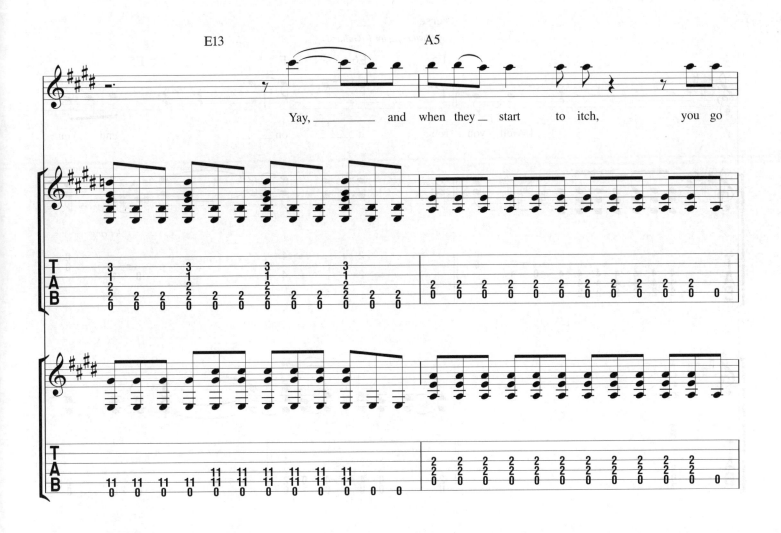

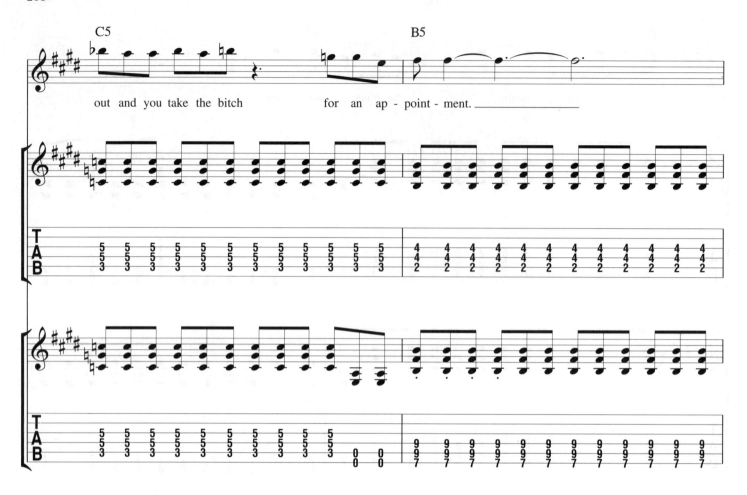

out and you take the bitch for an ap-point-ment. _____

Verse

w/Rhythm figure 1 (Guitar 1)

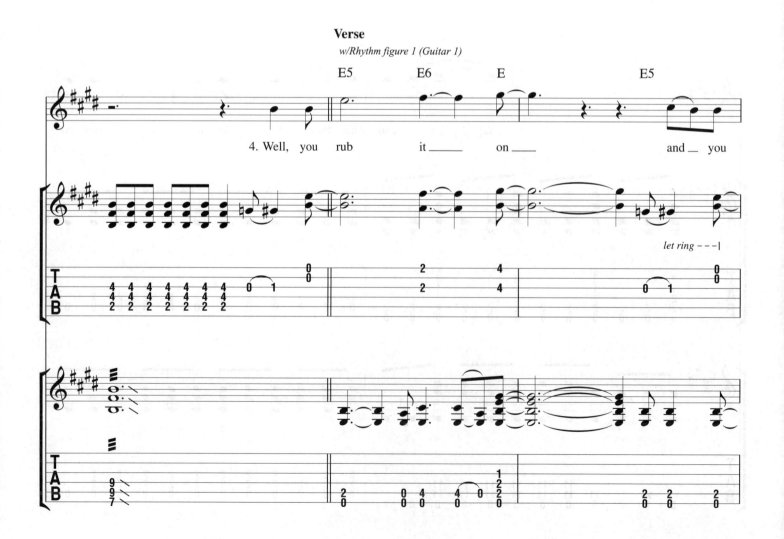

4. Well, you rub it ____ on ____ and ___ you

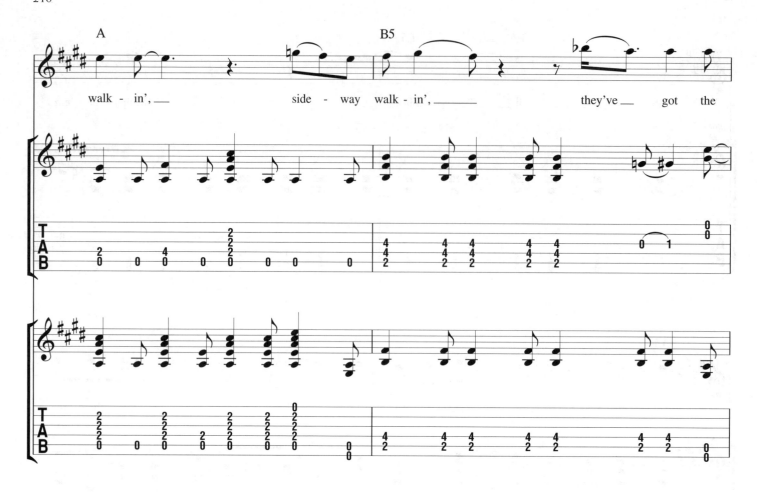

walk - in', _____ side - way walk - in', _____ they've _ got the

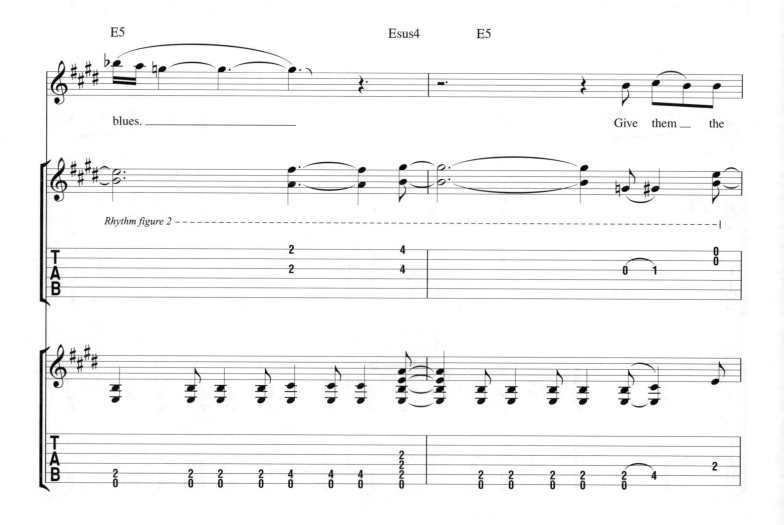

blues. _____ Give them _ the

Cover You In Oil

By Angus Young and Malcolm Young

hard,   she gon - na like it slow.____
rough,   she give it tough,—

All right, hon - ey,   come on let's__ go!
come on, hon - ey,   and strut your stuff!

Pre-chorus

Ba - by,____   feel what you want,____   it's the

guitars 1 & 2

216

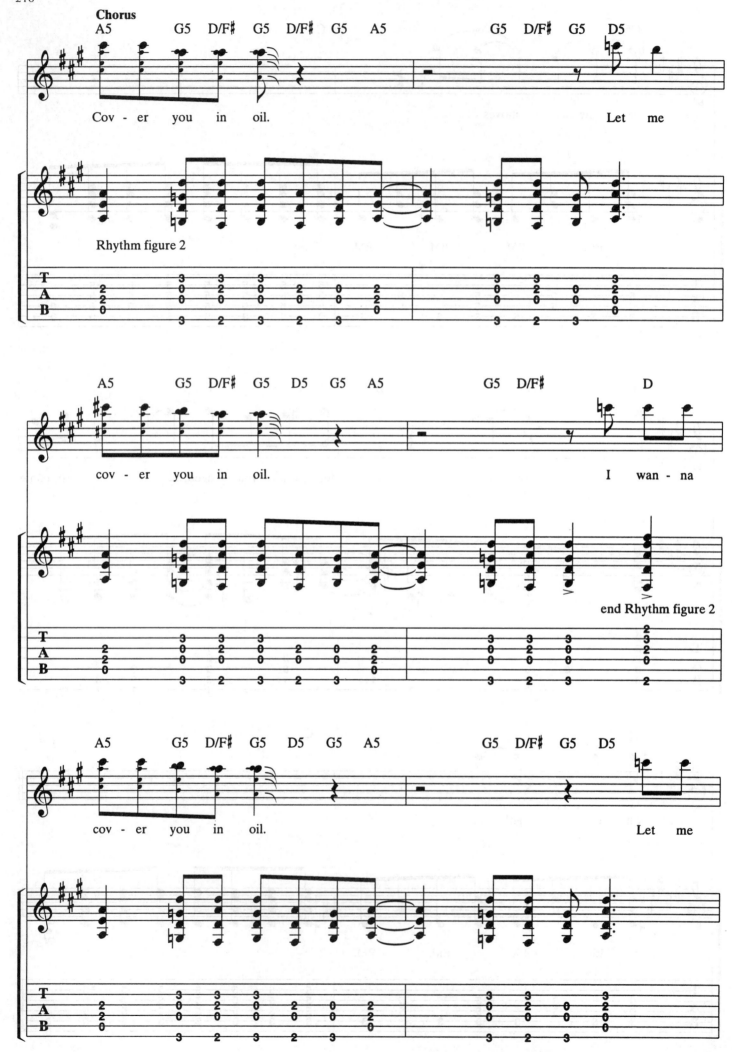

Guitar solo
guitars 1 & 2 with Rhythm figures 1 & 1a (two times)

220

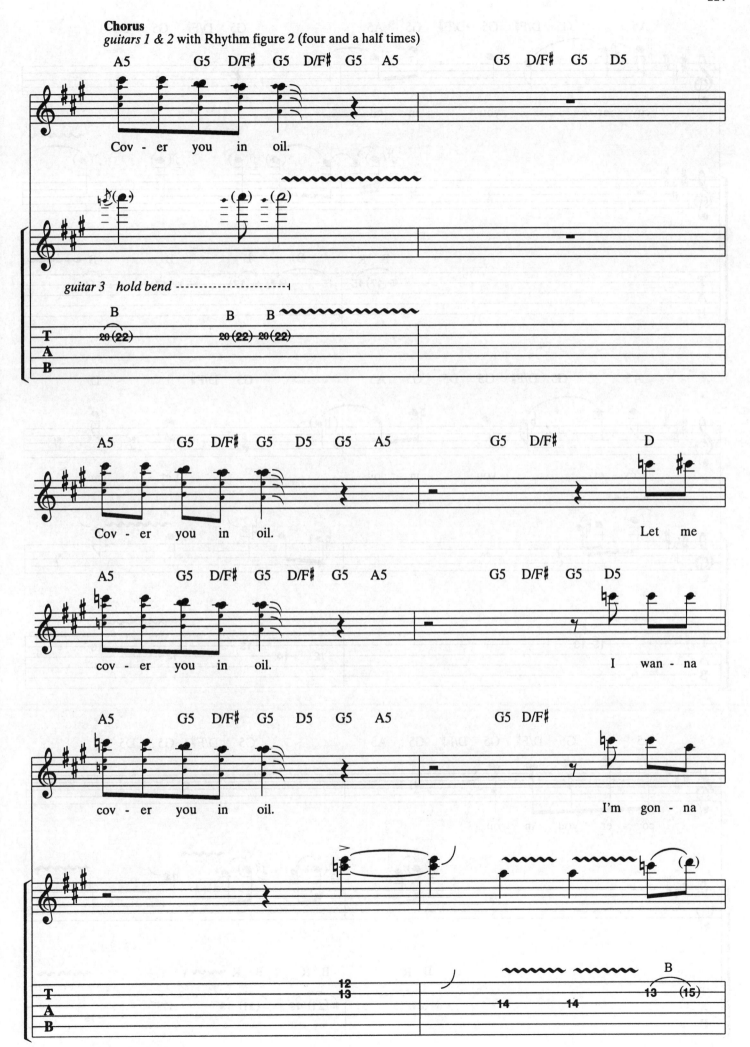

Dirty Deeds Done Dirt Cheap

By Angus Young, Malcolm Young and Bon Scott

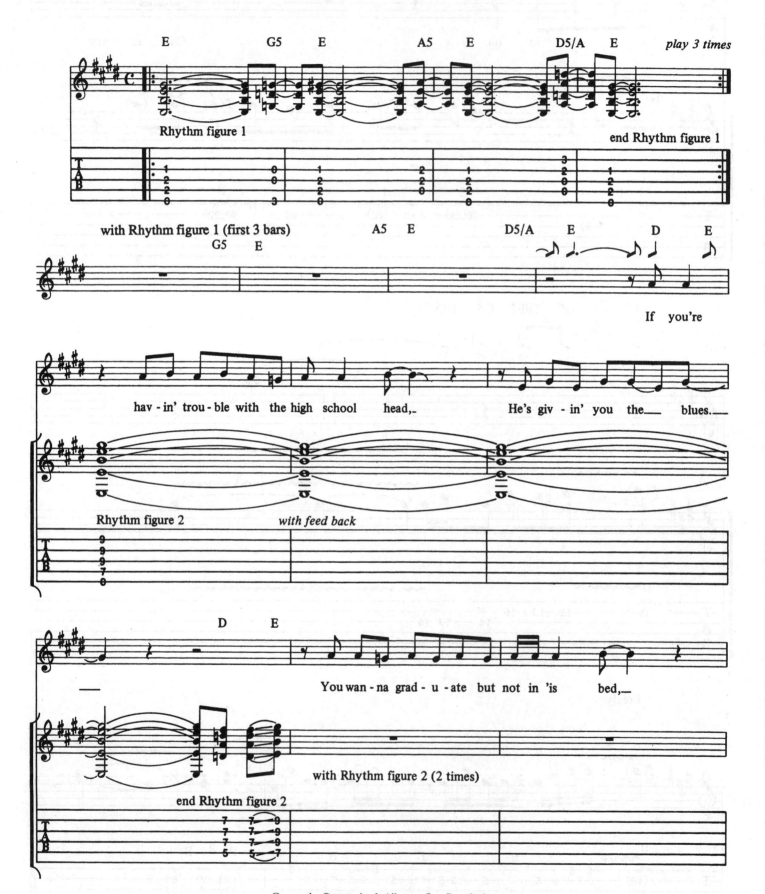

225

226

228

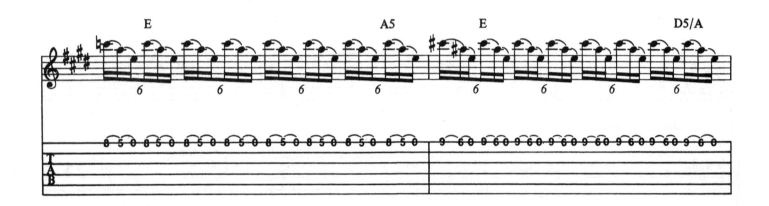

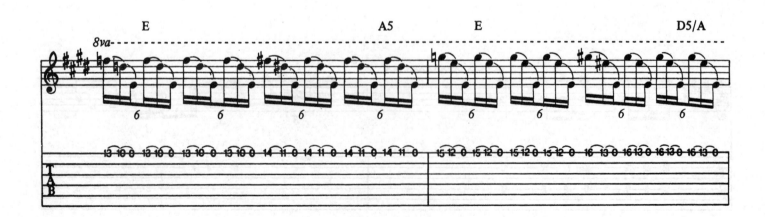

230

Dog Eat Dog

By Angus Young, Malcolm Young and Bon Scott

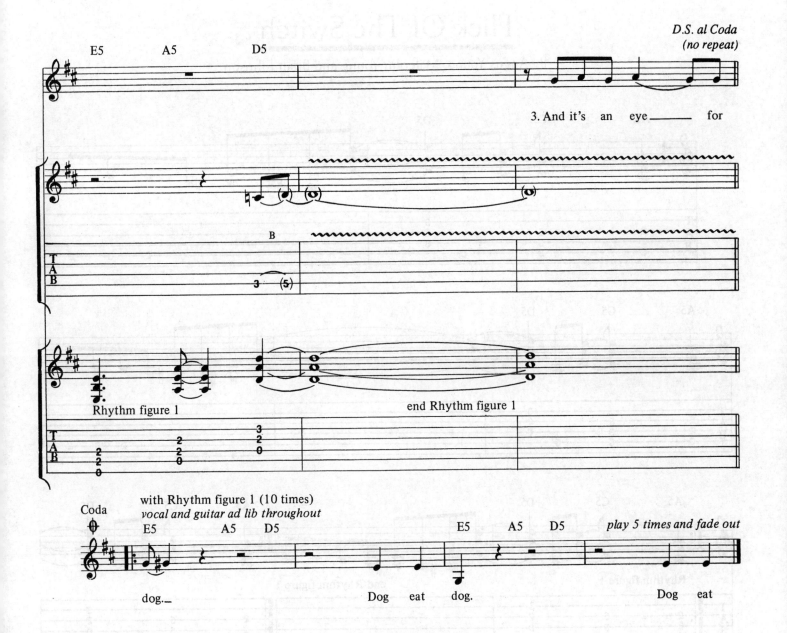

D.S. al Coda
(no repeat)

E5   A5   D5

3. And it's an eye_____ for

Rhythm figure 1

end Rhythm figure 1

Coda

with Rhythm figure 1 (10 times)
vocal and guitar ad lib throughout

E5   A5   D5   E5   A5   D5   *play 5 times and fade out*

dog.___   Dog   eat   dog.   Dog   eat

Additional Lyrics

2. Dog eat dog, read the news,
   Some will win, some will lose.
   Up's above and down's below,
   And middle's in between.
   Up you win and down you lose,
   It's anybody's game.

3. And it's a eye for eye, tooth for tooth,
   It's a lie, that's the truth.
   See the blind man on the street,
   Looking for something free.
   Well, the kind man asks his friends,
   "Hey, what's in it for me?"

Flick Of The Switch

By Angus Young, Malcolm Young and Brian Johnson

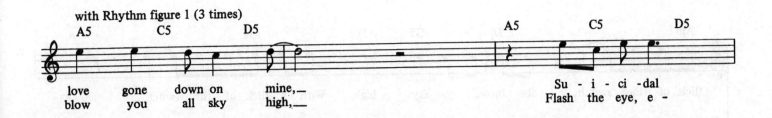

with Rhythm figure 1 (3 times)

love gone down on mine,—
blow you all sky high,—

Su - i - ci - dal
Flash the eye, e -

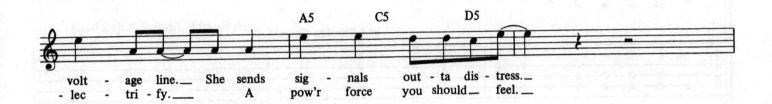

volt - age line.— She sends sig - nals out - ta dis - tress.—
- lec - tri - fy.— A pow'r force you should— feel.—

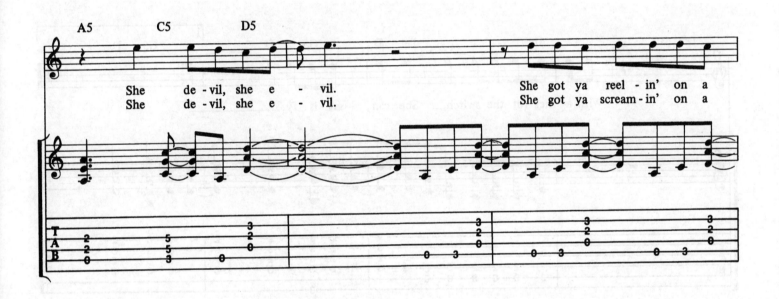

She de - vil, she e - vil.
She de - vil, she e - vil.

She got ya reel - in' on a
She got ya scream - in' on a

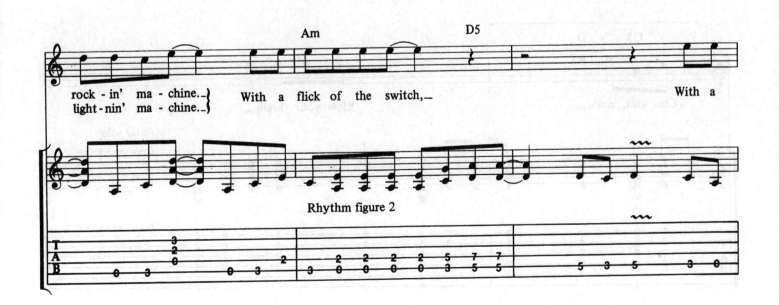

rock - in' ma - chine.—
light - nin' ma - chine.—

With a flick of the switch,—

With a

Rhythm figure 2

flick of the switch,_ She blow_ ya sky high. With a flick of the switch,_

end Rhythm figure 2   with Rhythm figure 2 (first 2 bars)

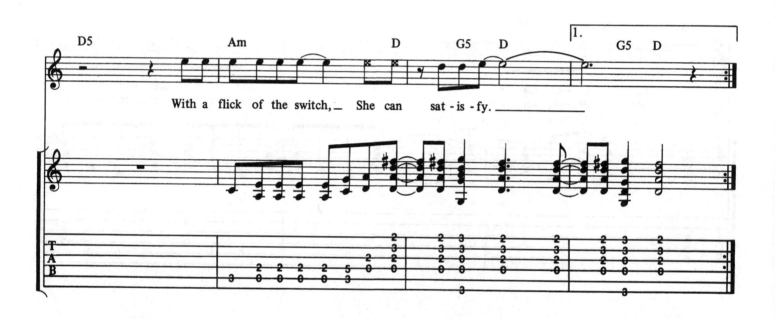

With a flick of the switch,_ She can sat-is-fy._

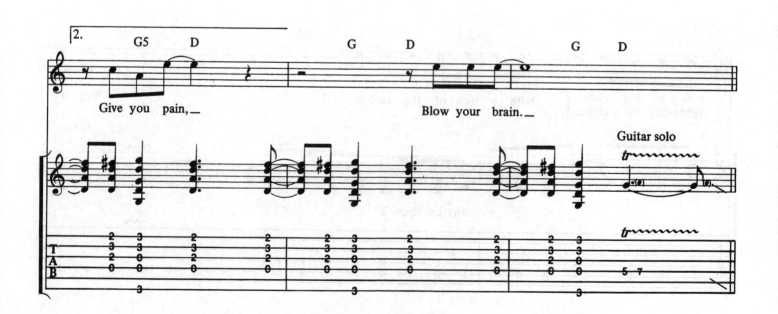

Give you pain,_   Blow your brain._

Guitar solo

240

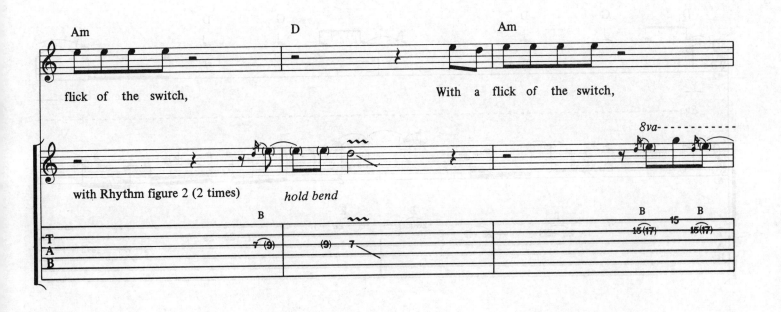

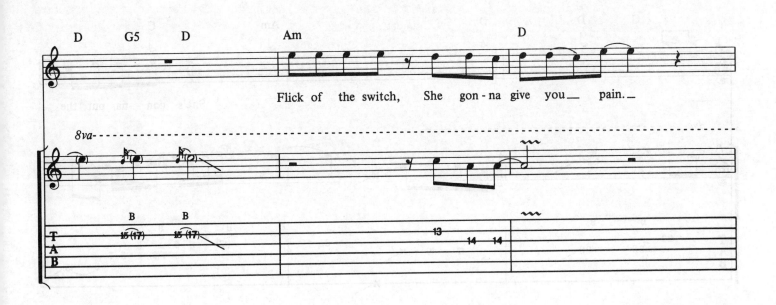

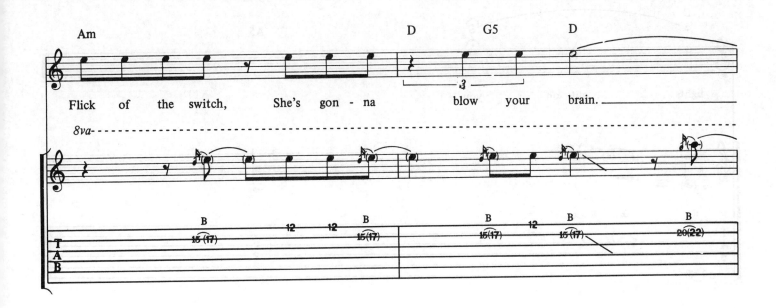

D G D G D
Blow your brain.
8va
G D D Am C
FREE
She's gon - na put the
8va
D A5
lights out on you.

Evil Walks

By Angus Young, Malcolm Young and Brian Johnson

244

ritard.

Additional lyrics

2. Black widow weaving new emotions,
   Dark secrets being spun in your web.
   You'll learn going down in your ocean,
   I can't swim, 'cause I'm tied to your back.

For Those About To Rock (We Salute You)

By Angus Young, Malcolm Young and Brian Johnson

Verse

254

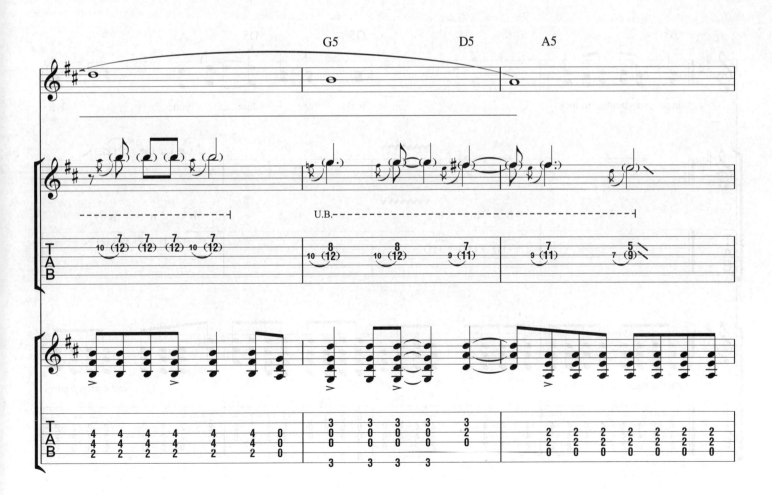

258

We sa - lute _____ you. _____

Given The Dog A Bone

By Angus Young and Malcolm Young and Brian Johnson

264

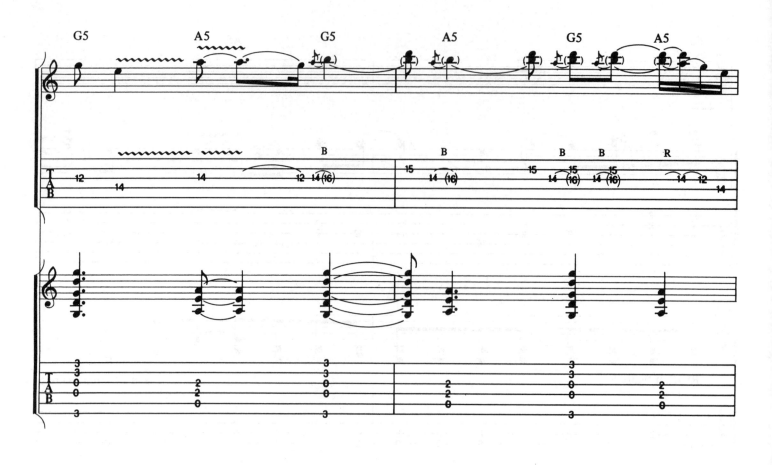

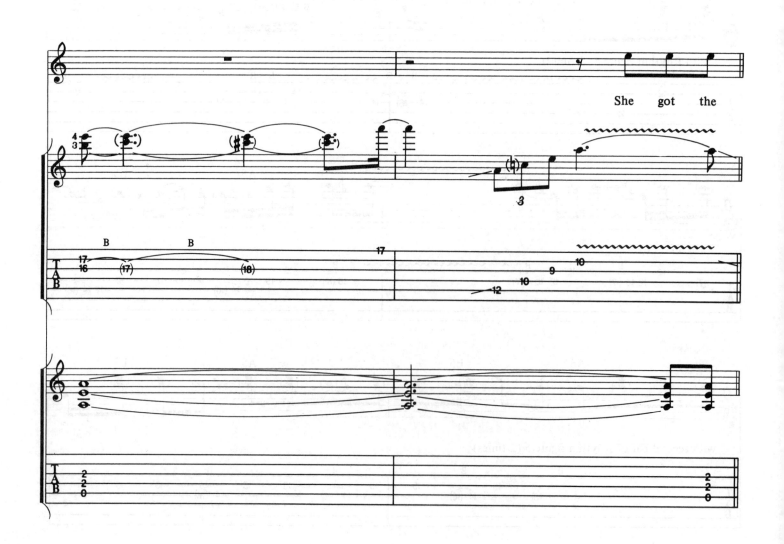

She got the

Get It Hot

By Angus Young, Malcolm Young and Bon Scott

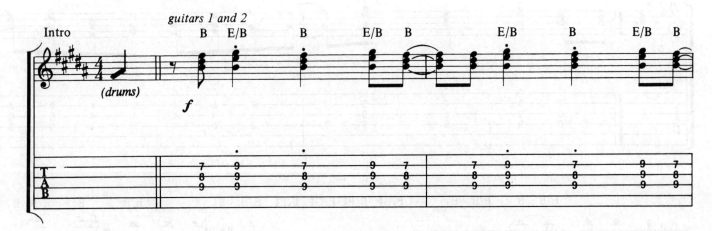

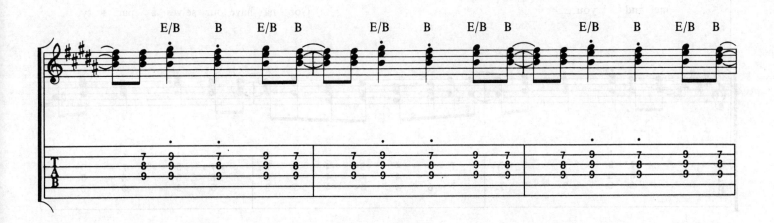

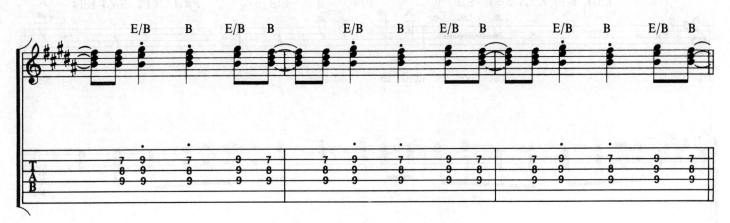

272

274

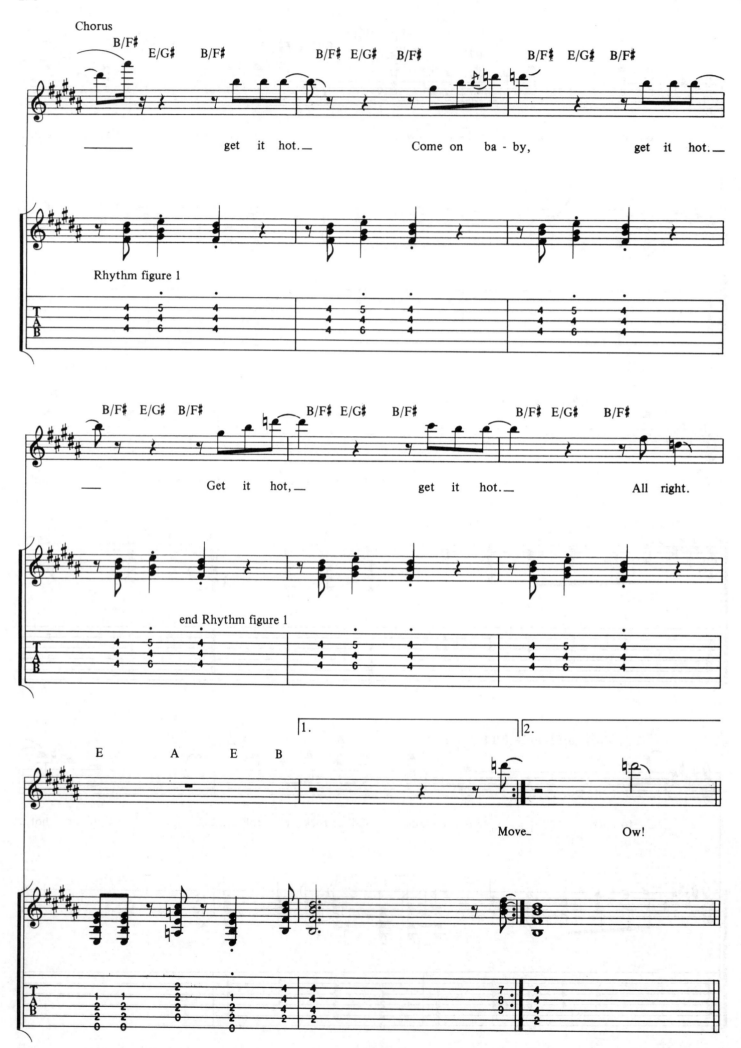

Additional Lyrics

2. Move around the motorway,
   Got a whole lotta booze.
   Got myself a sweet little number,
   Who's got nothin' to lose.
   Gonna bend you like a G string,
   Conduct you like a fire.
   So get your body in the right place,
   We'll set the world on fire.

Girls Got Rhythm

By Angus Young, Malcolm Young and Bon Scott

2. Guitar solo

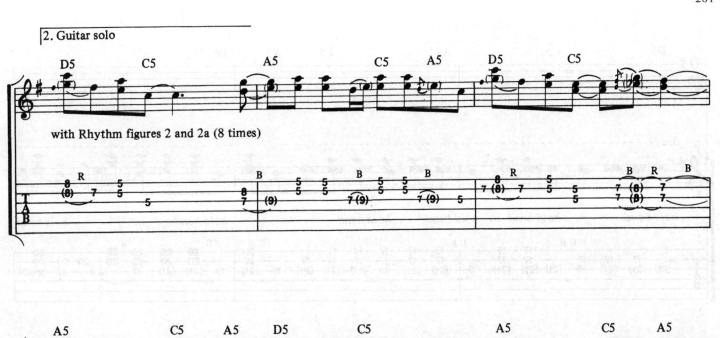

with Rhythm figures 2 and 2a (8 times)

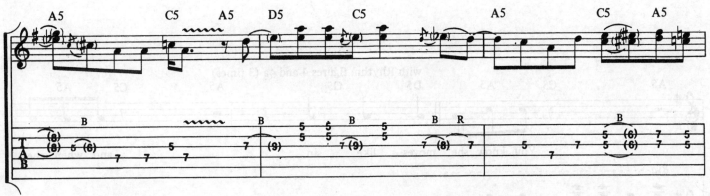

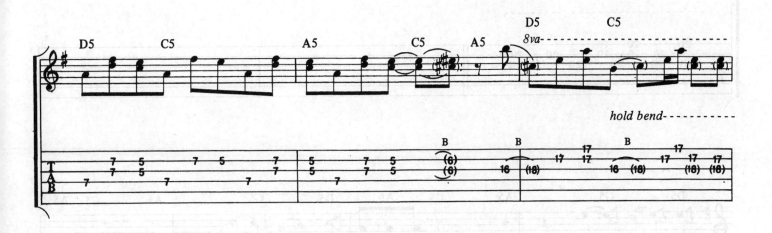

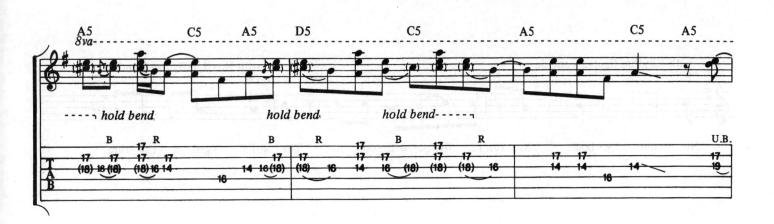

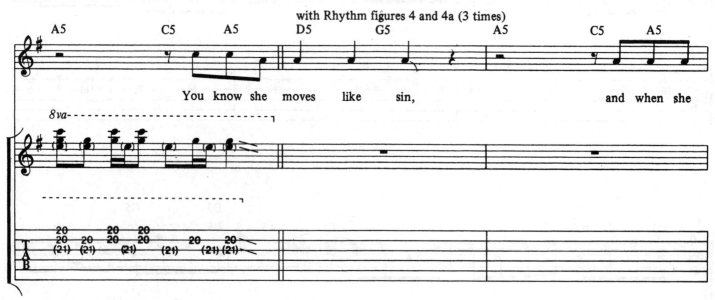

with Rhythm figures 4 and 4a (3 times)

You know she moves like sin, and when she

lets me___ in___ It's like a - liq - uid___ love.

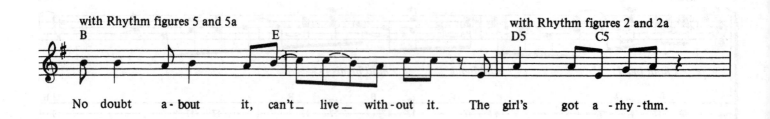

with Rhythm figures 5 and 5a

with Rhythm figures 2 and 2a

No doubt a - bout it, can't___ live___ with-out it. The girl's got a - rhy -thm.

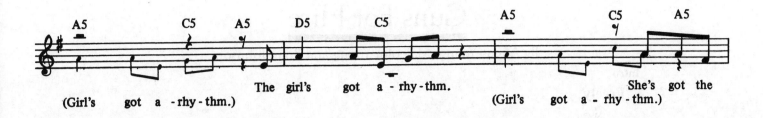

(Girl's got a - rhy-thm.)   The girl's got a - rhy-thm.   (Girl's got a - rhy-thm.)   She's got the

back seat a - rhy-thm.   (Back seat a - rhy-thm.)   The girl's got a - rhy-thm.__

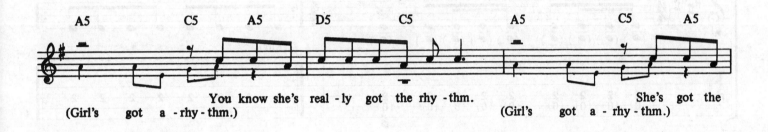

(Girl's got a - rhy-thm.)   You know she's real - ly got the rhy-thm.   (Girl's got a - rhy-thm.)   She's got the

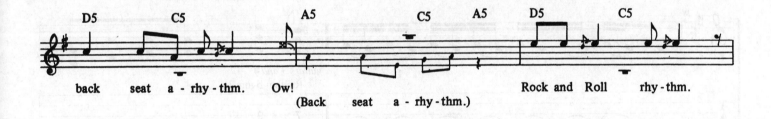

back seat a - rhy-thm. Ow!   (Back seat a - rhy-thm.)   Rock and Roll rhy-thm.

with Rhythm figures 3 and 3a

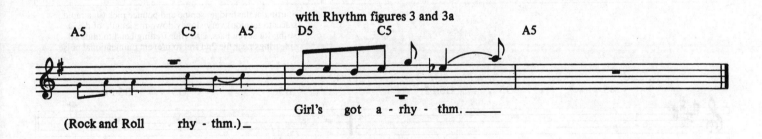

(Rock and Roll rhy - thm.) _   Girl's got a - rhy-thm. _____

Additional Lyrics

2. She's like a lethal brand, too much for any man.
She gives me first degree, she really satisfies me.
Loves me till I'm legless, achin' and sore.
Enough to stop a freight train or start the third world war.
You know I'm losin' sleep but I'm in too deep,
Like a body needs blood.

Guns For Hire

By Angus Young, Malcolm Young and Brian Johnson

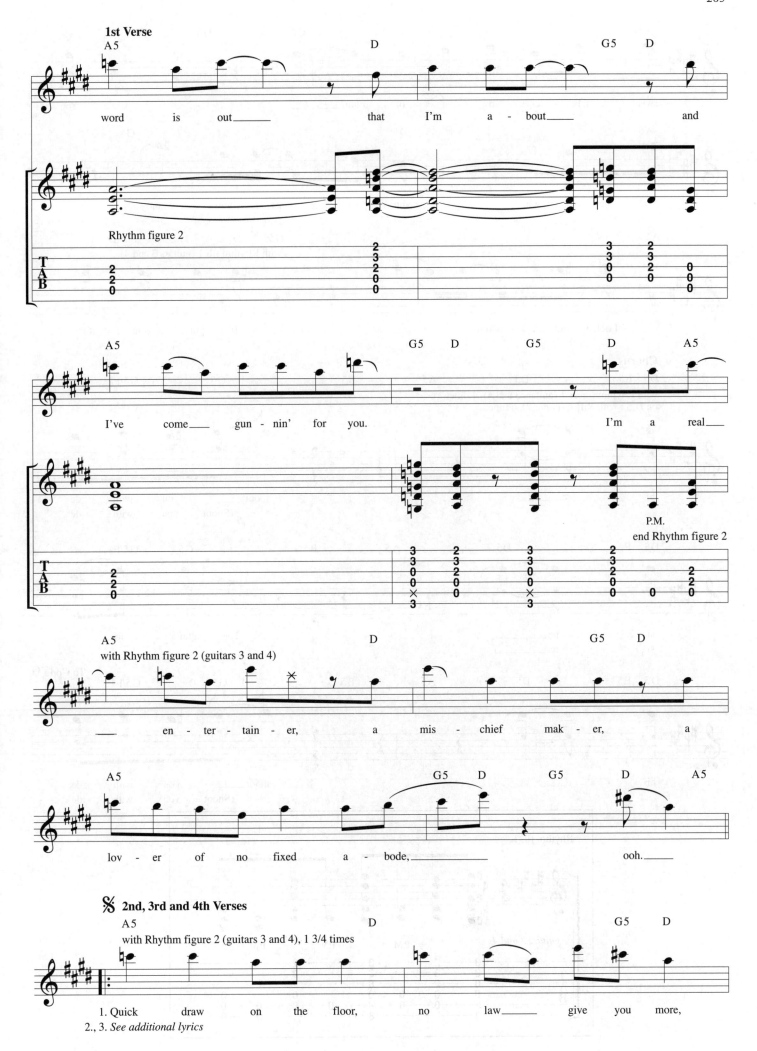

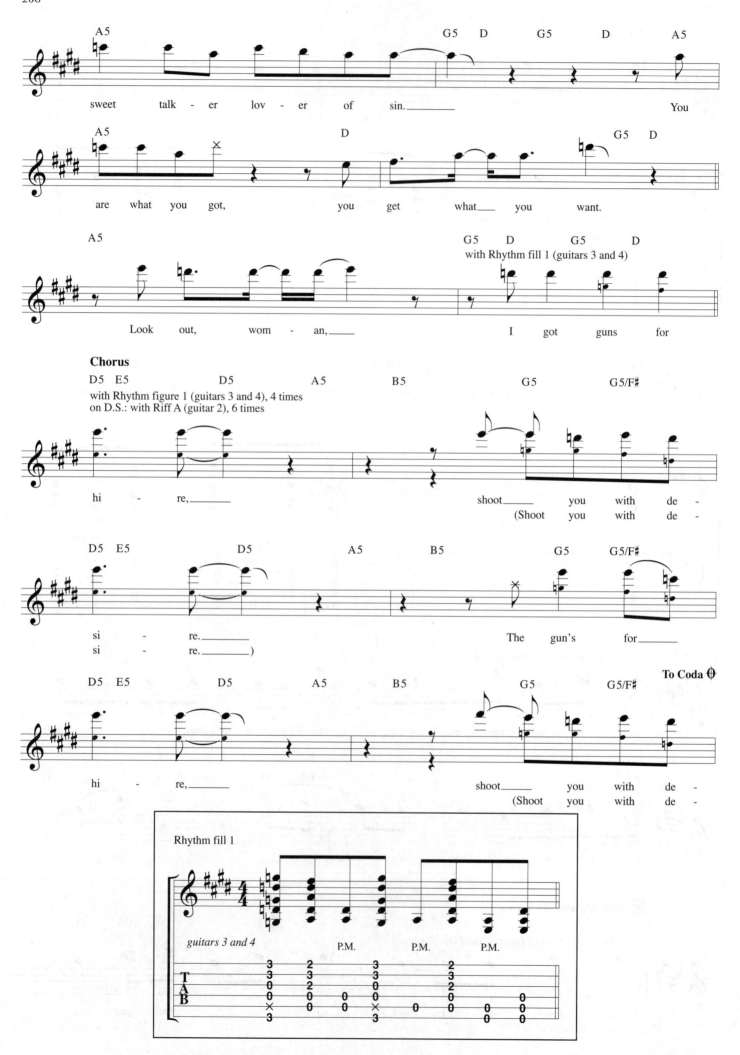

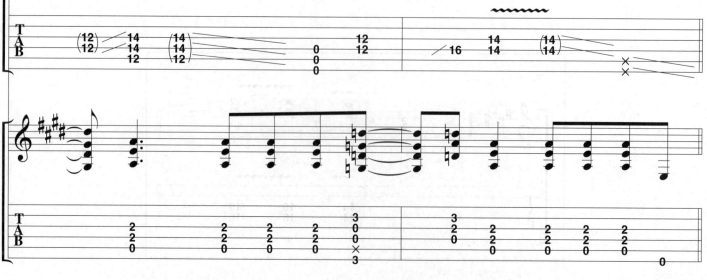

Guitar Solo

Outro Chorus

Freely

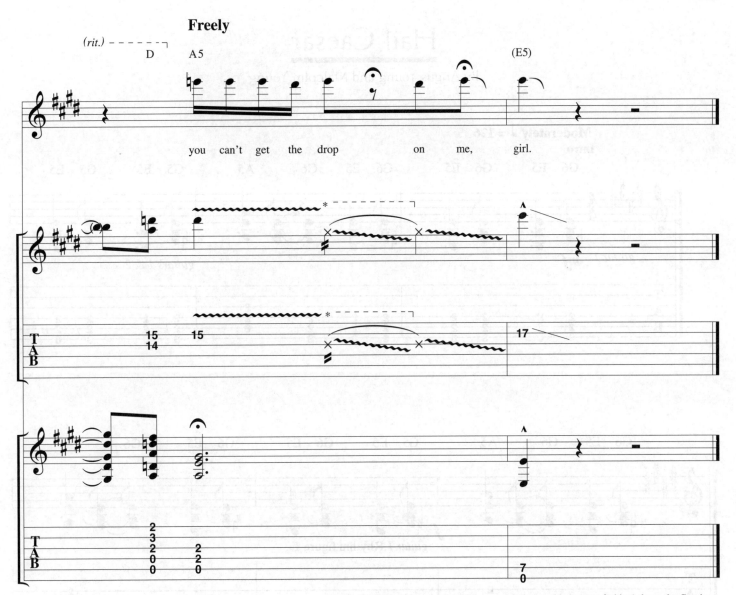

you can't get the drop on me, girl.

*Starting at the bridge, scrape and bounce pick (in a rapid, staccato fashion) down the G string, gradually moving over the pickups. On beat 4, continue pick scrape in regular fashion.

Additional Lyrics

2. I'm a wanted poster, a needed man,
   Running right across the land.
   I'm a smooth operator, a big dictator,
   Gonna mark you with my brand.
   My gun's for...

3. Hot to trot, big shot, take a lot,
   Never get the drop on me.
   I'm a real entertainer, mischief maker,
   Lover in seven languages.
   My gun's for...

Hail Caesar

By Angus Young and Malcolm Young

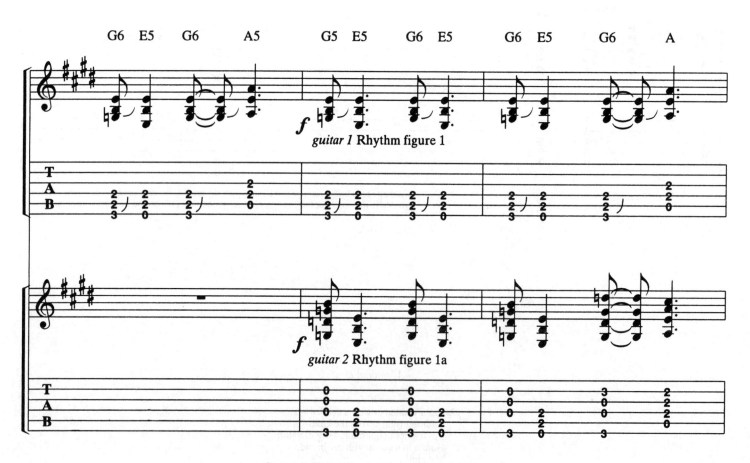

end Rhythm figure 1

end Rhythm figure 1a

Chorus

302

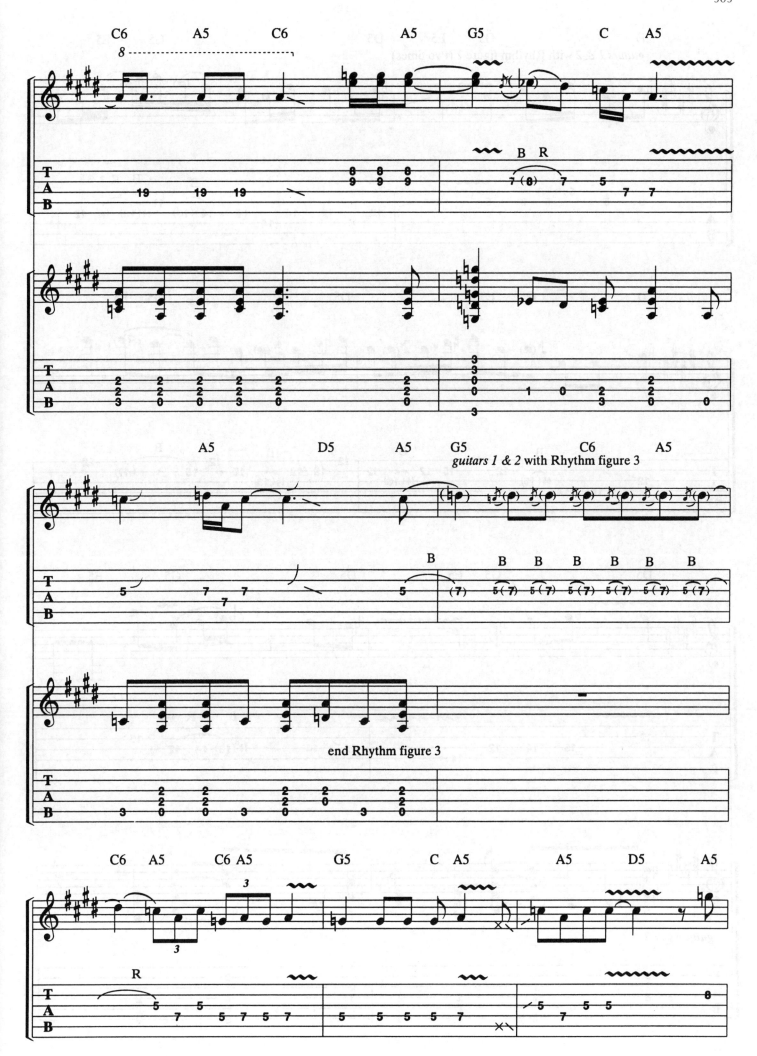

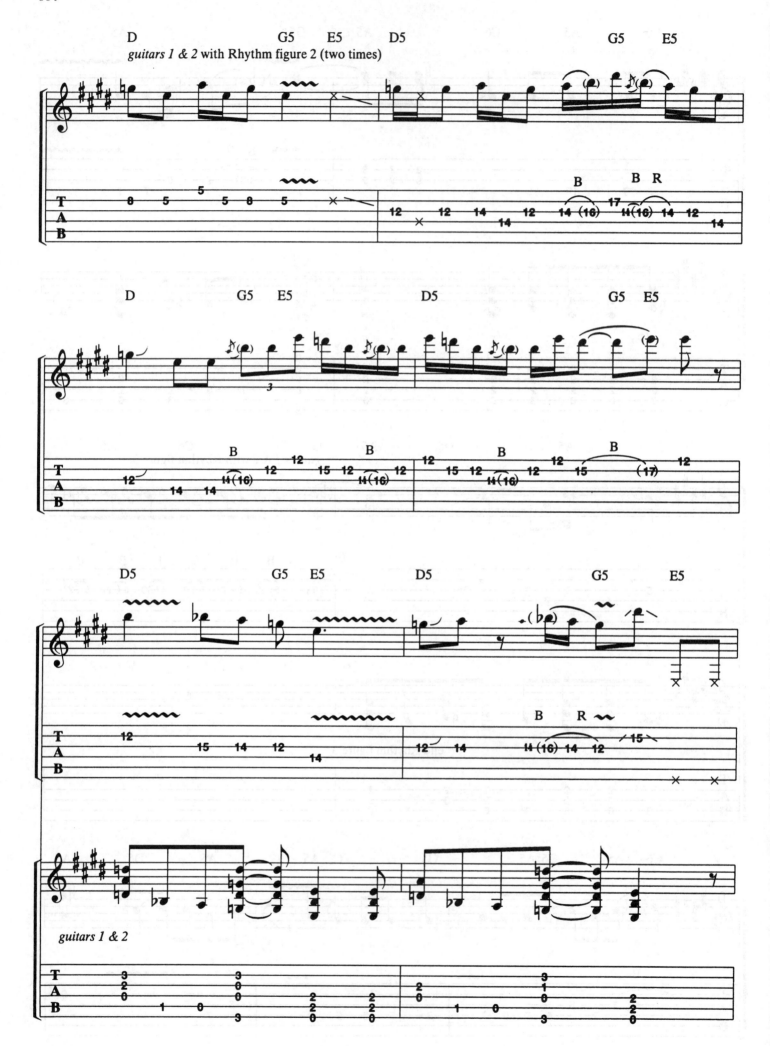

306

Verse 3

Down   at   the   ep - i - cen - ter

guitars 1 & 2

flip toggle switch as fast as possible

bass arranged for guitar

314

You need eyes—— on the back of your head, boy.

You're dead.

*flip toggle switch.

*slide while trilling and flipping
toggle switch as fast as possible.

If You Want Blood (You've Got It)

By Angus Young, Malcolm Young and Bon Scott

Additional Lyrics

2. It's animal,
   Livin' in a human zoo.
   Animal,
   The shit that they toss to you.
   Feelin' like a Christian,
   Locked in a cage.
   Thrown to the lions,
   On the second page.

Hard As A Rock

By Angus Young and Malcolm Young

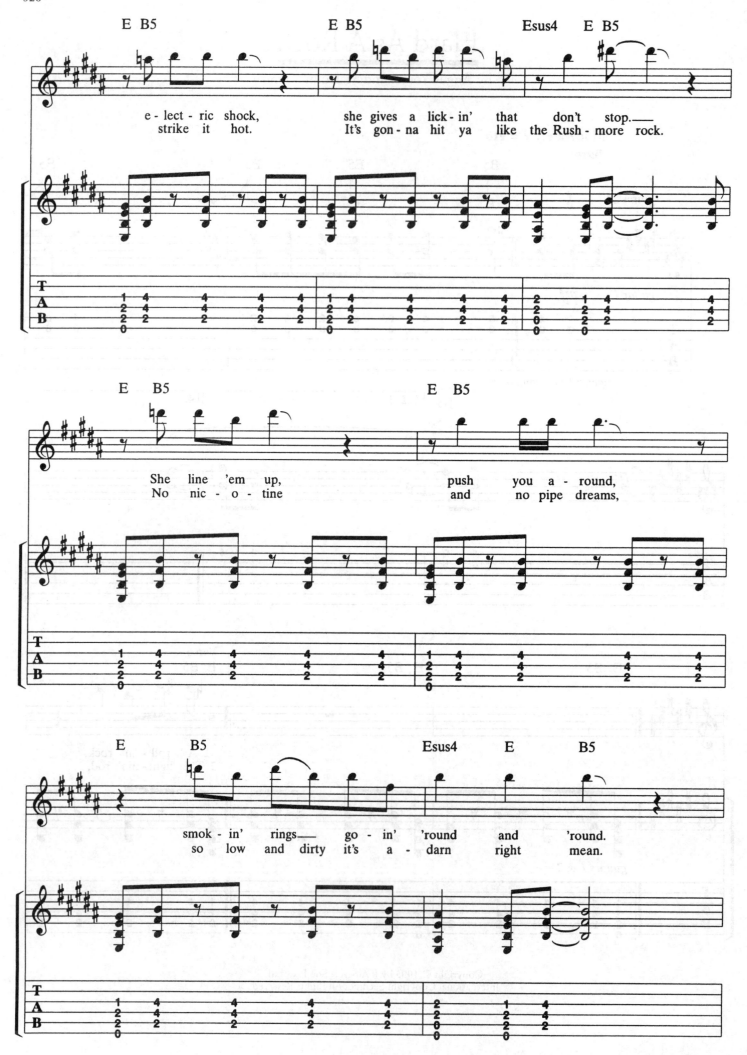

Guitar solo
guitar 1 with Riff A

Fill 1

334

Hard - er than a rock.

Well, I'm hard - er than a rock.

Hard-

Fill 2

guitar 1

Have A Drink On Me

By Angus Young and Malcolm Young and Brian Johnson

Heatseeker

By Angus Young, Malcolm Young and Brian Johnson

heat - seek - er,   I don't need no

life pre-serv - er.   I don't need no   one to hose_ me_ down,_

with Rhythm figure 1

to hose   me down._   Ooh,_____ they get - tin'

with Rhythm figure 1 (first 3 bars)

_   Ah,   you got it.

351

Hell Ain't A Bad Place To Be

By Angus Young, Malcolm Young and Bon Scott

Don't mind ya play-in' de-mon,_

As long as it's with me.   If this is hell,_ then

you could say,   It's heav-en-ly.   Hell ain't a bad place to

be.

Guitar solo

Rhythm figure 3   end Rhythm figure 3

Hells Bells

By Angus Young, Malcolm Young and Brian Johnson

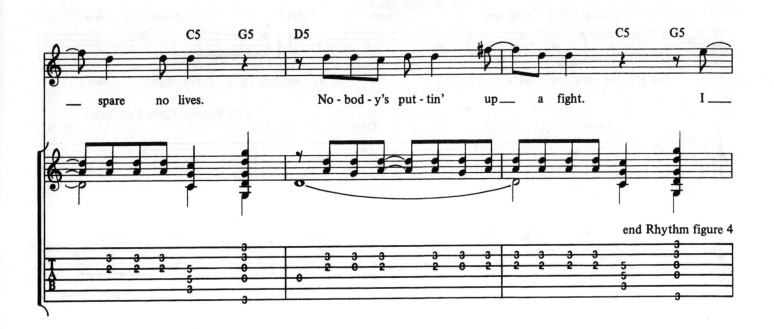

360

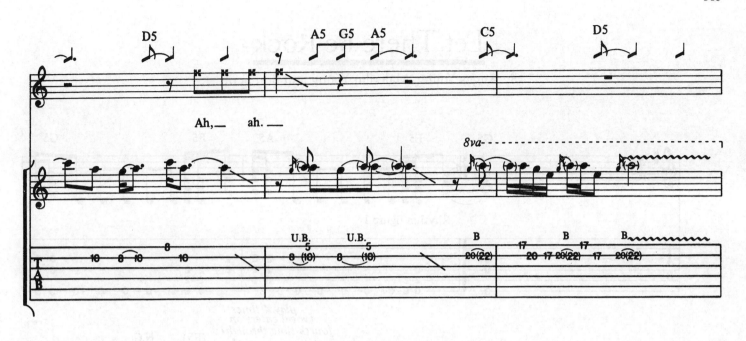

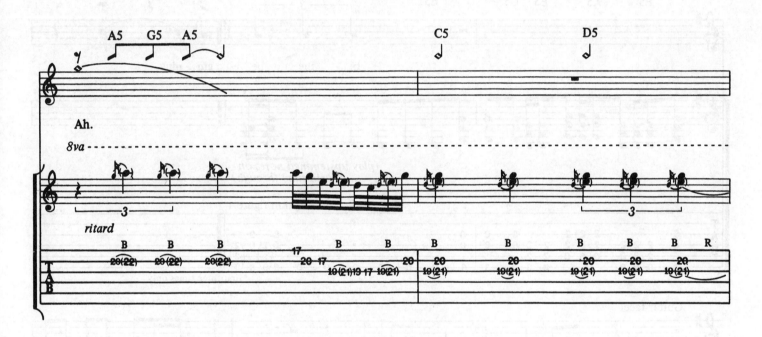

Let There Be Rock

By Angus Young, Malcolm Young and Bon Scott

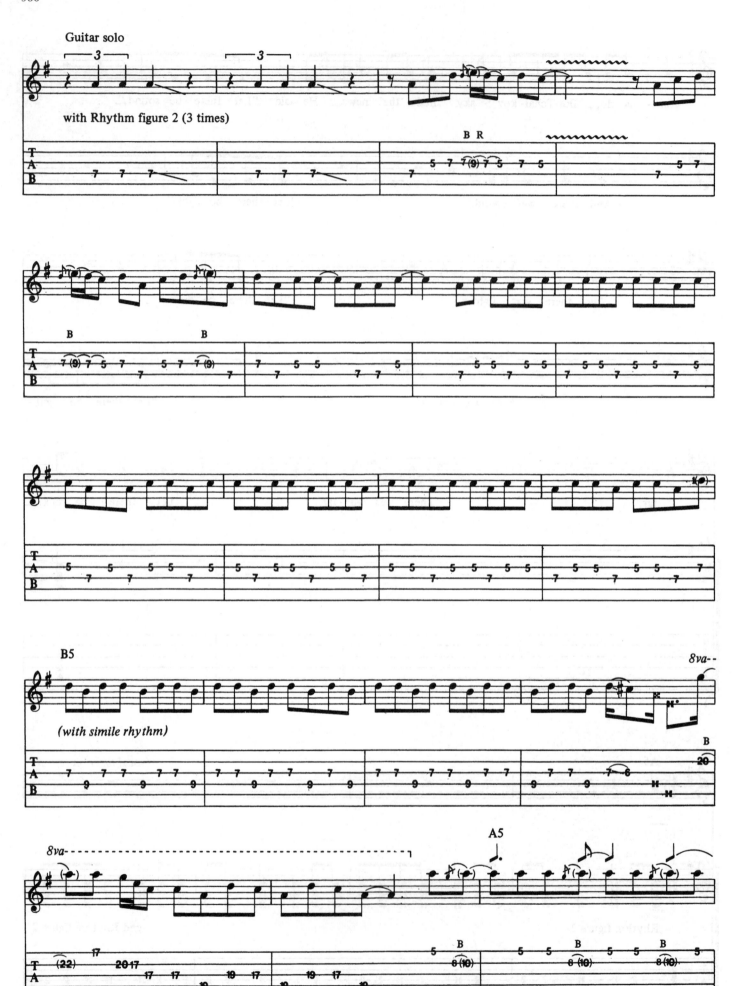

370

(with simile rhythm)

B5

A5

G5

with feedback

a tempo
with Rhythm figure 1 (4 times)

play 4 times
(vocal enters on
fourth time through)

One

High Voltage

By Angus Young, Malcolm Young and Bon Scott

374

Highway To Hell

By Angus Young, Malcolm Young and Bon Scott

379

Hold Me Back

By Angus Young and Malcolm Young

Moderate rock
Intro

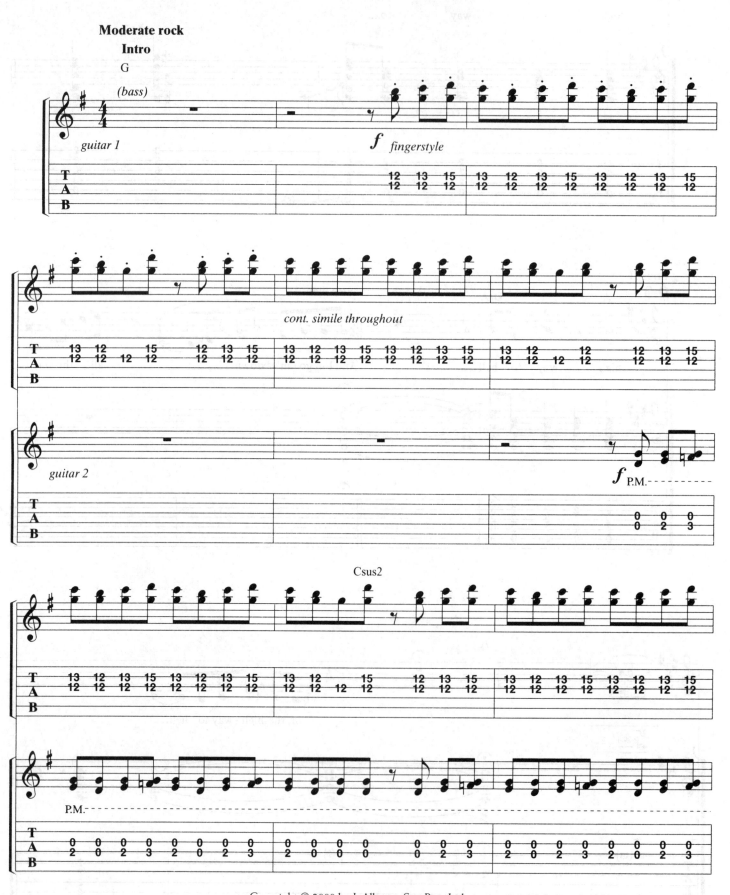

Verse
guitars 1 & 2 play Rhythm figures 1 & 1A on repeat

1. I got a big fat Cad - il - lac built for you, I got a
2. *See additional lyrics*

honk that - 'll blow— the av - e - nue. Got a hot dog kick-in' all

Rhythm figure 1

Rhythm figure 1A

384

Chorus

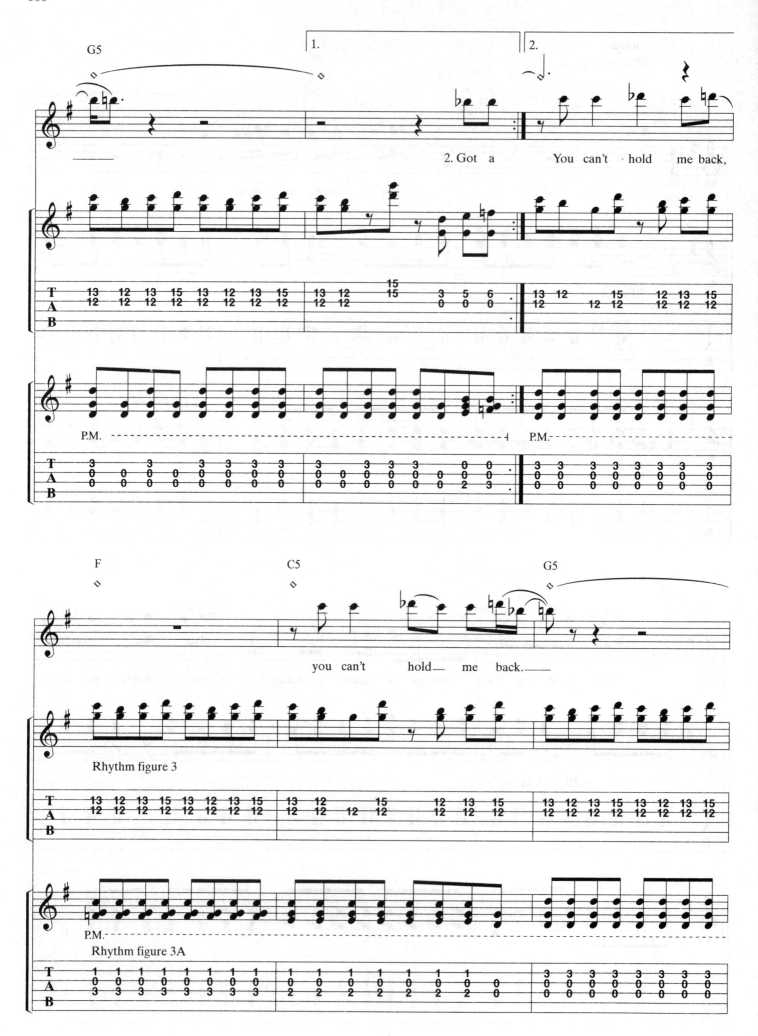

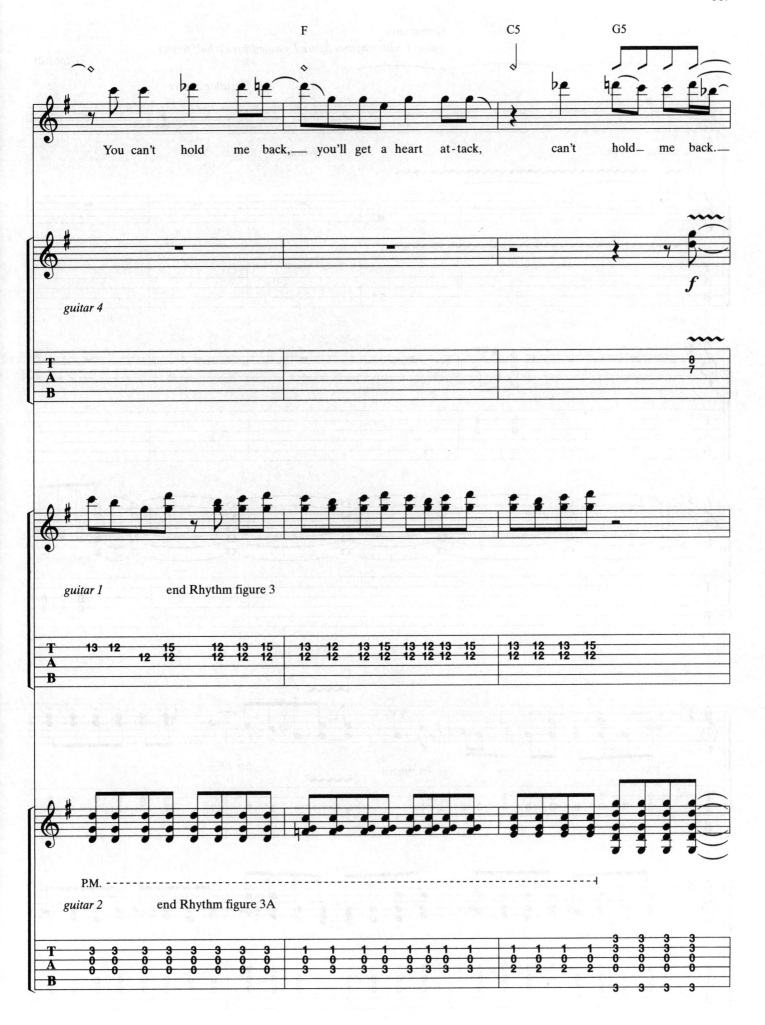

You can't hold me back,— you'll get a heart at-tack, can't hold— me back.—

guitar 4

guitar 1   end Rhythm figure 3

guitar 2   end Rhythm figure 3A

388

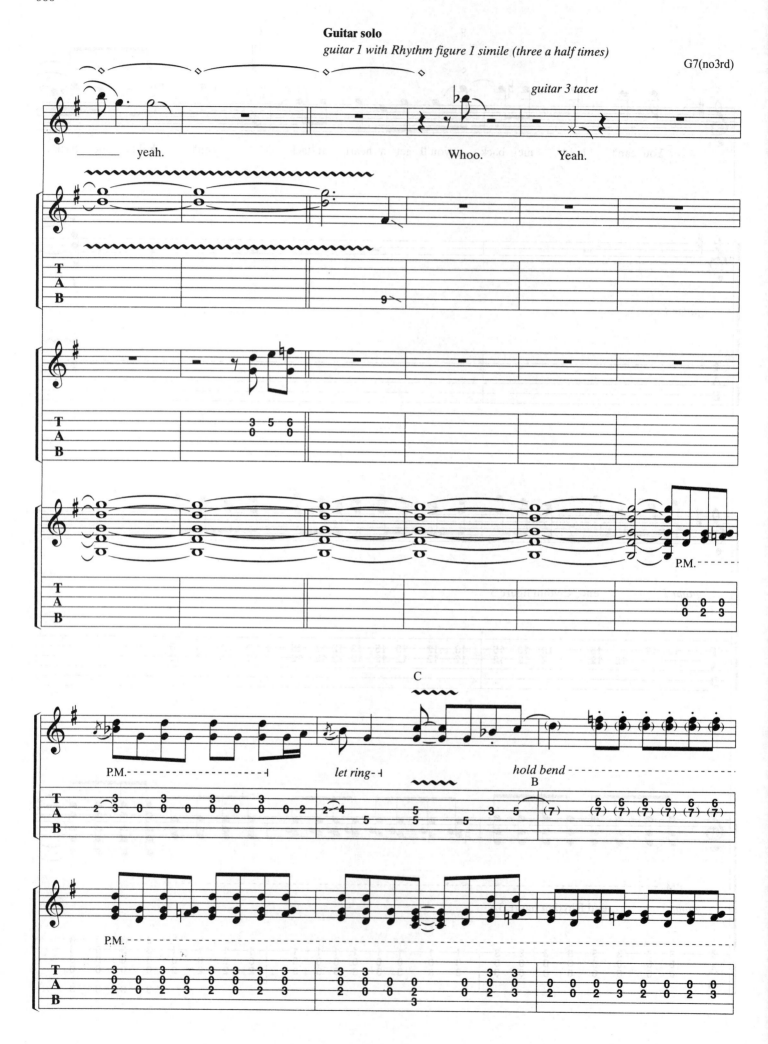

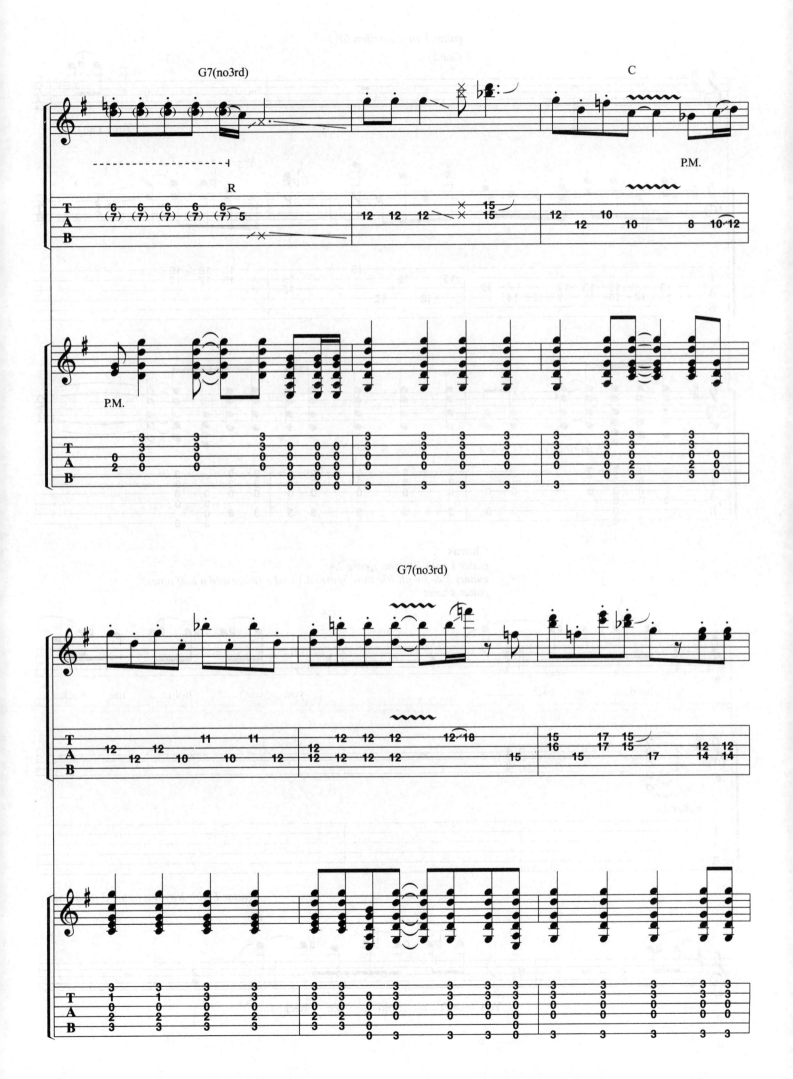

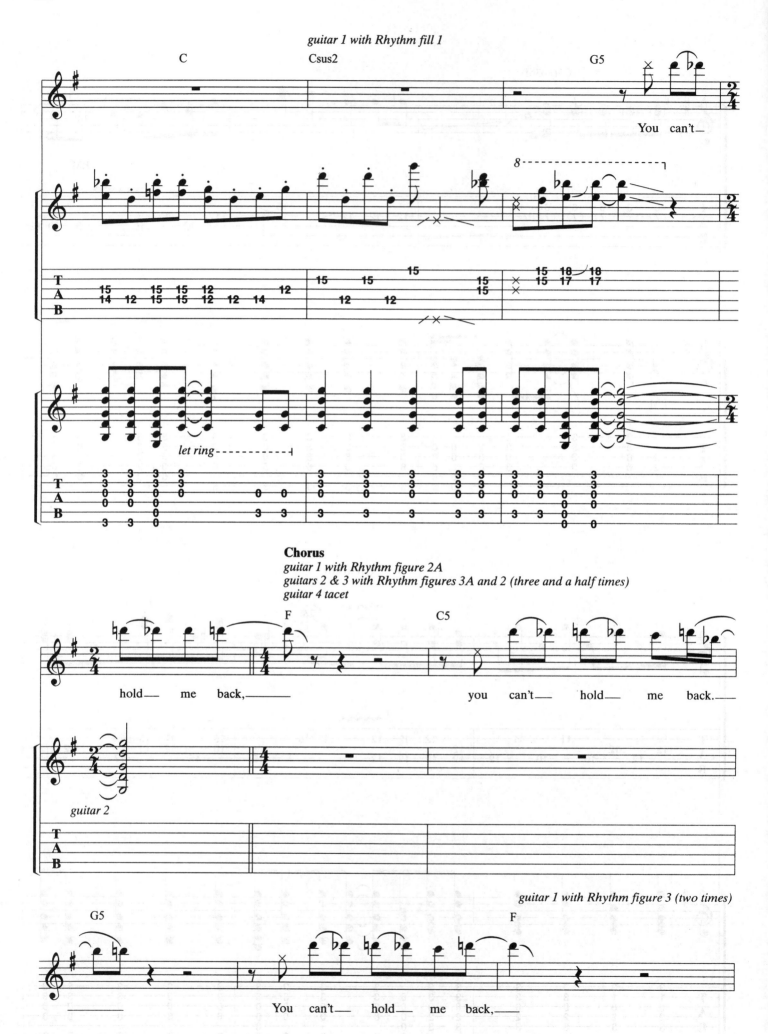

392

Outro

with Vocal figure 1 (three and a half times)
guitar 1 with Rhythm figure 1 simile (three and a half times)

394

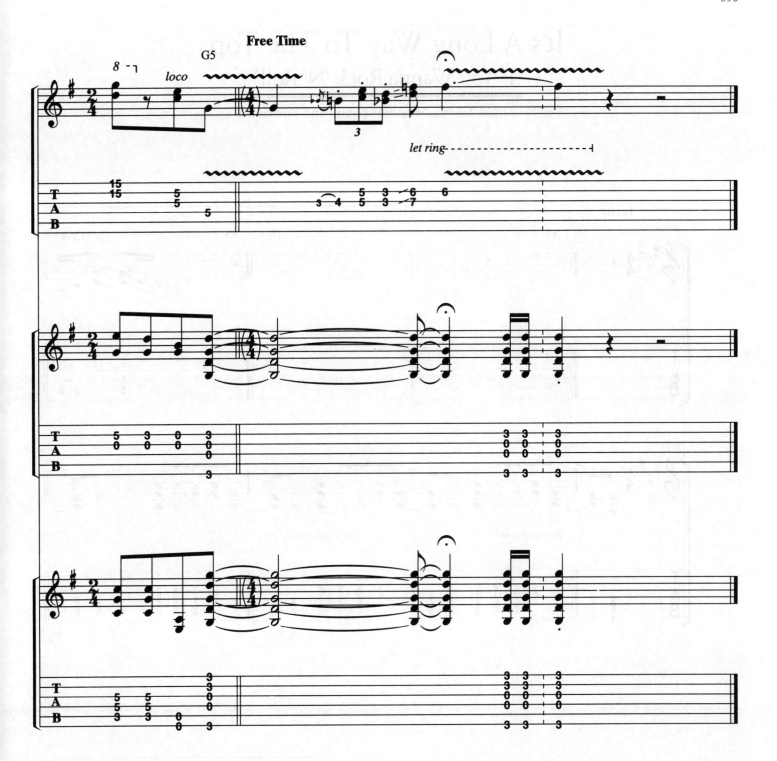

Additional lyrics

2. Got a honky tonk big ball hit to thrill,
   I got a sugar boot money baby that'll kill.
   A honky dog fifteen golden mile,
   Got a bald headed woman loaded in the town
   You can get me to the ball man, drivin' in
   And don't balk the kill, call in the 'ville.
   You gotta map the wrong town, hit the road;
   You got the whole boppa movin' on down the road.
   (to Chorus)

It's A Long Way To The Top
(If You Wanna Rock 'N' Roll)

By Angus Young, Malcolm Young and Bon Scott

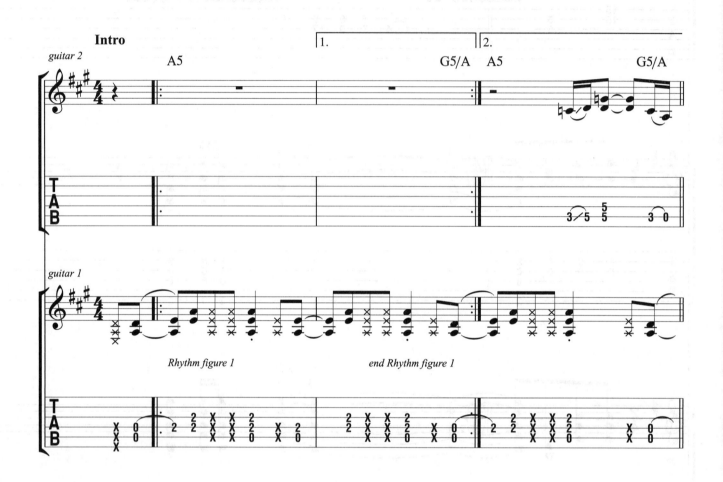

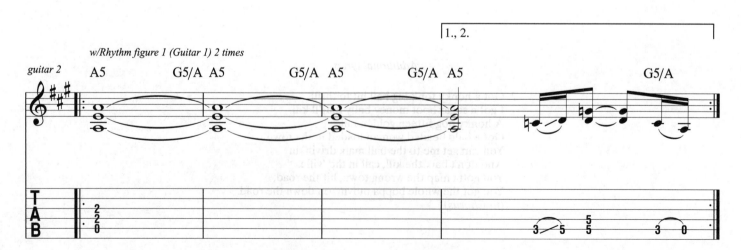

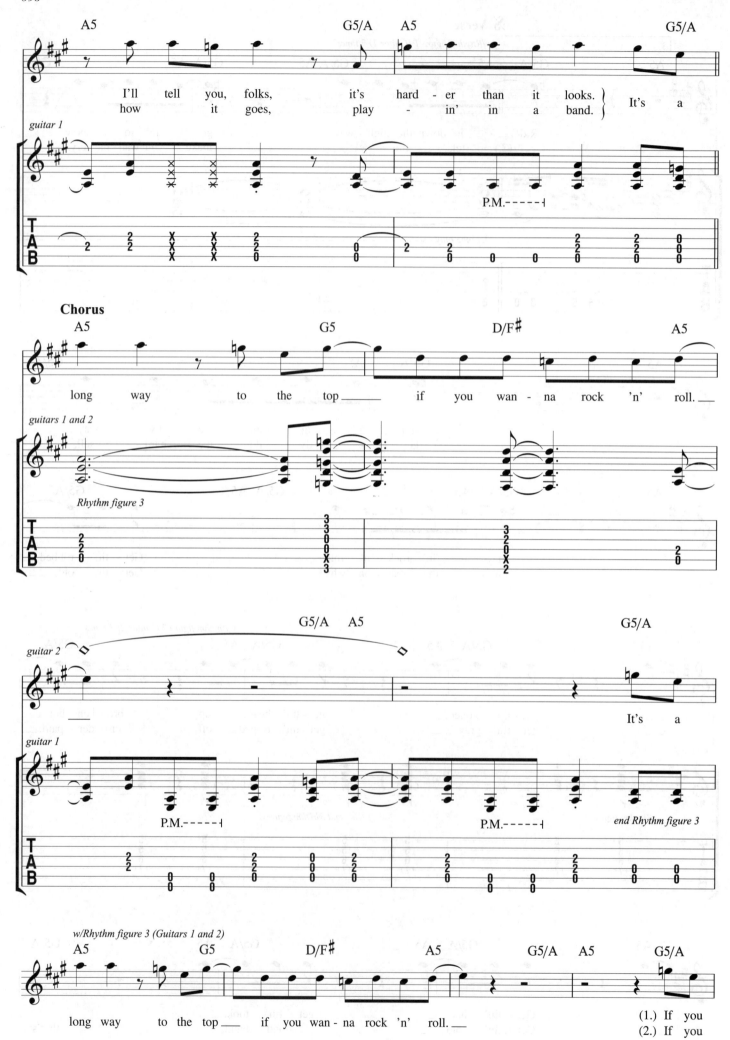

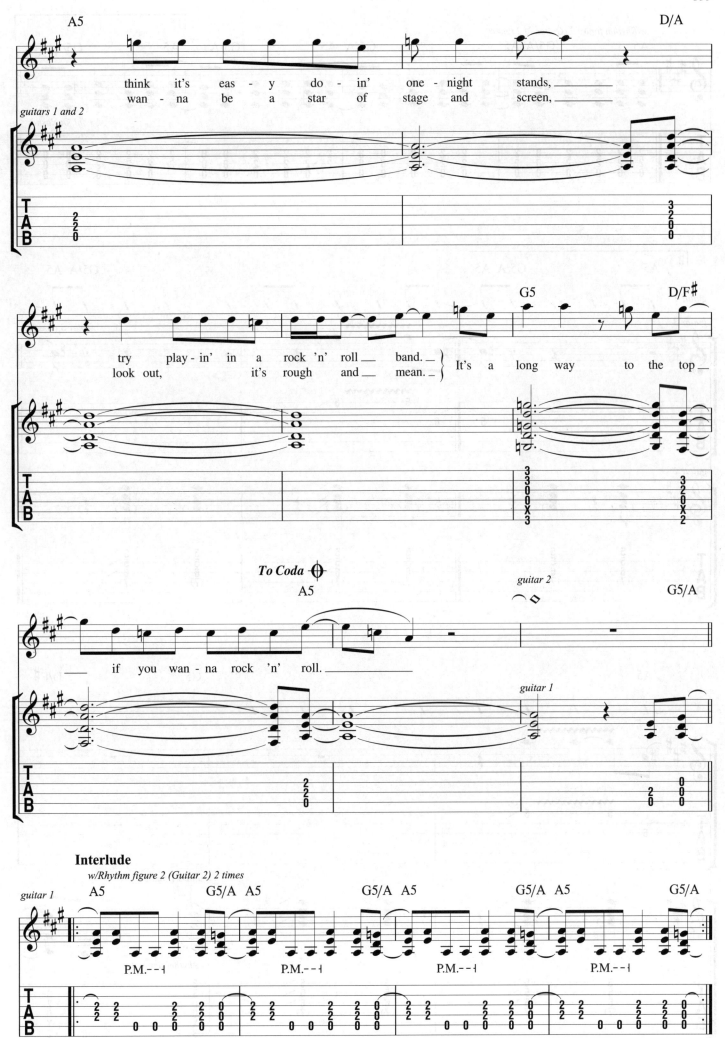

400

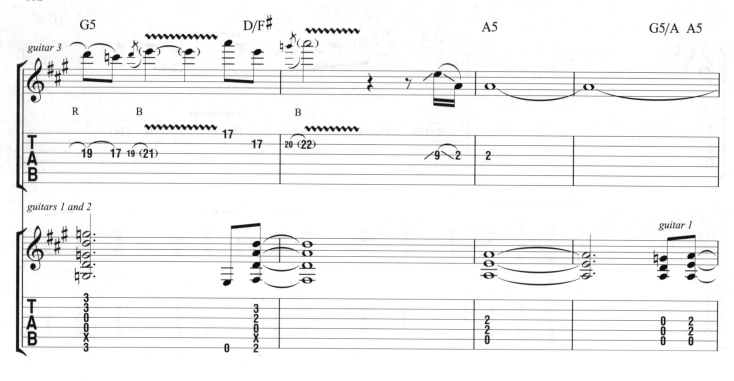

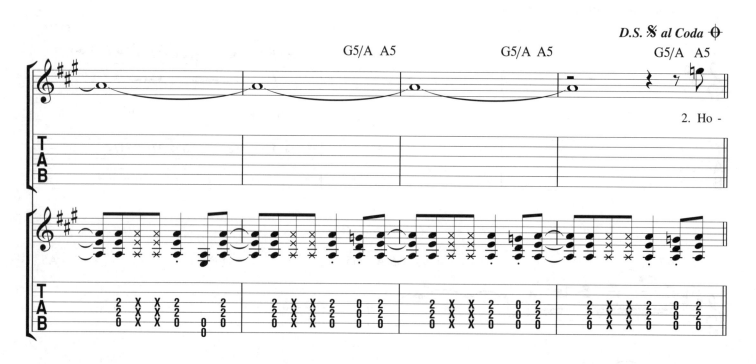

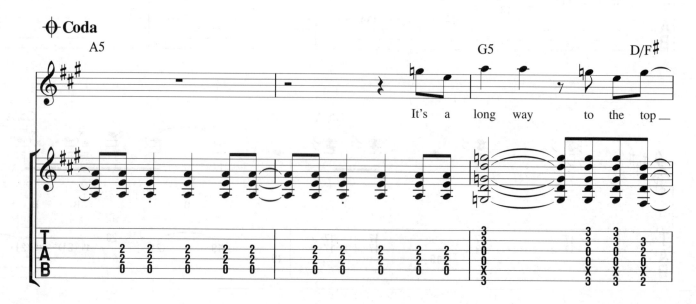

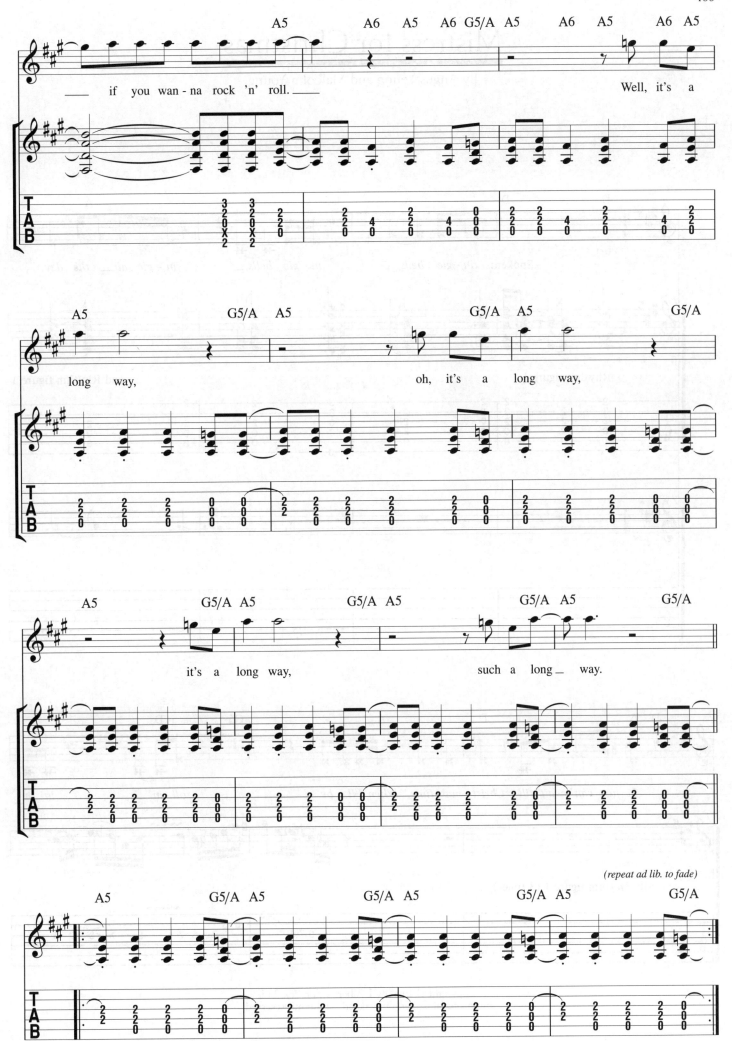

(repeat ad lib. to fade)

Mistress for Christmas

By Angus Young and Malcolm Young

408

mis - tress___ for Christ - mas.___

with Rhythm figure 1 (2 times)

I wan - na mis - tres___ for Christ - mas.___

Ah, yeah.

Spoken: *You know what I'm talkin' about.*

The Jack

By Angus Young, Malcolm Young and Bon Scott

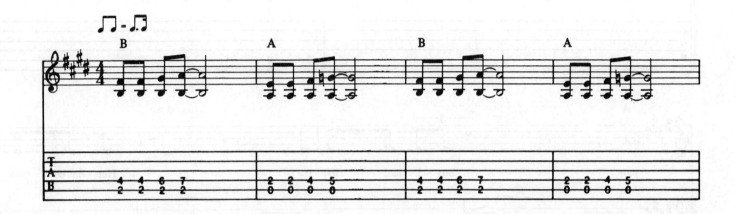

415

416

418

Pok - er face was her name,   pok - er face was her

na - ture, Pok - er straight was her game, if she knew she could get you. She played 'em

A

fast, and she played 'em hard, She could close her eyes, and feel ev - 'ry

E

card. But how was I to know, that she'd been shuf - fled be - fore,— Said she'd

nev - er had a roy - al flush, but I should have known, That

A

all the cards were com - in', from the bot - tom of the pack, And if I'd

D.S. al Coda I

known what she was deal - in' out, I'd have dealt it back. She's got the

Coda I

B

*play chorus 3 times
(take Coda II third time)*

She's got the

Coda II

E

jack.

ritard

F **E**

Jailbreak

By Angus Young, Malcolm Young, Bon Scott

Intro

Verse

w/Rhythm figure 1 (Guitar 2) 1½ times

friend of mine__ on__ mur - der

and the judg-e's gav - el__ fell.__

__ Ju - ry found __ him __ guilt-y,__ gave him

six - teen__ years__ in hell!_____ He said,

*turn 6th-string tuning peg down gradually

421

Verse

w/Rhythm figure 1 (Guitar 2) 4 times

1. I ain't spend-in' my life ___ here,   I ain't liv-in' a-lone. ___   Ain't
2. *See additional lyrics*

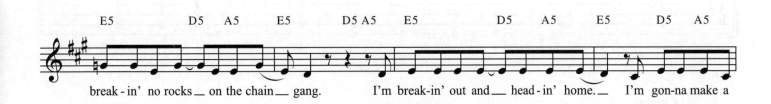

break-in' no rocks ___ on the chain ___ gang.   I'm break-in' out and ___ head-in' home. ___ I'm gon-na make a

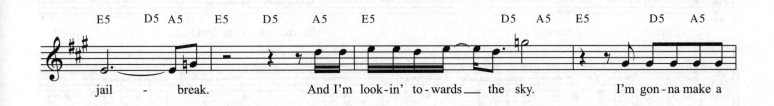

jail - break.   And I'm look-in' to-wards ___ the sky.   I'm gon-na make a

jail - break.   Oh, how I ___ wish that I could ___ fly!

Pre-Chorus

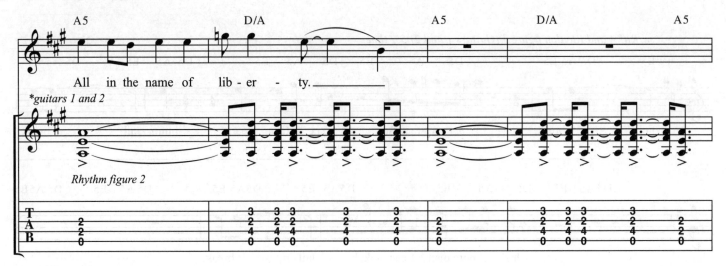

All in the name of lib-er-ty. ___

guitars 1 and 2

Rhythm figure 2

*Composite arrangement

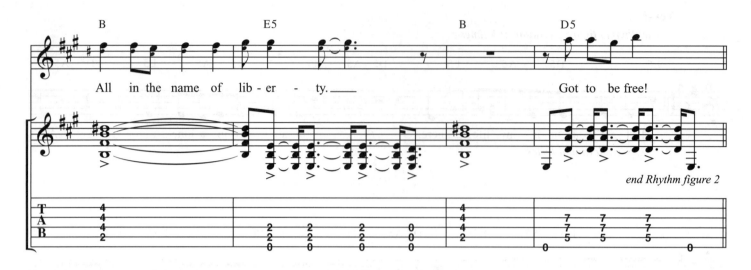

Chorus

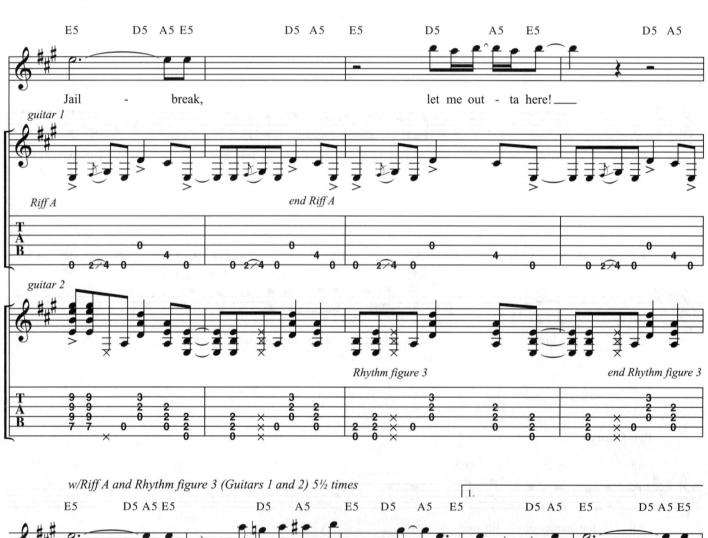

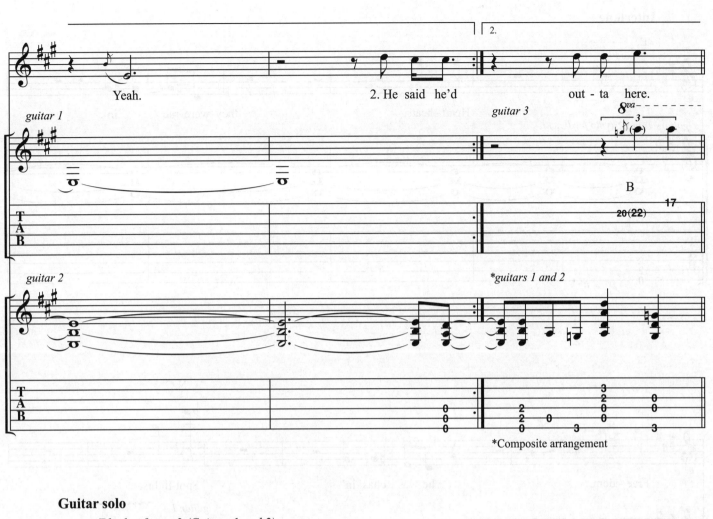

Yeah.　　2. He said he'd　out - ta here.

*Composite arrangement

Guitar solo

w/Rhythm figure 2 (Guitars 1 and 2)

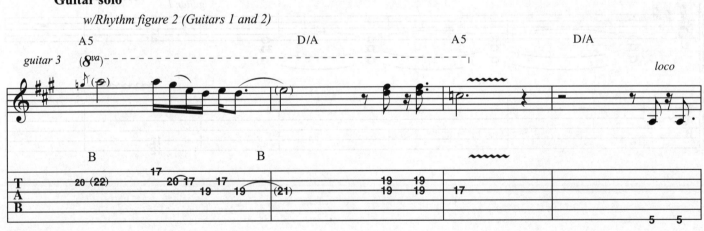

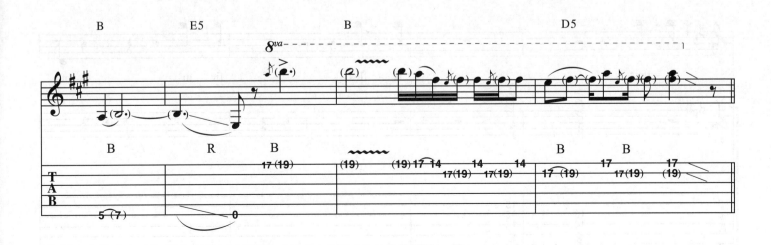

Interlude

Heart-beats, they were rac - in'.

guitars 1 and 2 (with feedback)

N.C.

Free - dom, he was chas-in'. Spot-lights,

guitar 1

si - rens, ri - fles fir - in', but

he made it out   with a bul - let in his back!

Outro Chorus

w/Riff A (Guitar 1) 2 times
w/Rhythm figure 3 (Guitar 2) 2 times
guitar 3 ad lib.

E5   D5   A5 E5   D5   A5   E5   D5   A5 E5   D5   A5

(repeat and fade)

Jail   -   break.

Additional lyrics:

2. He said he'd seen his lady being fooled with by another man.
   She was down and he was up.
   He had a gun in his hand.
   Bullets flying everywhere and people started to scream.
   Big man lying on the ground with a hole in his body
   Where his life had been.
   But it was...

Let Me Put My Love Into You

By Angus Young and Malcolm Young and Brian Johnson

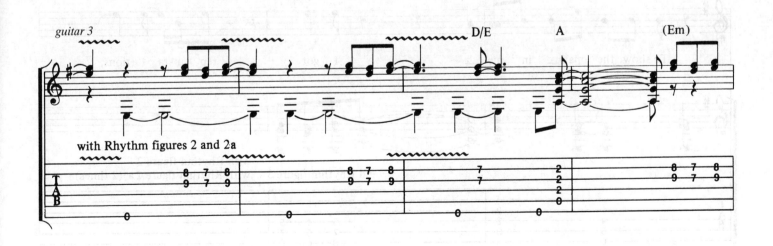

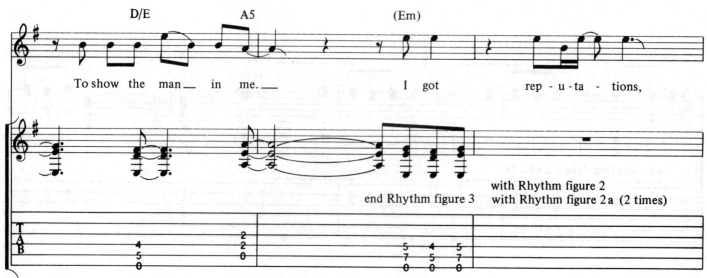

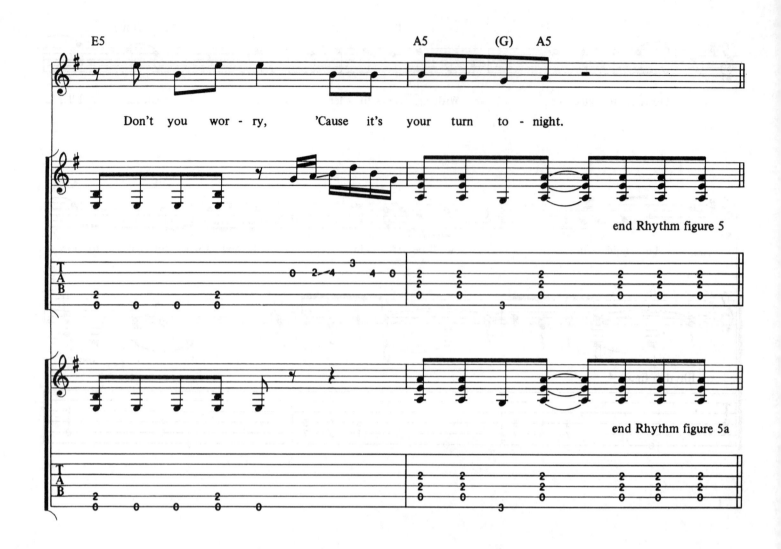

Don't you wor - ry, 'Cause it's your turn to - night.

end Rhythm figure 5

end Rhythm figure 5a

Let me put my love in - to you— babe,   Let me put my love on the line.—

Rhythm figure 6

431

432

434

Live Wire

By Angus Young, Malcolm Young and Bon Scott

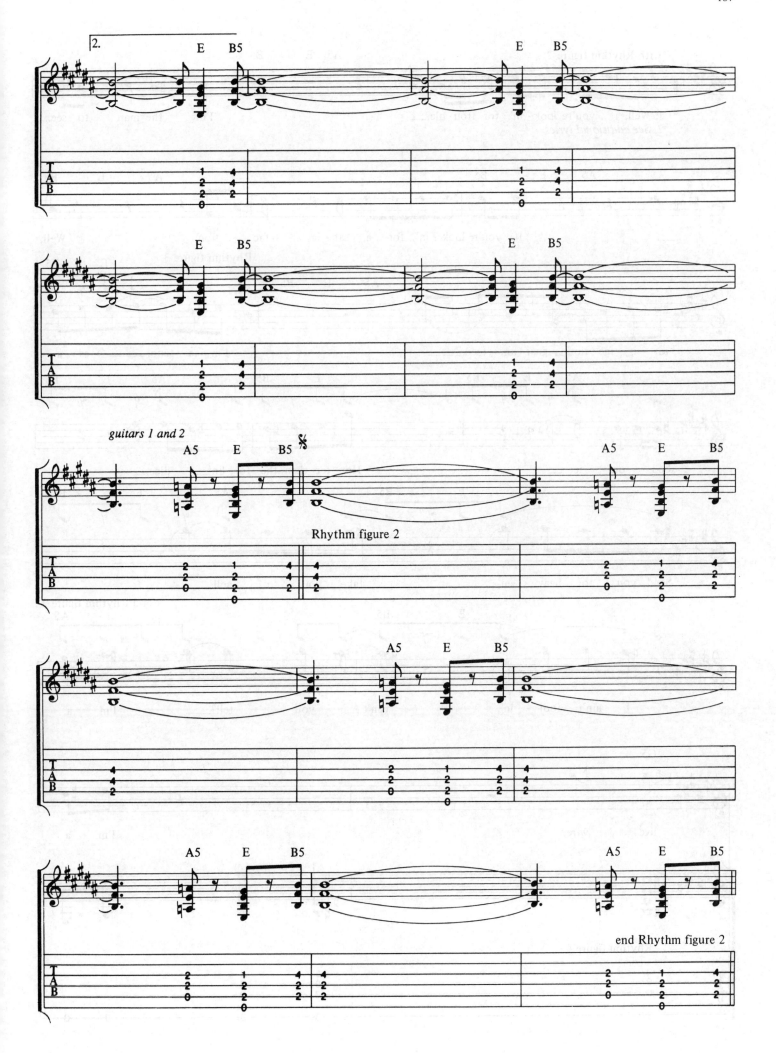

438

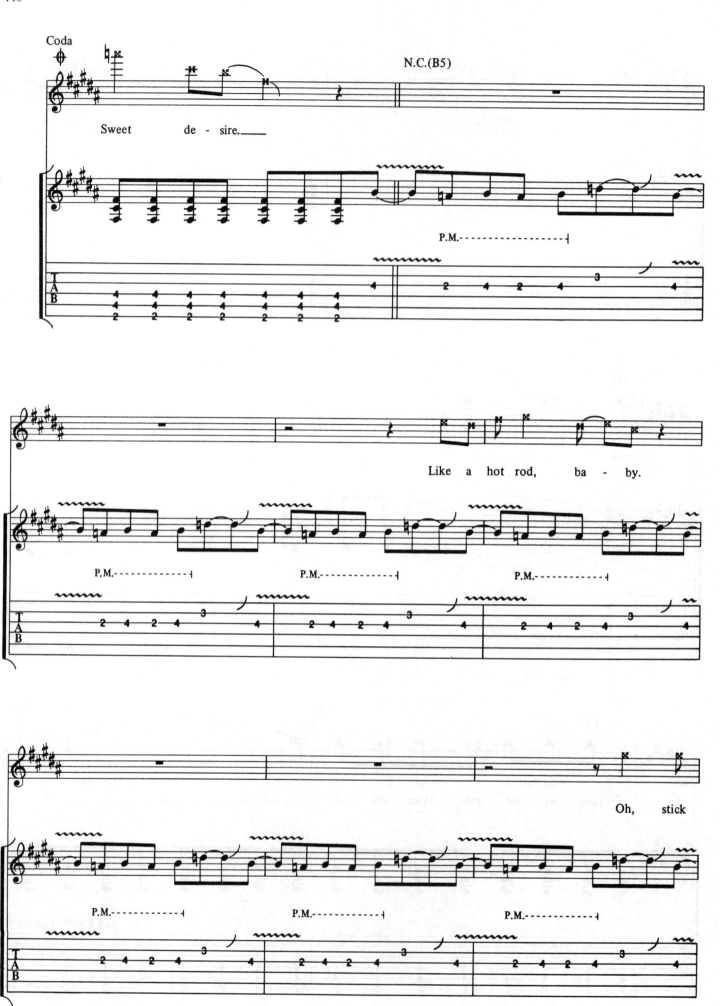

442

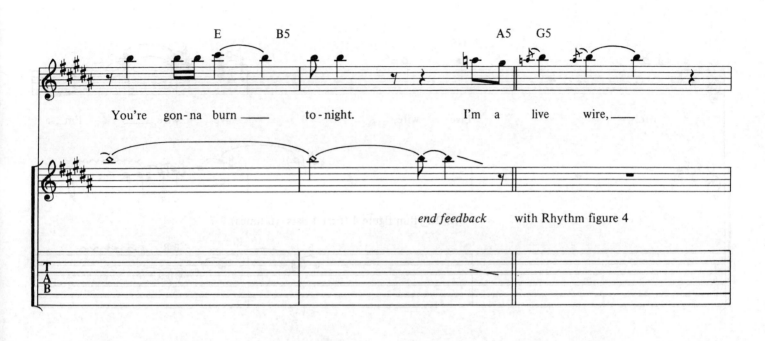

You're gon-na burn ____ to-night.   I'm a live wire, ____

end feedback   with Rhythm figure 4

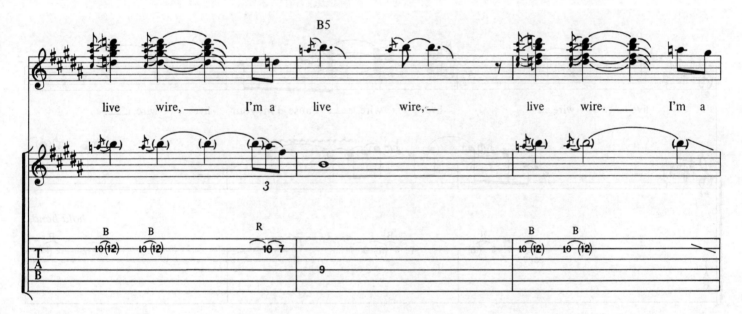

live wire, ____ I'm a live wire, ____ live wire. ____ I'm a

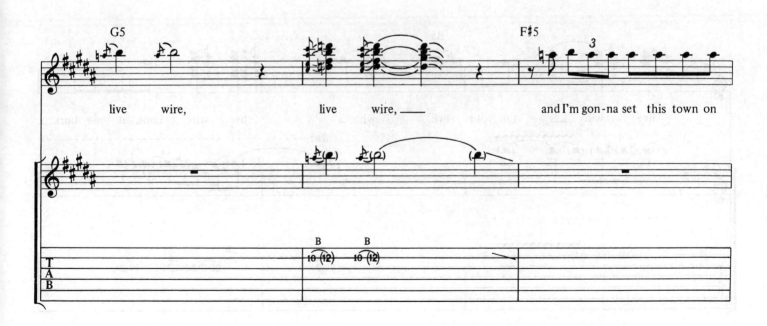

live wire,   live wire, ____   and I'm gon-na set this town on

fire!   Live   wire,   live   wire,____   I'm a

with Rhythm figure 4 (first 4 bars) (6 times)

live   wire,__   live   wire. __ 'Cause I'm your   live   wire,____

hold bend...

live   wire, __   I'm your   live   wire,_   live   wire.   Look   at   me   burn._

8va--

448

Additional Lyrics

2. And if you need some lovin',
And if you need some man,
You've got the phone and the number,
And I've got no future plans.
Oh, come on honey,
You got nothin' to lose.
You've got the thirst,
And I've got the booze.
Give you an inch, take you a mile,
I'm gonna make you fry.

Love At First Feel

By Angus Young, Malcolm Young and Bon Scott

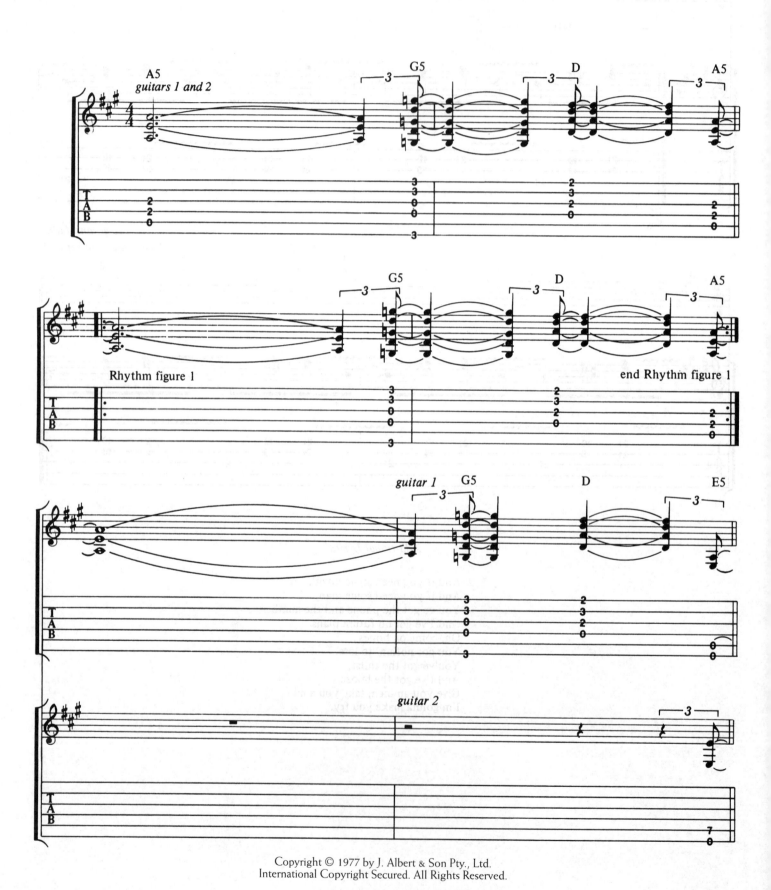

Rhythm figure 2

1. You nev - er told me where you came from,
2. See additional lyrics

Rhythm figure 2a

You nev - er told me your name,

end Rhythm figure 2

end Rhythm figure 2a

452

Guitar solo
A5

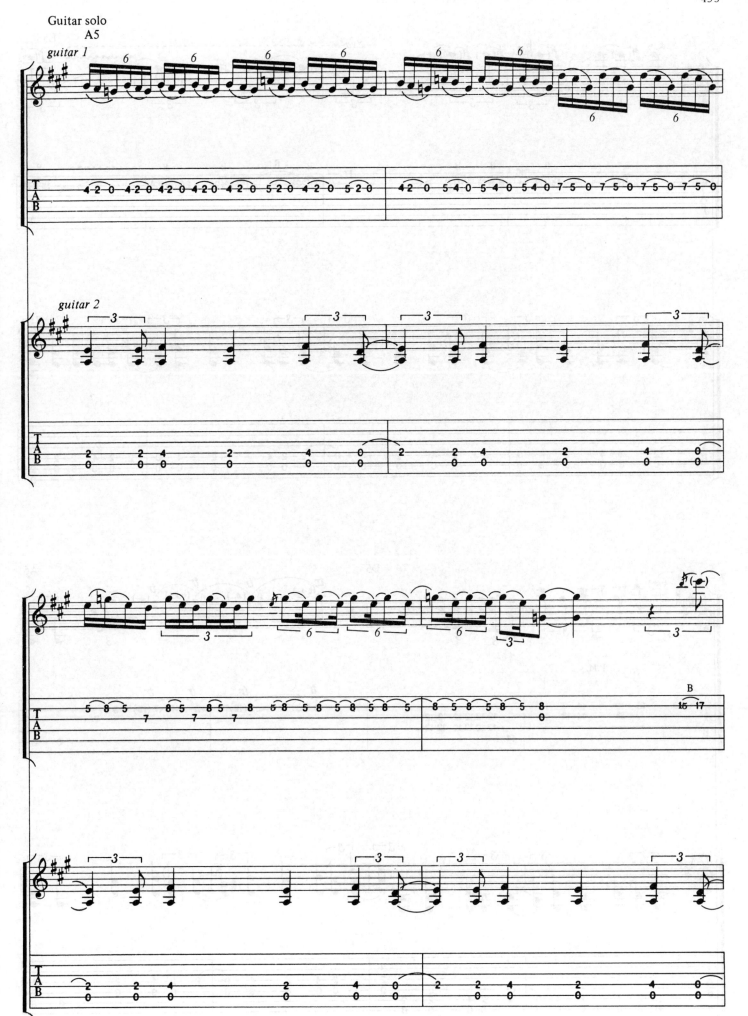

Additional Lyrics

2. They told me it was disgustin,
   They told me it was a sin,
   They saw me knocking on your front door,
   Saw me smile when you let me in.
   You and me, baby, we's all alone.
   Let's get something goin', while your mom and dad ain't home.

Love Hungry Man

By Angus Young, Malcolm Young and Ronald Scott

460

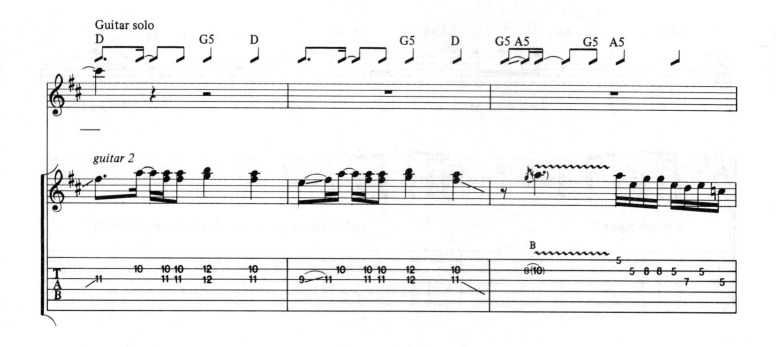

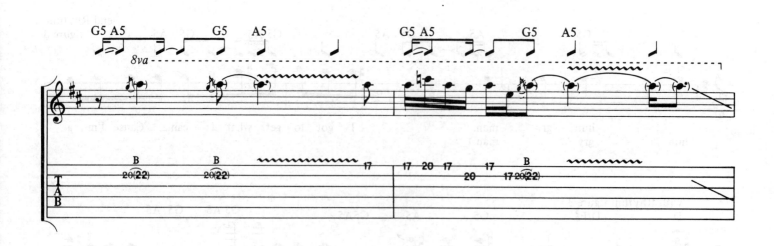

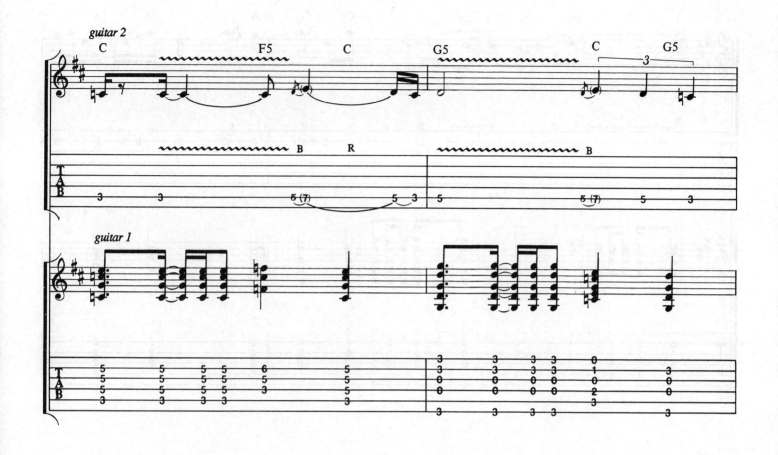

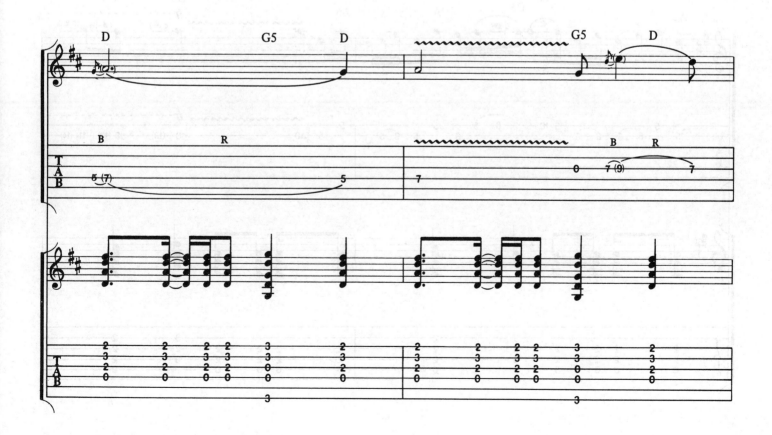

462

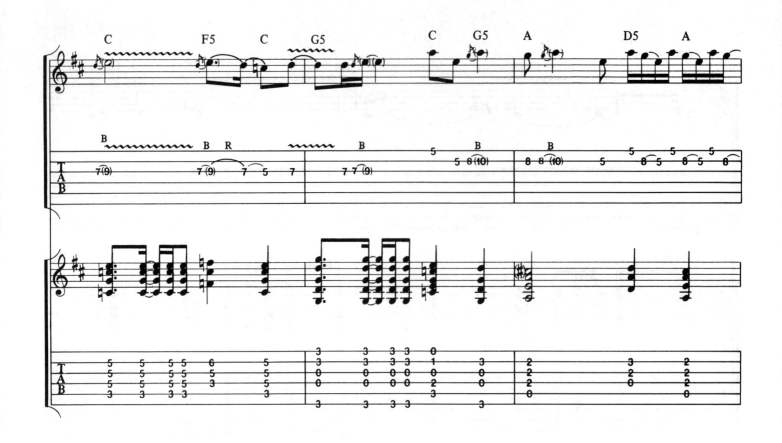

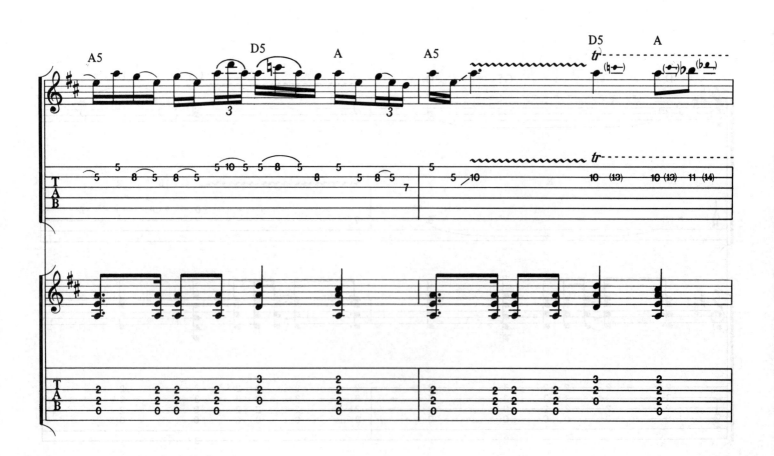

Ooh,   love hun-gry   man!

Money Talks

By Angus Young and Malcolm Young

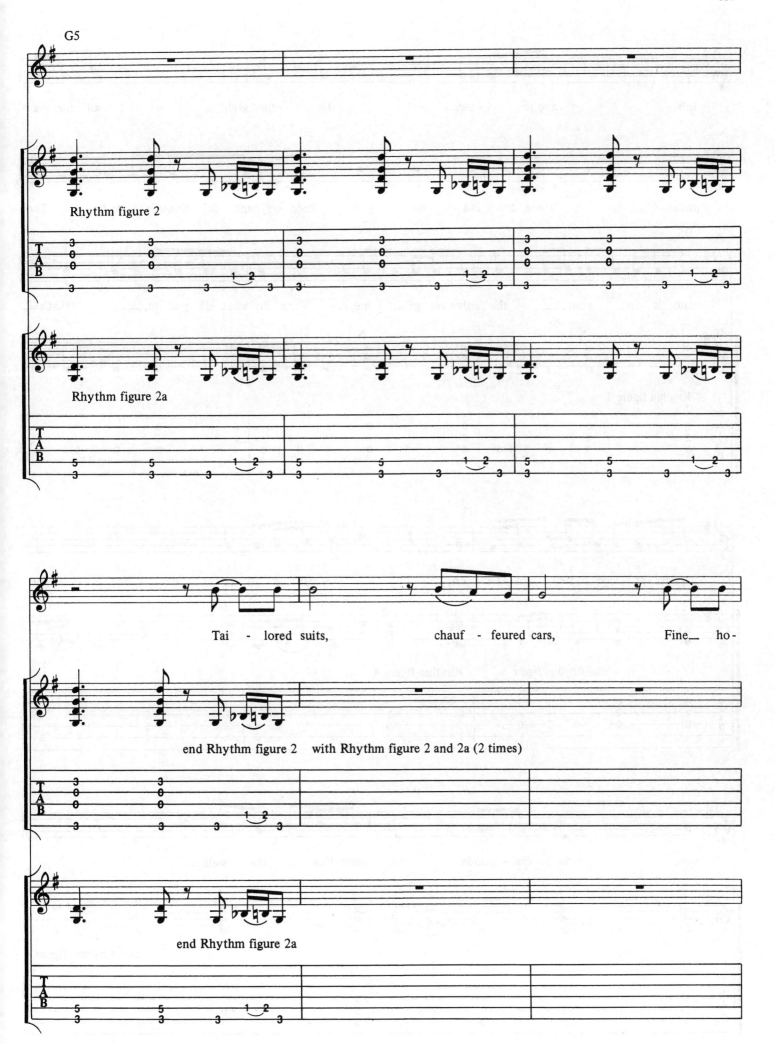

468

tels, and big ci - gars. Up for grabs, all for a

price, Where the red hot girls keep on danc - in' through the night. The

D5

claim is on__ you,___ the sights are on__ me,___ So what do you do,____ that's

Rhythm figure 3

__ guar - an - teed?__ Hey__ lit - tle girl, you want it all, ___ The

C5

end Rhythm figure 3   Rhythm figure 4

furs, the dia - monds, the paint - ings on the wall. ___

end Rhythm figure 4

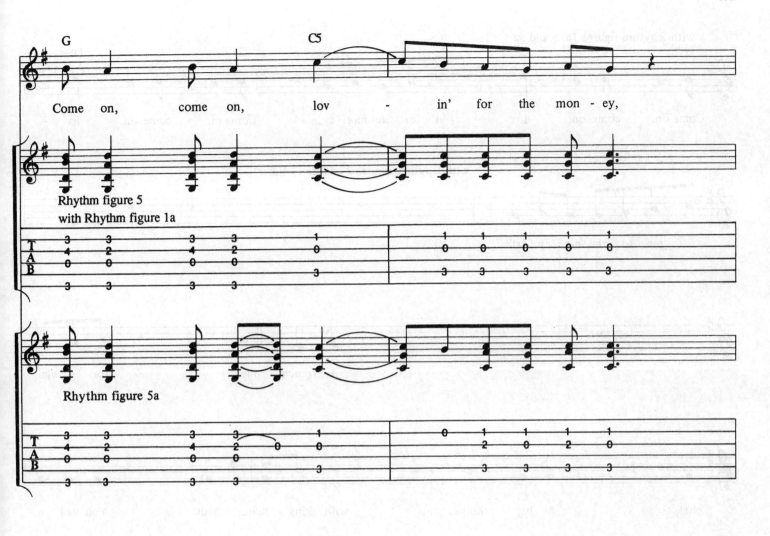

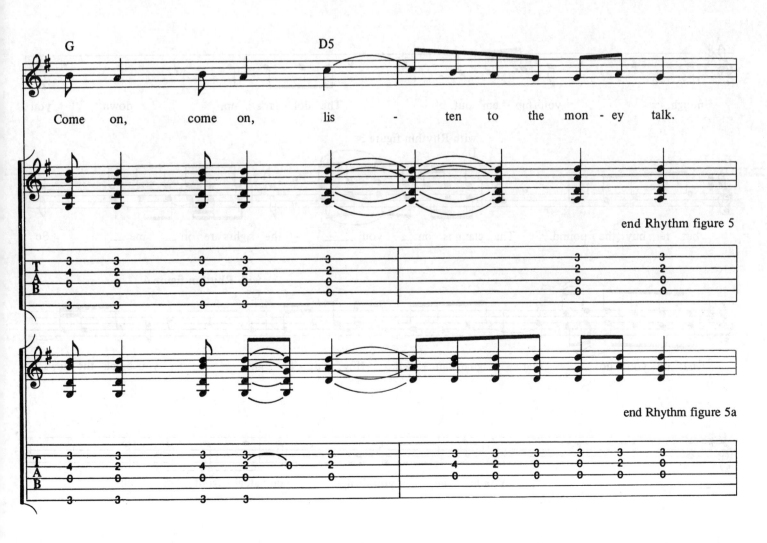

470

471

hold bend

with Rhythm figure 3

with Rhythm figure 4

474

The Razors Edge

By Angus Young and Malcolm Young

Rhythm figure 1

with simile rhythm (14 bars)

end Rhythm figure 1

476

Rhythm figure 3

Rhythm figure 3a

end Rhythm figure 3

end Rhythm figure 3a

with Rhythm figure 2 (2 times)

To raise__ the dead.__   To cut to__ shreds.__

(Ra - zor's edge.)   (ra - zor's edge.)

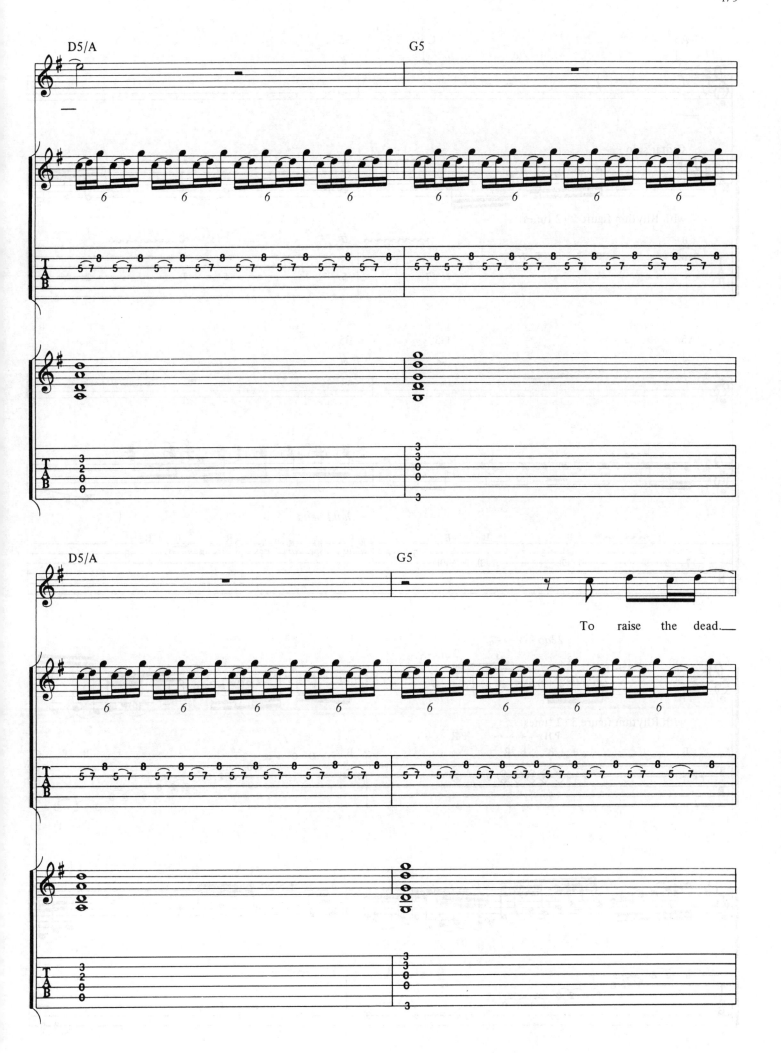

To raise the dead.___

hold bend

with Rhythm figure 2 (2 times)

Here comes the ra - zor's edge.

with Slide guitar figure

Here comes the ra - zor's edge.

Well, here it comes,

482

Money Made

By Angus Young & Malcolm Young

Intro

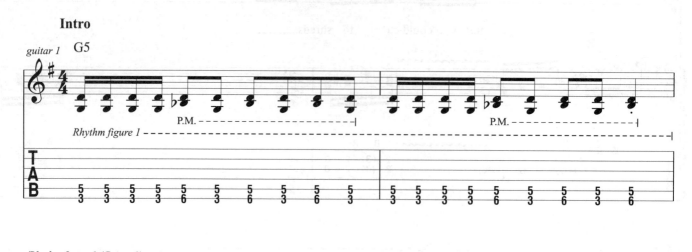

Chorus

*Background vocals sing middle notes 1st & 3rd time and bottom notes 2nd & 4th time.

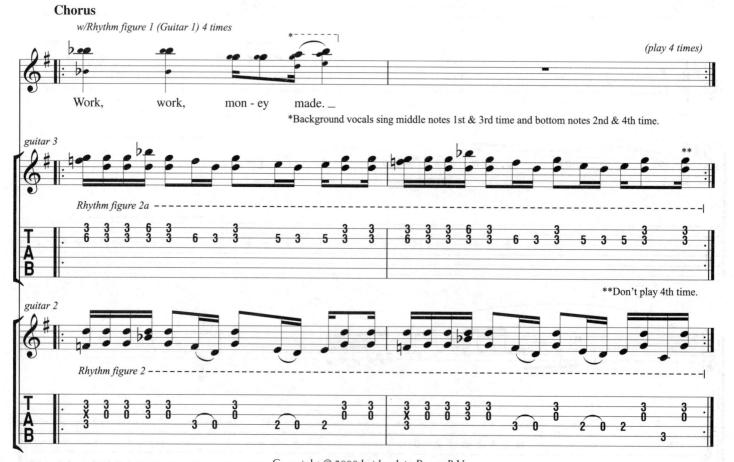

1st and 2nd Verses

1. They went down ___ to L. A.,
2. *See additional lyrics*

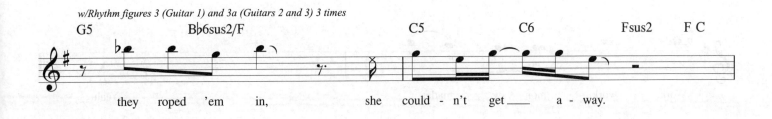

they roped 'em in, she could - n't get ___ a - way.

Spread - in' cash ___ all a - bout, ___ yeah,

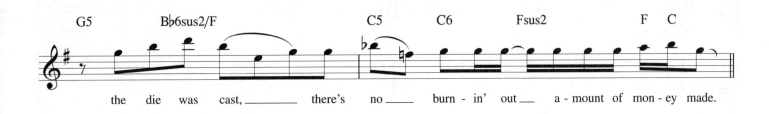

the die was cast, ___ there's no ___ burn - in' out ___ a - mount of mon - ey made.

486

Chorus

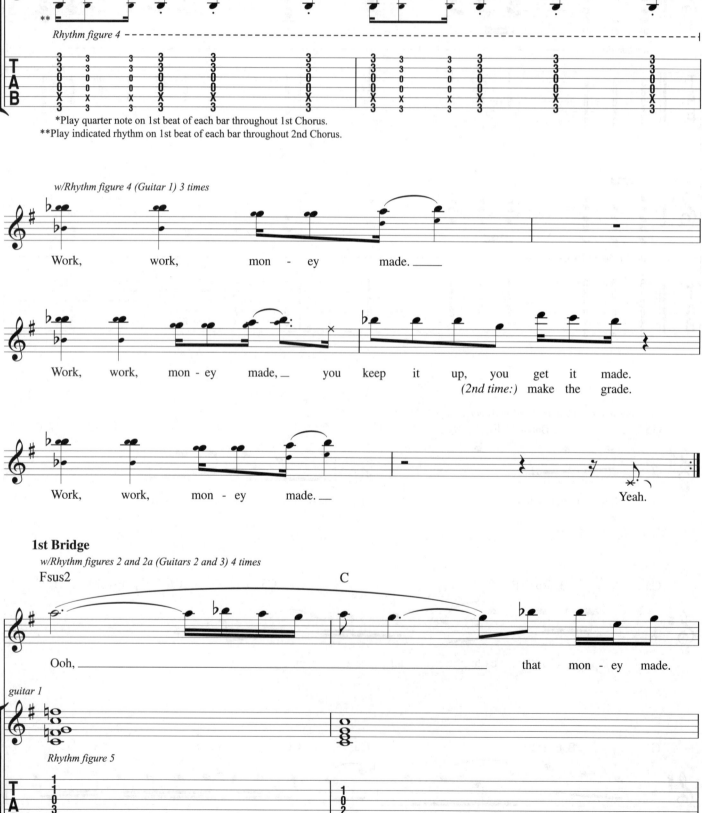

*Play quarter note on 1st beat of each bar throughout 1st Chorus.
**Play indicated rhythm on 1st beat of each bar throughout 2nd Chorus.

1st Bridge

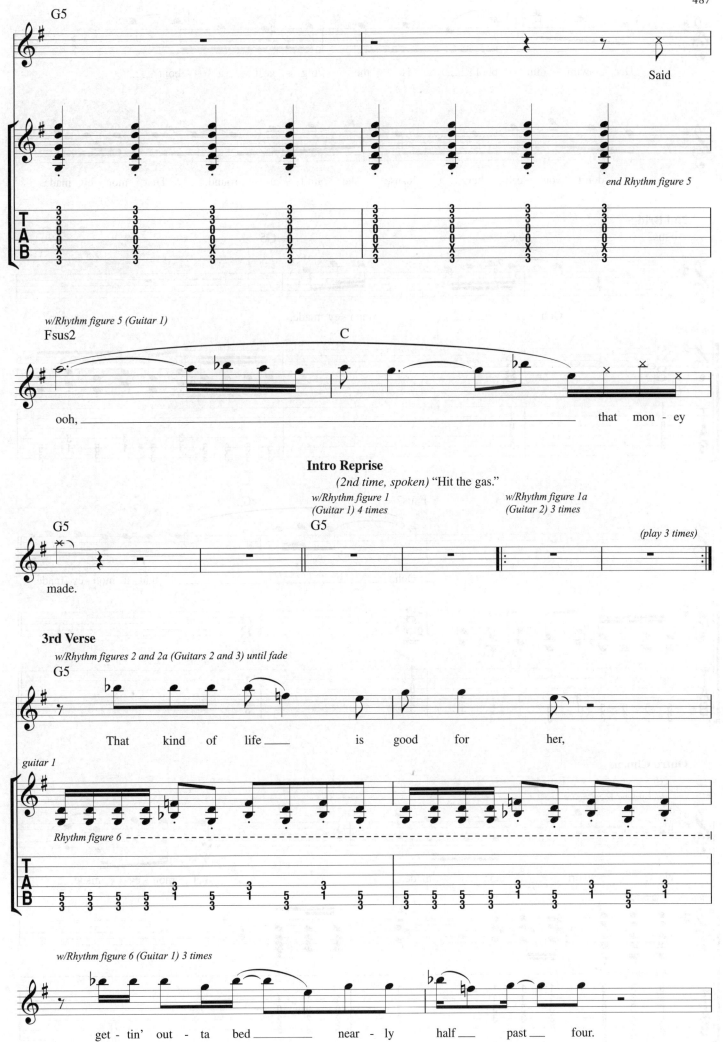

Additional lyrics

2nd Verse:
Can't bring me into Hollywood
See you livin' it up, it feels mighty good
Recommendations all around
Come taste the sweet life, that's what it's all about
That money made

Nervous Shakedown

By Angus Young, Malcolm Young, Brian Johnson

Intro

*guitars 1 and 2

*Composite arrangement

Rhythm figure 1

end Rhythm figure 1

Verse

w/Rhythm figure 1 (Guitars 1 and 2) 3 ½ times

1. "Freeze!" said the man cruis - in' the beat.
2. *See additional lyrics*

You got your

hands up, spread your feet. "Don't you move an inch," I heard him say.

"Or you'll be do - in' time un - til the judg - ment day."

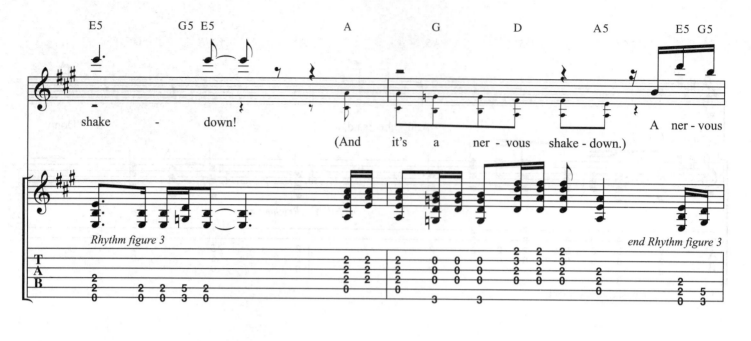

shake - down!

(And it's a ner - vous shake - down.)

A ner - vous

Rhythm figure 3

end Rhythm figure 3

w/Rhythm figure 3 (Guitars 1 and 2) 2½ times

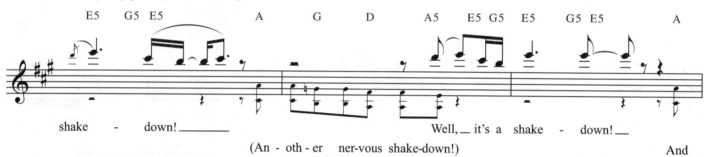

shake - down!____

(An - oth - er ner-vous shake-down!)

Well,__ it's a shake - down!__

And

w/Fill A (Guitars 1 and 2)

it's a ner-vous shake-down.)

We got a shake - down!_____

An - oth-er ner-vous shake-down!

Interlude

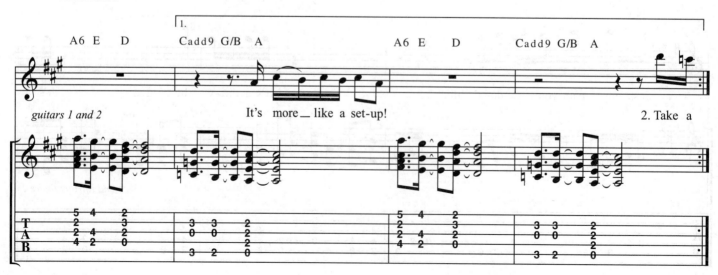

It's more__ like a set-up!

guitars 1 and 2

2. Take a

The law__ is gon - na__get you this__time and throw a-way the key!

Guitar solo

w/Rhythm figure 4 (Guitars 1 and 2) 2 times

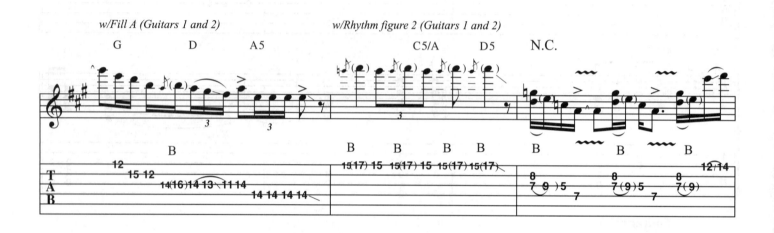

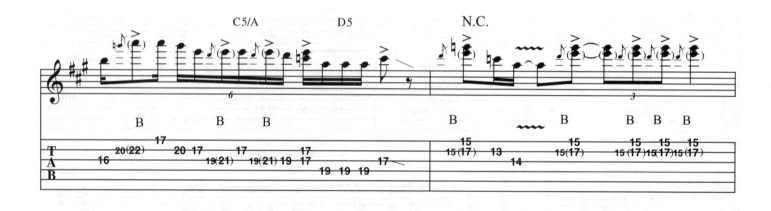

Outro Chorus *(vocals ad lib. on repeats)*

w/Rhythm figure 1 (Guitars 1 and 2) 4 times

Additional lyrics

2. "Take a dime," said the man, "you can make one call."
   "You go a one-way ticket to the County Hall."
   Well, the judge looked high and I looked low.
   And when he smiled at me it was a one-man show.
   He said, "Two to five, the jury decides."
   "Double parole if you survive."
   It's a dirty lie.

Night Of The Long Knives

By Angus Young, Malcolm Young, Brian Johnson

498

Additional lyrics

2. Oh, where is that savior?
   Where is that blade,
   When you're prayin'
   For your life?
   Who's that fighting
   Back to back?
   Who's defending
   Whose attack?

Night Prowler

By Angus Young, Malcolm Young and Bon Scott

504

506

night (Night prowl - er, ____ prowl - er. ____) when you shut out the light.

508

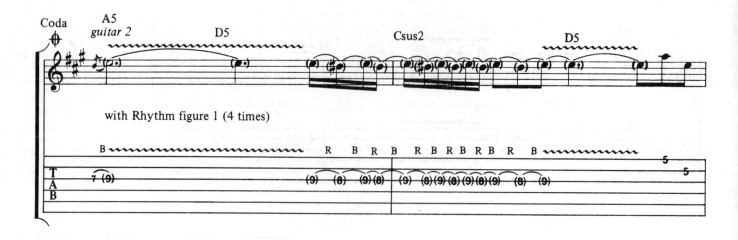

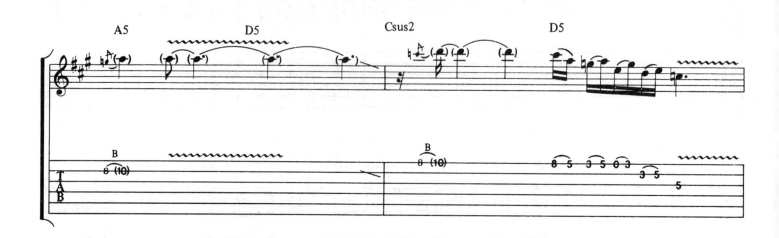

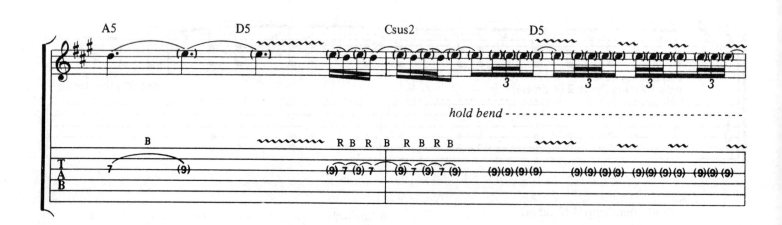

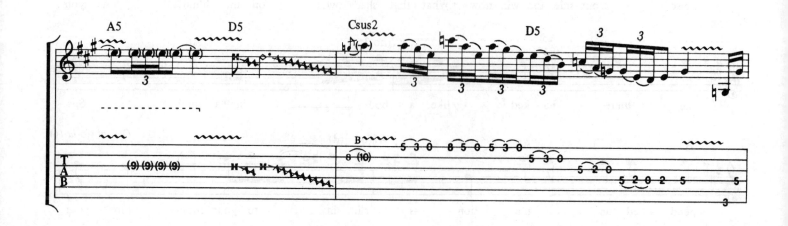

510

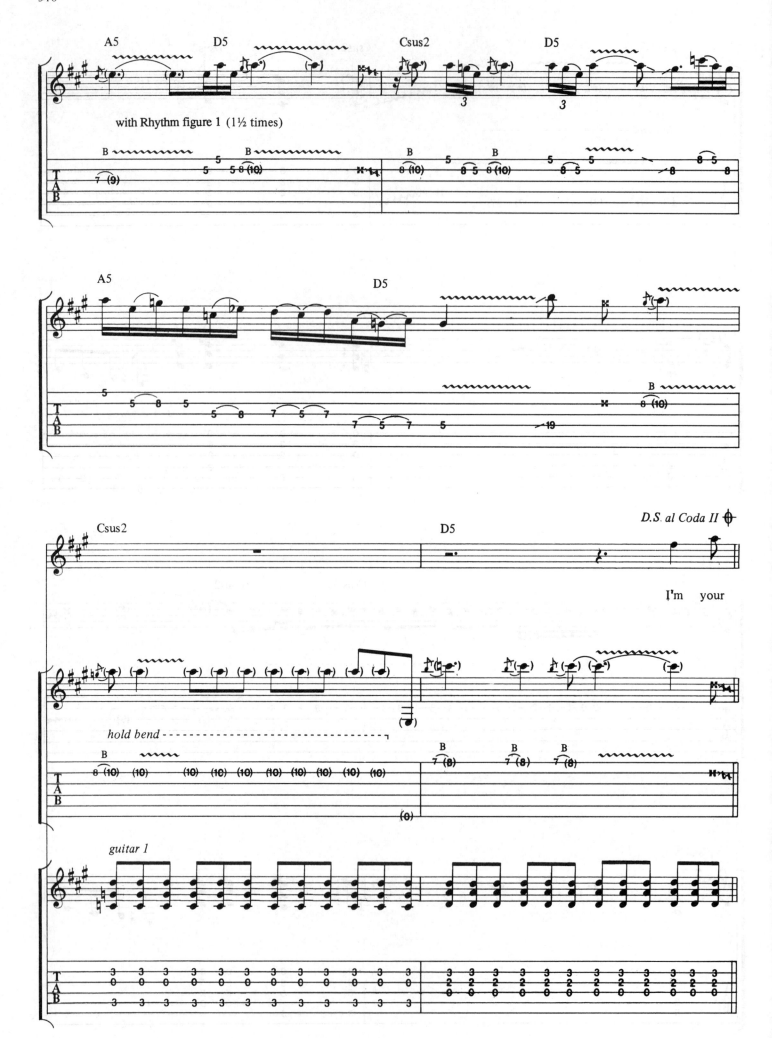

with Rhythm figure 1 (1½ times)

D.S. al Coda II

I'm your

hold bend -

guitar 1

Coda II

you torn out the light. I'm your night prowl - er,____ oh.
(Night prowl - er,____

let ring - - - - - - ┐

Csus2 D5 A5 D5

I'm your night prowl - er.____ I'm the
break down your door.__) (Night prowl - er,____ crawl - in' 'cross your floor.)

Csus2 D5 A5 D5 Csus2 D5

night prowl - er,____ yes I will.__
(Night prowl - er,____ make a mess of you.__)

A5 D5 Csus2 D5

Night prowl - er,____ and I'm tel - in' this to you, There ain't noth - in',
(Night prowl - er.____)

A5 D5 Csus2

let ring - ┐

There ain't noth - in', oh! A - noth - in' you can do._____

D5 A5

Problem Child

By Angus Young, Malcolm Young and Bon Scott

Guitar solo

515

516

Additional lyrics

2. Make my stand
   No man's land
   On my own
   Man in blue
   It's up to you
   The seed is sown
   What I want I stash, what I don't I smash
   And you're on my list
   Dead or alive, I got a .45
   And I never miss
   I'm a problem child…

3. Every night
   Street light
   I drink my booze
   Some run
   Some fight
   When I win they lose
   What I need I like, what I don't I fight
   And I don't like you
   Say bye-bye while you're still alive
   Your time is through
   'Cause I'm a problem child…

Ride On

By Angus Young, Malcolm Young and Bon Scott

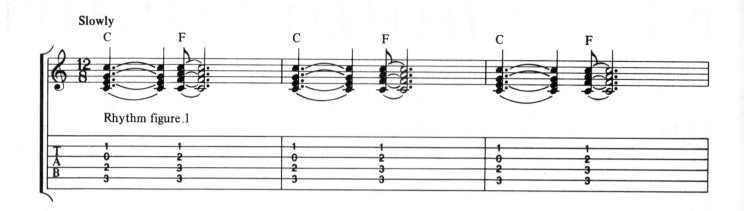

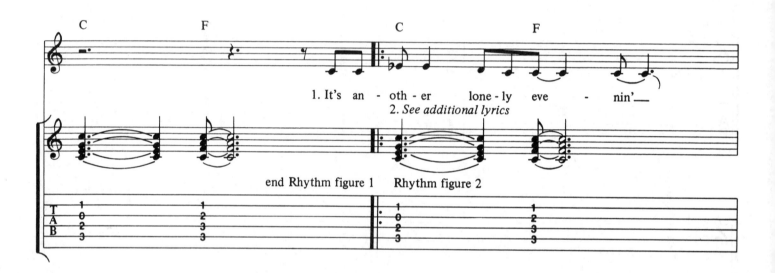

530

Additional Lyrics

2. Got another empty bottle,
And another empty bed,
Ain't too young to admit it,
And I'm not too old to lie,
I'm just another empty head.

Riff Raff

By Angus Young, Malcolm Young and Bon Scott

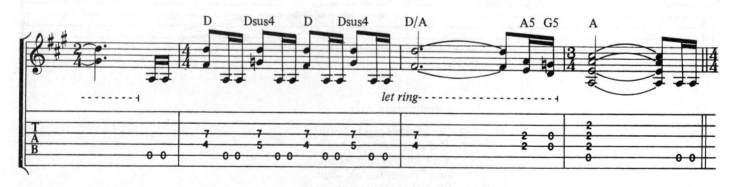

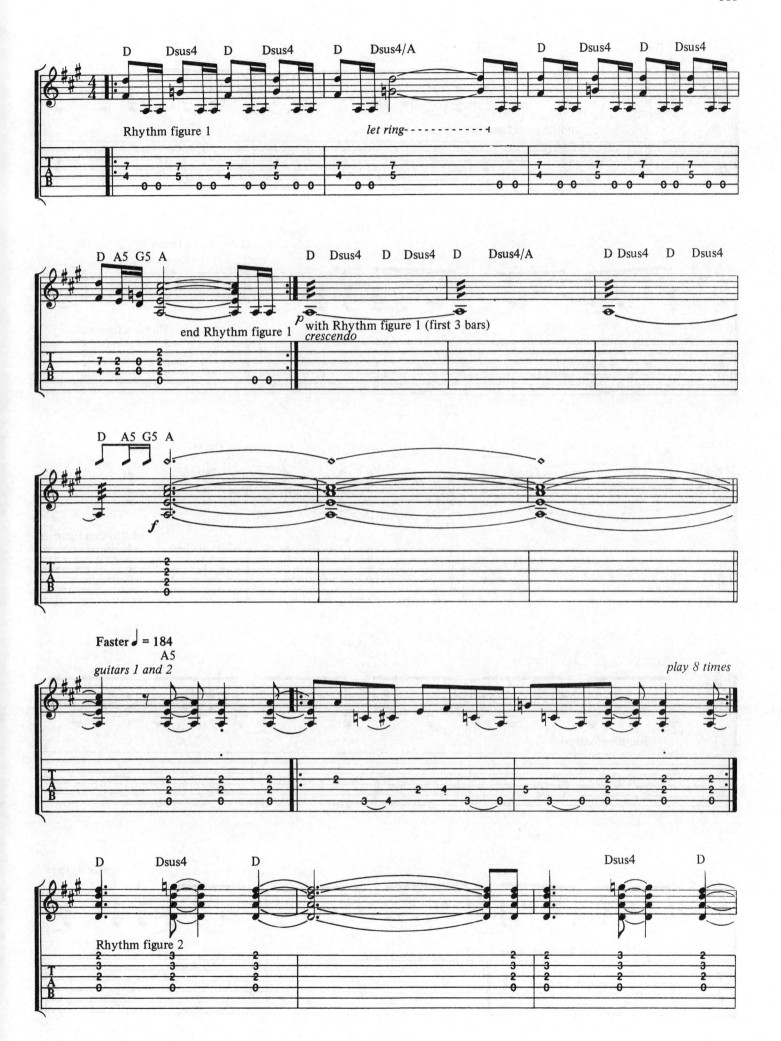

534

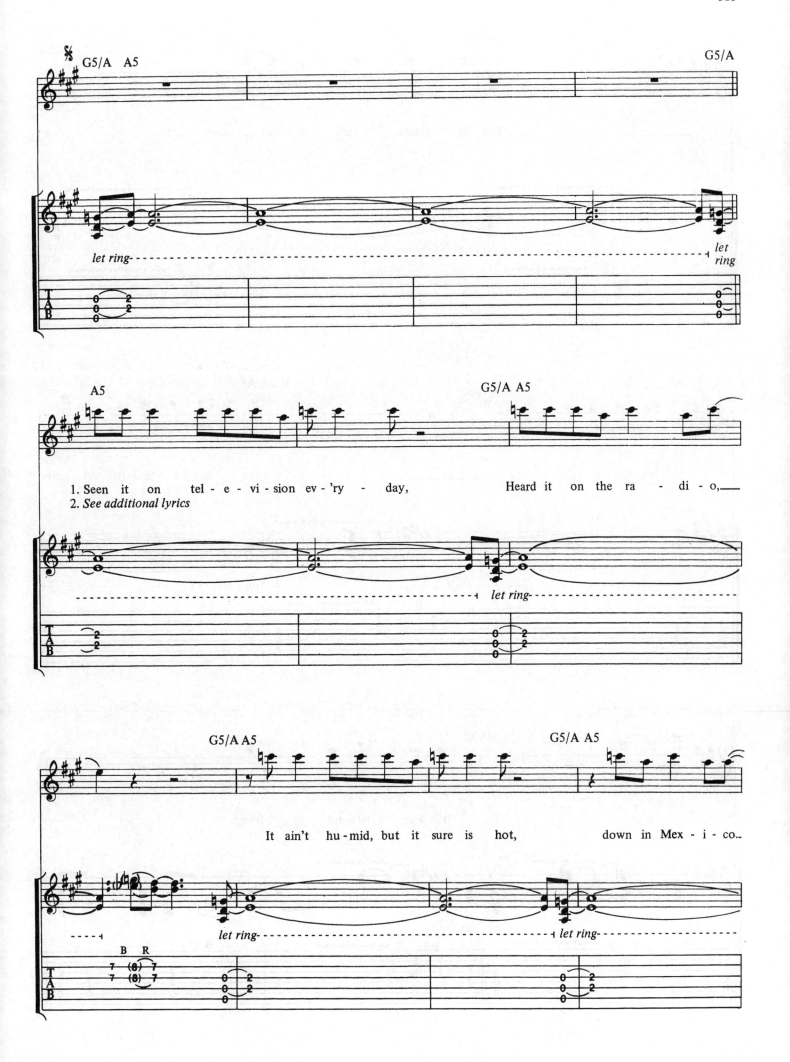

1. Seen it on tel-e-vi-sion ev-'ry - day,   Heard it on the ra - di - o,___
2. *See additional lyrics*

It ain't hu - mid, but it sure is hot,   down in Mex - i - co..

Guitar solo 1

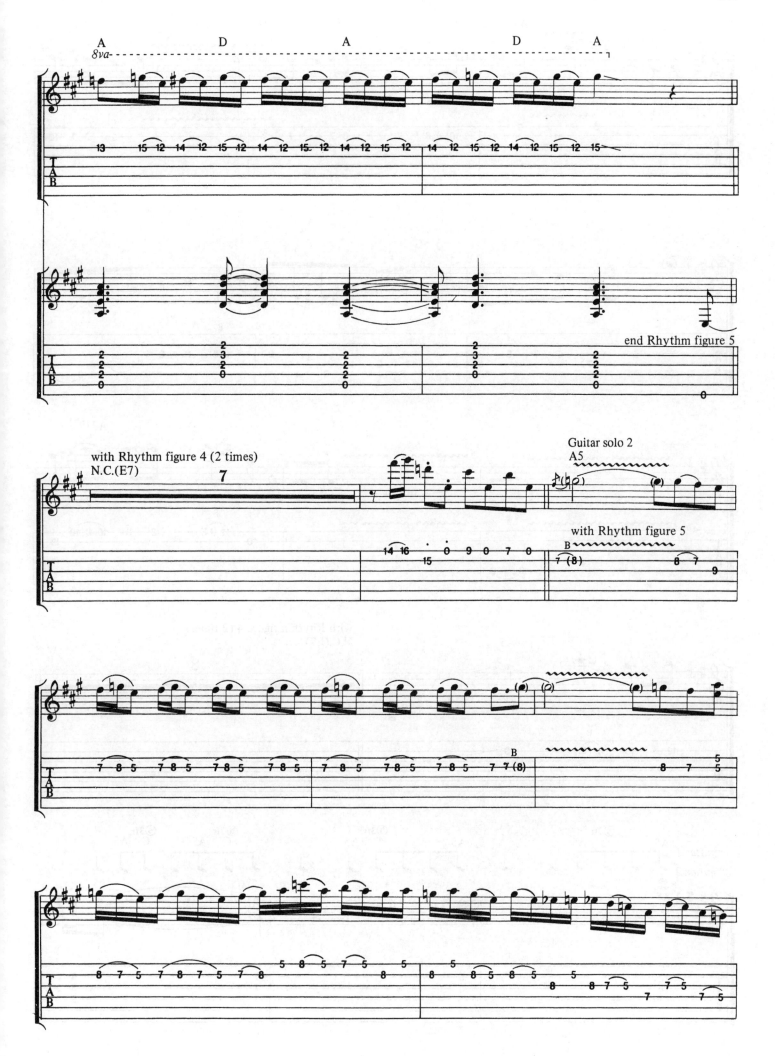

D.S. al Coda

544

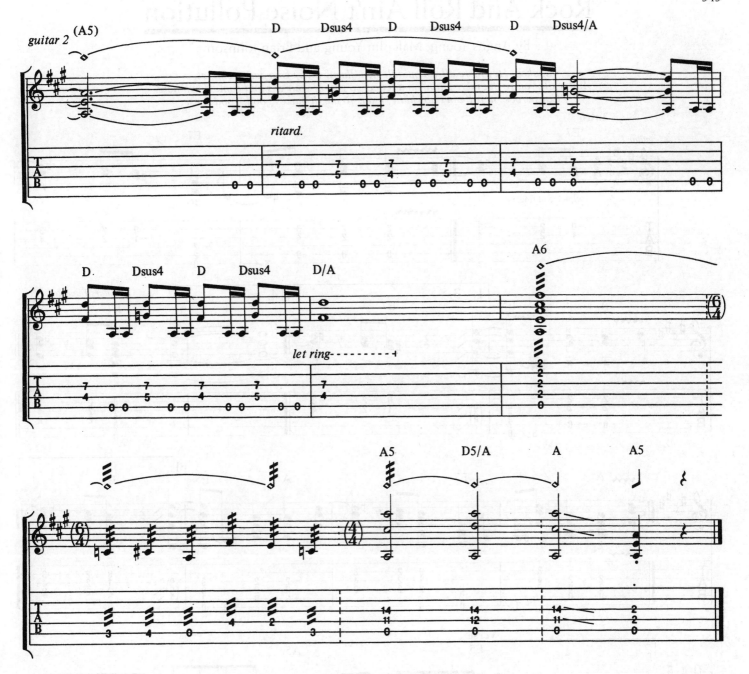

Additional lyrics

2. Now I'm the kind of guy who keeps his big mouth shut,
   It don't bother me,
   Somebody kicking me when I'm up,
   Living in misery.
   I never shot nobody,
   Don't even carry a gun,
   I ain't done nothing wrong,
   I'm just having fun.

Rock And Roll Ain't Noise Pollution

By Angus Young, Malcolm Young and Brian Johnson

Spoken: Hey there all you middlemen, throw away your fancy clothes.
And while you're out there sittin' on a fence, so get off your ass and come down here.
'Cause rock 'n' roll ain't no riddle, man. To me, it makes good, good sense.

548

550

Guitar solo

w/Rhythm figures 1 and 1a (Guitars 1 and 2)

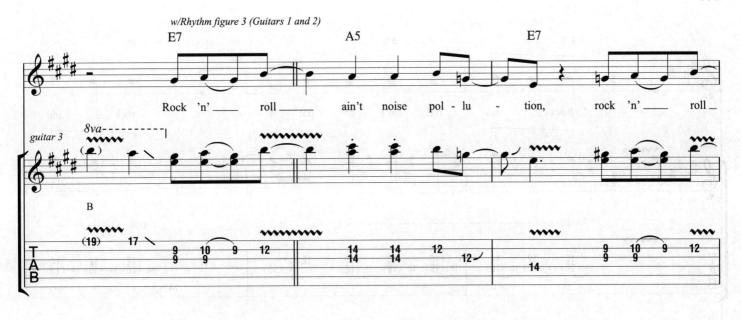

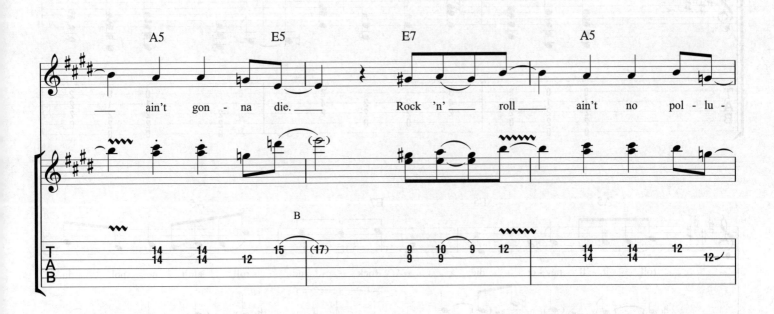

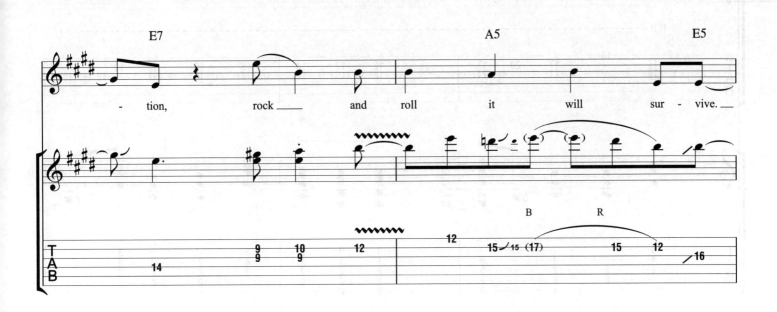

552

Rock 'N' Roll Damnation

By Angus Young, Malcolm Young and Bon Scott

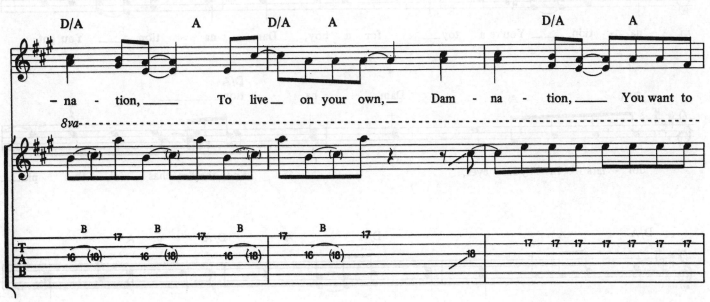

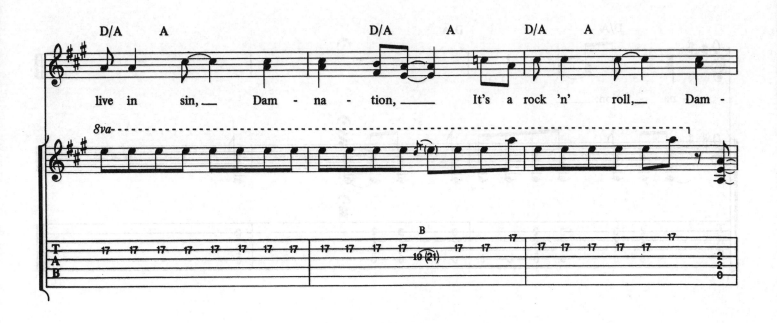

558

Rock 'N' Roll Singer

By Angus Young, Malcolm Young and Bon Scott

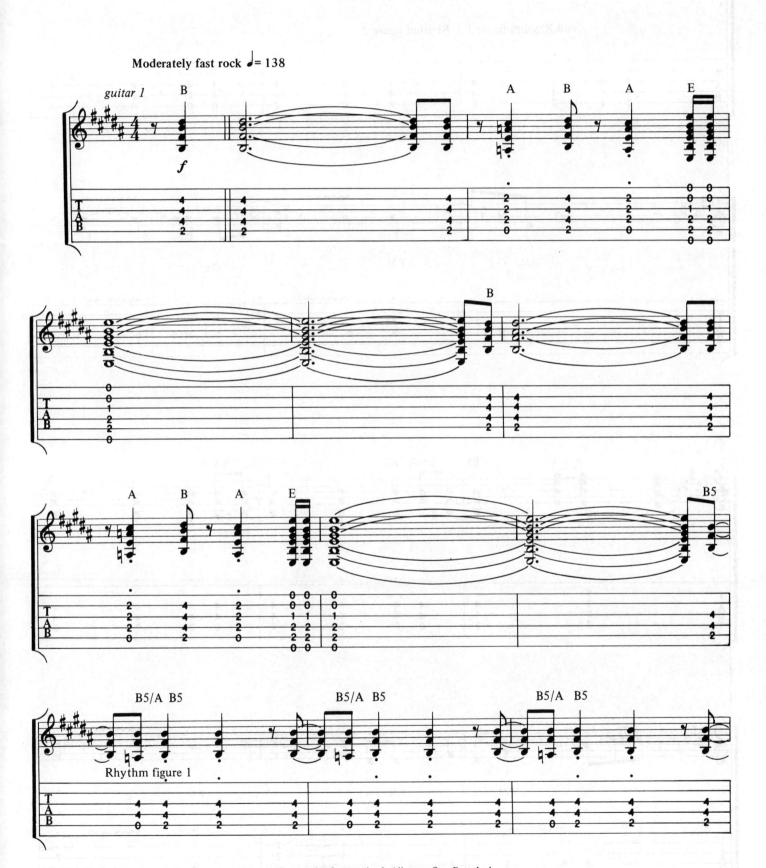

566

stick your gol - den hand - shake, And you can stick your_ sil - ly

rules, And all the oth - er shit, That ya'

teach the kids in school.__ 'Cause I__ ain't

__ no__ fool.__ Gon - na be a rock__

Yes, I are!

Additional Lyrics

2. Well, I worked real hard and got myself
A rock'n roll guitar,
I'm gonna be on top someday,
I'm gonna be a star.
I can see my name in lights,
And I can see the cue,
I got the devil in my blood,
Tellin' me what to do.
And I'm all ears.

Rock N Roll Train

By Angus Young & Malcolm Young

*chord played by guitar 1 only

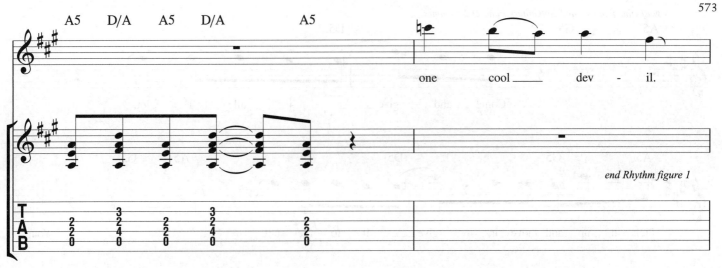

one cool____ dev - il.

end Rhythm figure 1

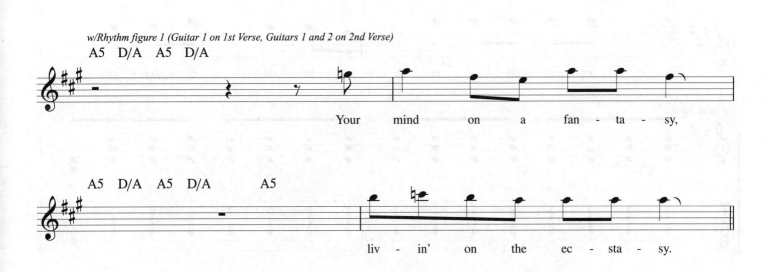

w/Rhythm figure 1 (Guitar 1 on 1st Verse, Guitars 1 and 2 on 2nd Verse)

Your mind on a fan - ta - sy,

liv - in' on the ec - sta - sy.

Pre-Chorus

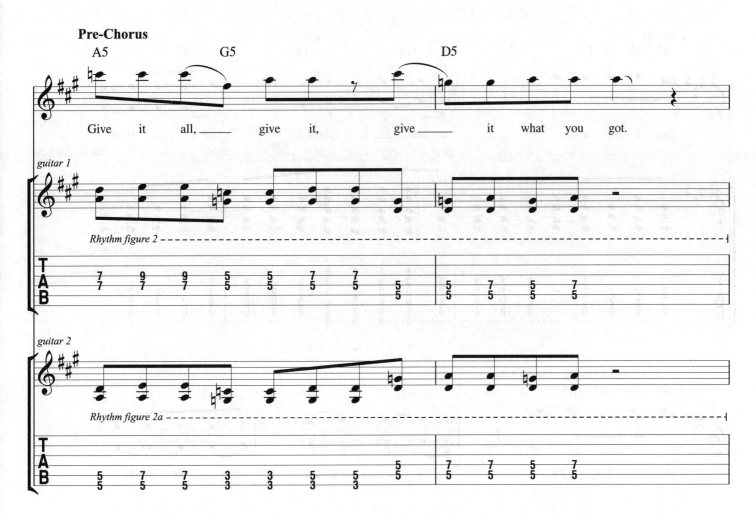

Give it all,____ give it, give____ it what you got.

guitar 1

Rhythm figure 2 - ⌐

guitar 2

Rhythm figure 2a - ⌐

574

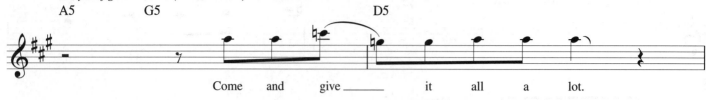

w/Rhythm figures 2 and 2a (Guitars 1 and 2) 2 1/2 times

A5   G5   D5

Come and give ____ it all a lot.

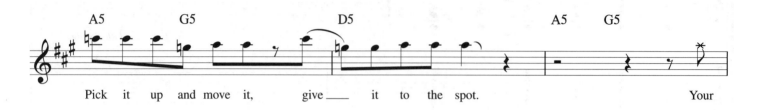

A5   G5   D5   A5   G5

Pick it up and move it, give ____ it to the spot.   Your

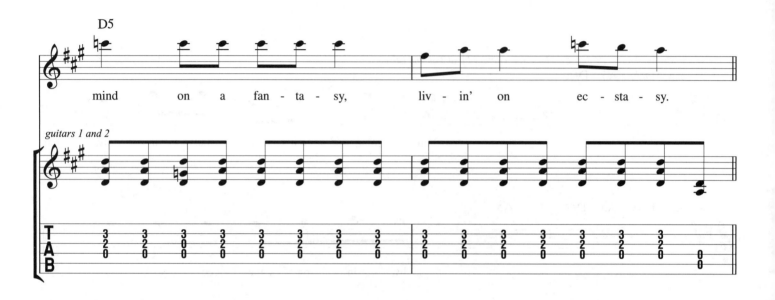

D5

mind   on a fan - ta - sy,   liv - in' on ec - sta - sy.

guitars 1 and 2

Chorus

A5 D5 A5 D5   G5   D5   A5

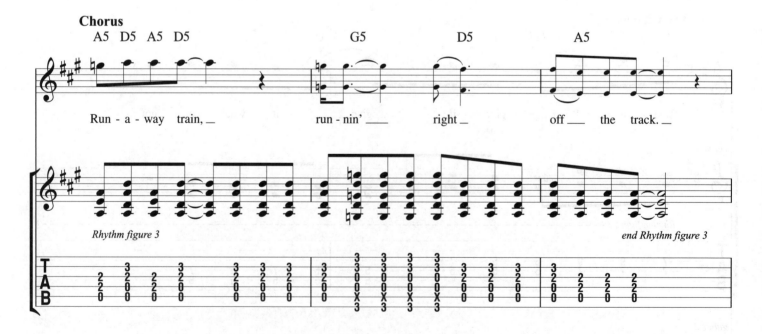

Run - a - way train, __   run - nin' ____ right __   off ____ the track. __

Rhythm figure 3   *end Rhythm figure 3*

w/Rhythm figure 3 (Guitars 1 and 2) 3 times

A5 D5 A5 D5   G5   D5   A5

Run - a - way train, __   run - nin' ____ right __   off ____ the track. __

Run - a - way train, __ run - nin' __ right __ off __ the track. __ Got a

run - a - way train, run - nin' _____ right _____

1.

off _____ the track. _____

guitars 1 and 2

2.

Guitar solo

run - nin' ___ right __ off __ the track. __

guitar 3

pick scrape - - - - -|

Rapidly bounce pick along strings while scraping.

guitars 1 and 2

Rhythm figure 4 -|

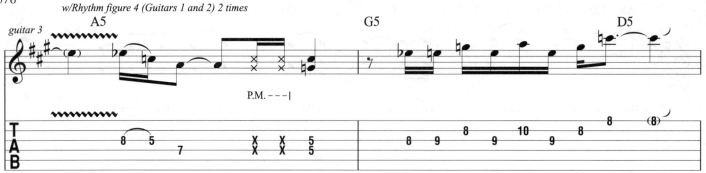

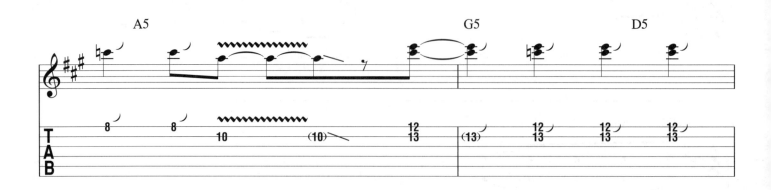

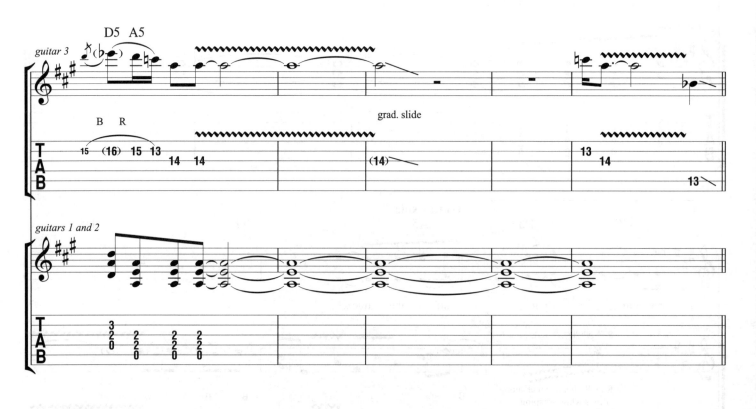

3rd Verse

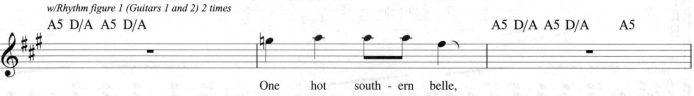

One   hot   south - ern   belle,

son   of   a   dev - il,   a   school - boy's   spell - ing   bee,

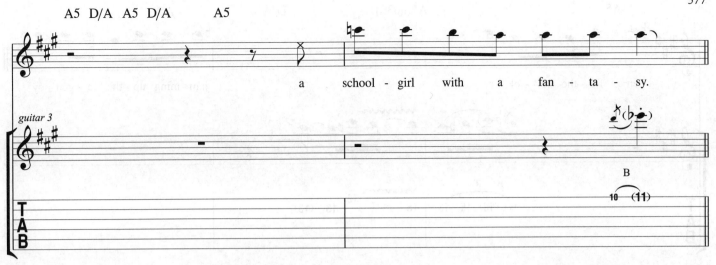

a school-girl with a fan-ta-sy.

4th Verse

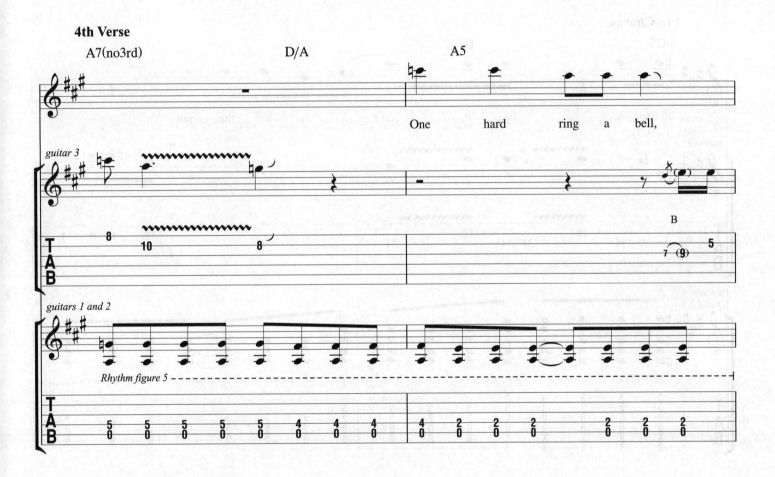

One hard ring a bell,

all screwed up. ___

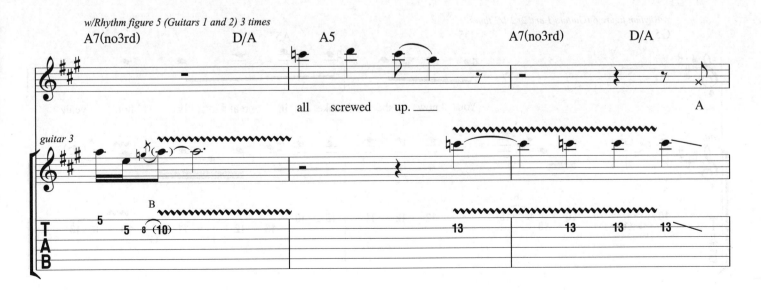

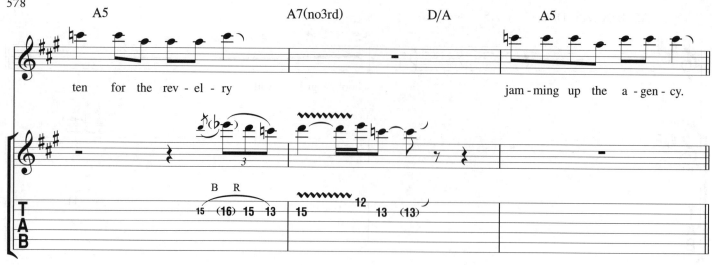

Pre-Chorus

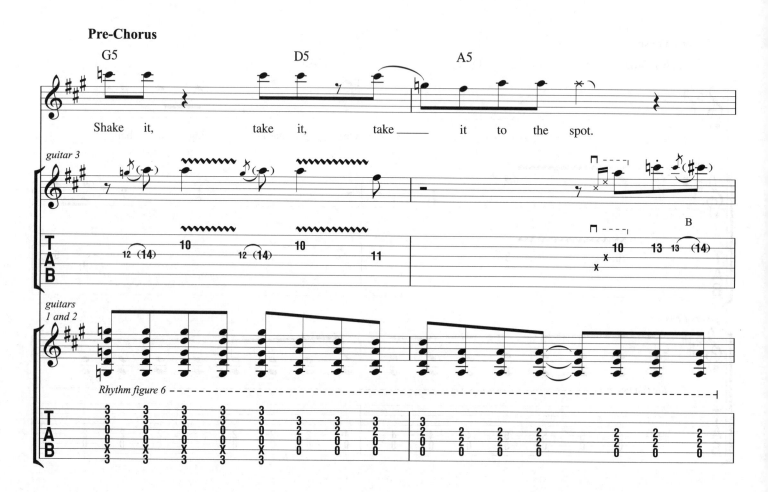

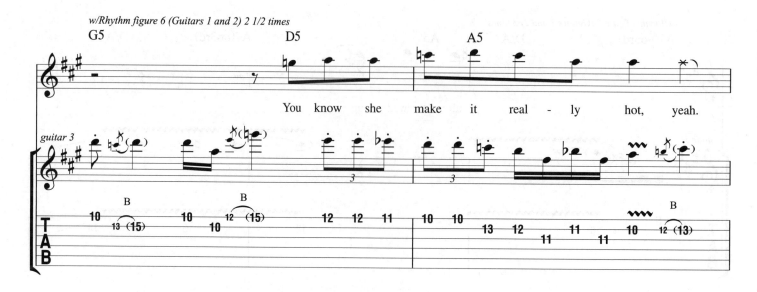

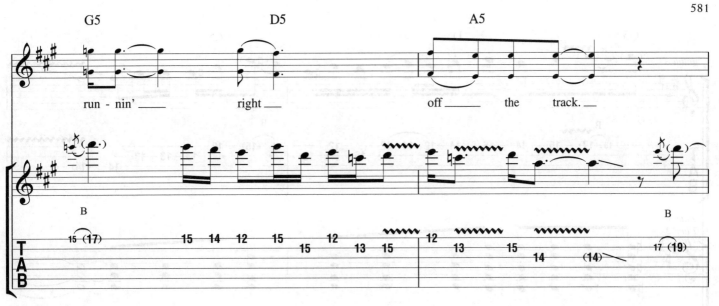

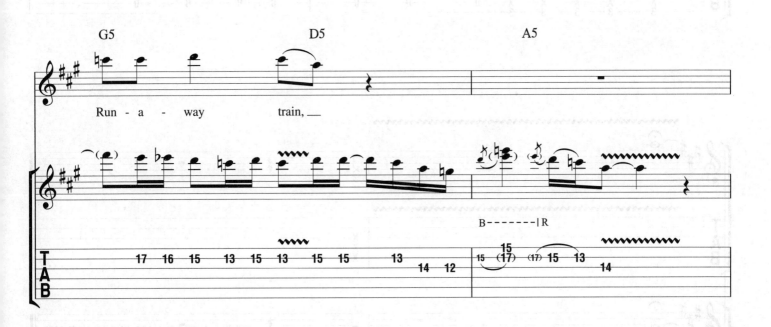

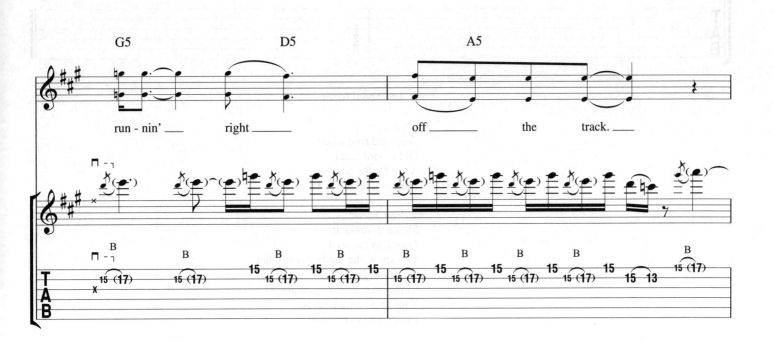

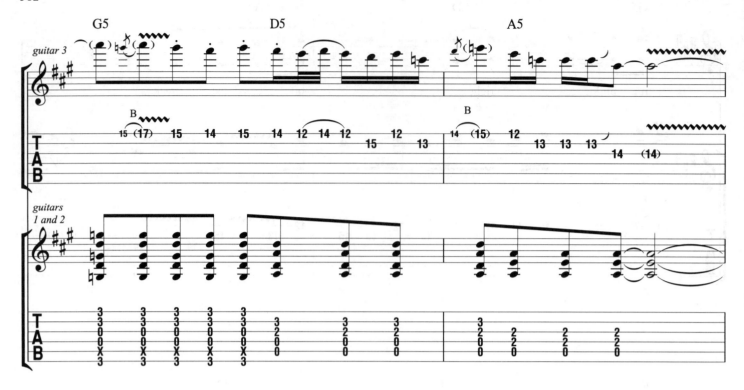

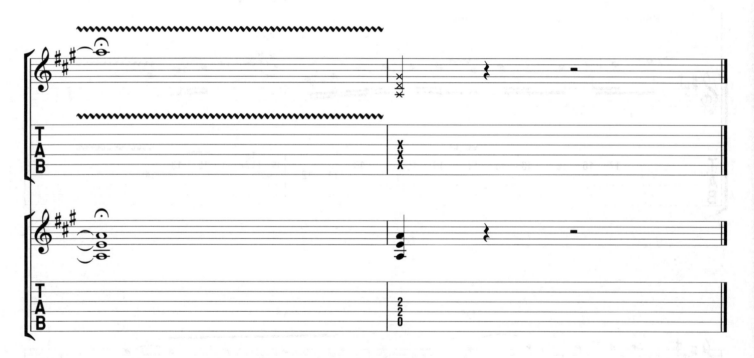

Additional lyrics

2nd Verse:
One hard ring a bell
Old school rebel
A ten for the revelry
Jamming up the agency

2nd Pre-Chorus:
Shake it, shake it
Take it to the spot
You know she made it really hot
Get it on, give it up
Come on give it all you got
Your mind on a fantasy
Living on the ecstasy

Rocker

By Angus Young, Malcolm Young and Bon Scott

Tune down 1/2 step:
⑥ = Eb ③ = Gb
⑤ = Ab ② = Bb
④ = Db ① = Eb

Guitar Solo (ad lib. on repeats)

guitar 2 with Rhythm figure 1

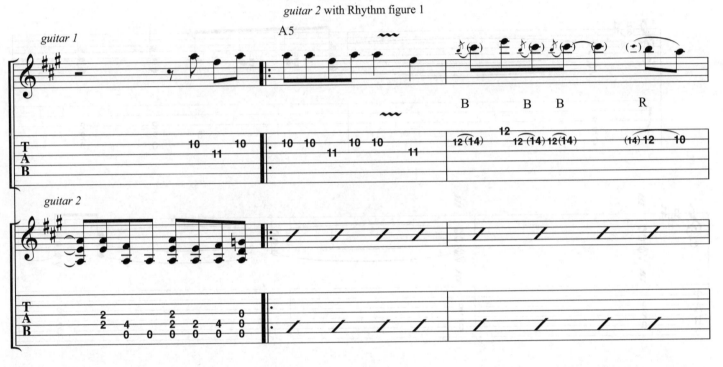

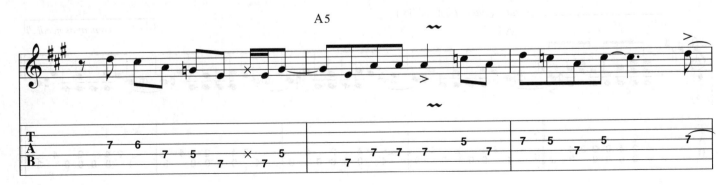

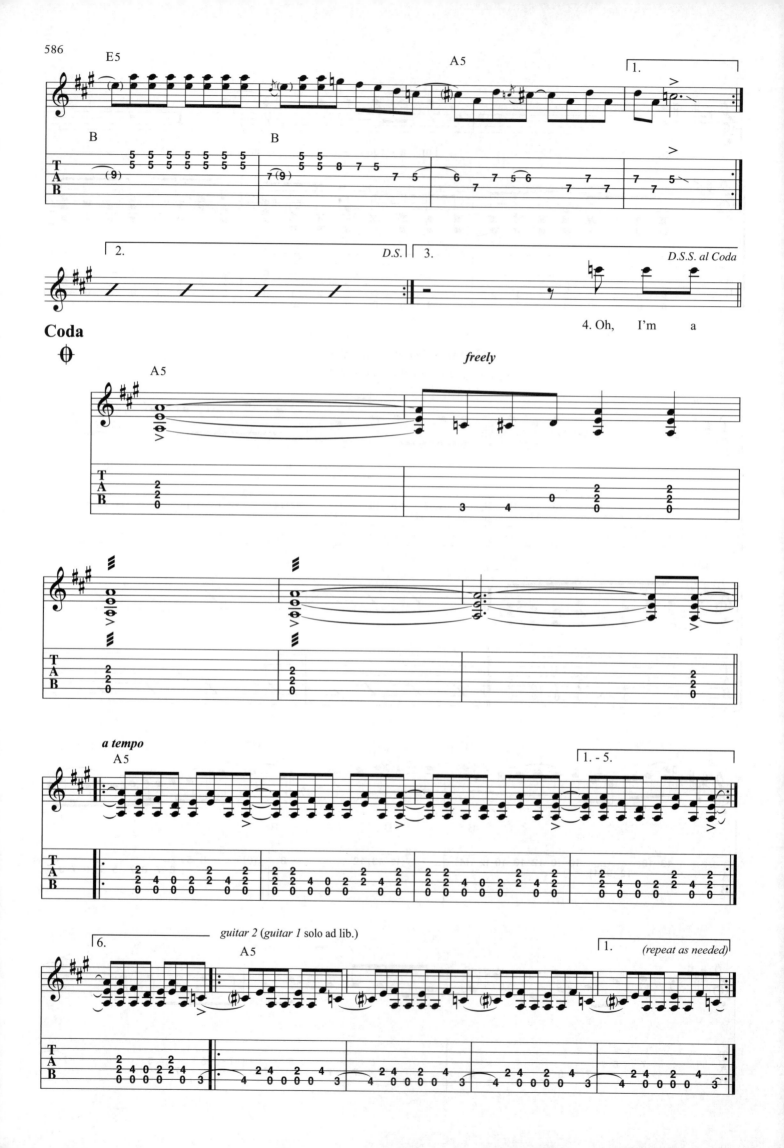

4. Oh,   I'm   a

Coda

freely

a tempo

guitar 2 (guitar 1 solo ad lib.)

(repeat as needed)

Outro Chorus
guitars 1 & 2 with Rhythm figure 1 (*vocal* ad lib. on repeat)

I'm a rock - er, roll - er, rock - er, roll,___ roll, roll-er.

Rock - er, roll - er. Yeah, I'm a rock, rock, rock 'n' roll - er. Rock-

er! Rock 'n' roll - er. Rock - er! Rock 'n' roll -

guitars 1 & 2

freely

accel. poco a poco

Additional Lyrics:

3. Got lorex socks,
   Blue suede shoes,
   And tattoos...

4. I'm a rocker,
   I'm a roller...
   A rock 'n' roll man...

Rocking All The Way

By Angus Young & Malcolm Young

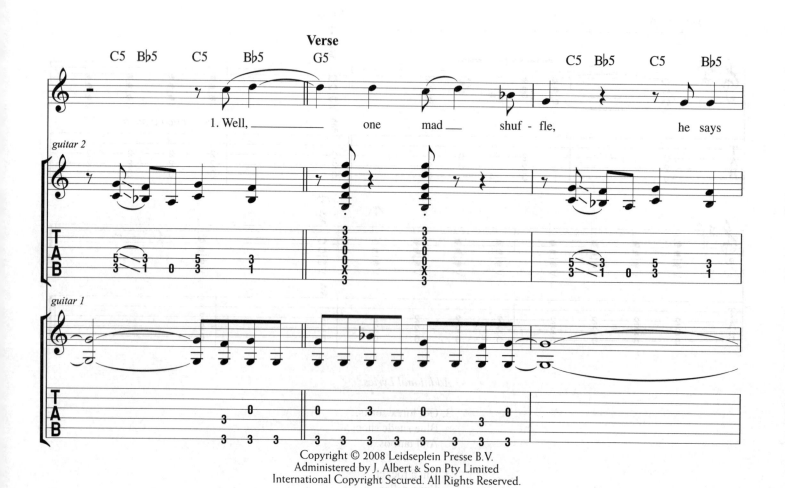

590

591

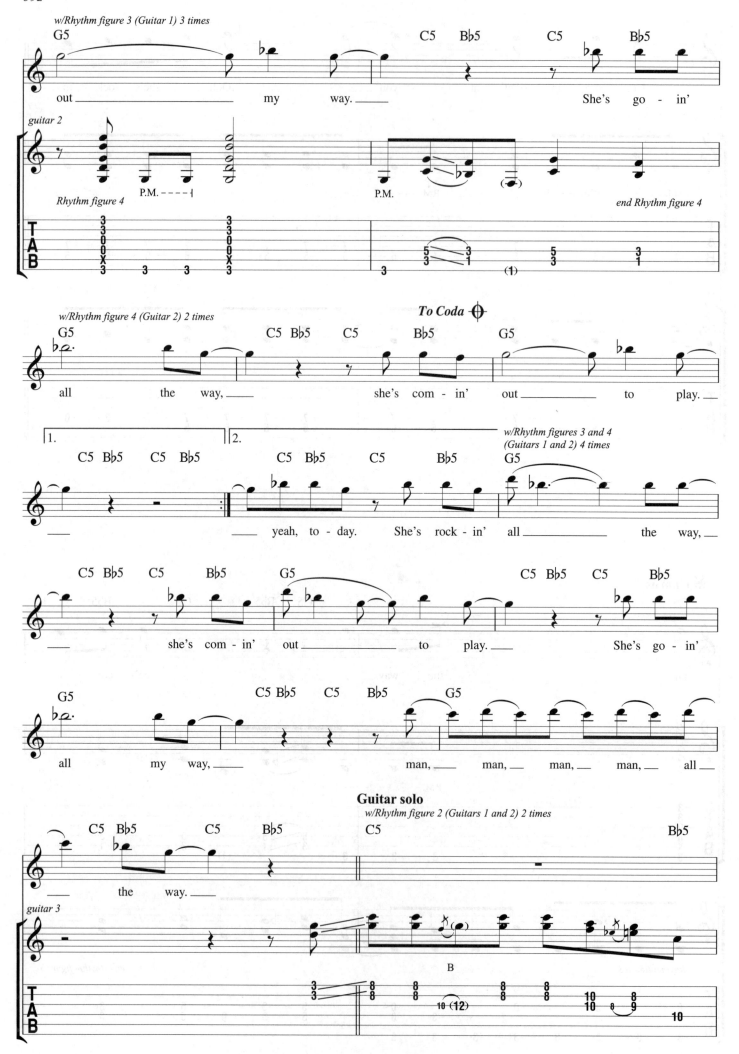

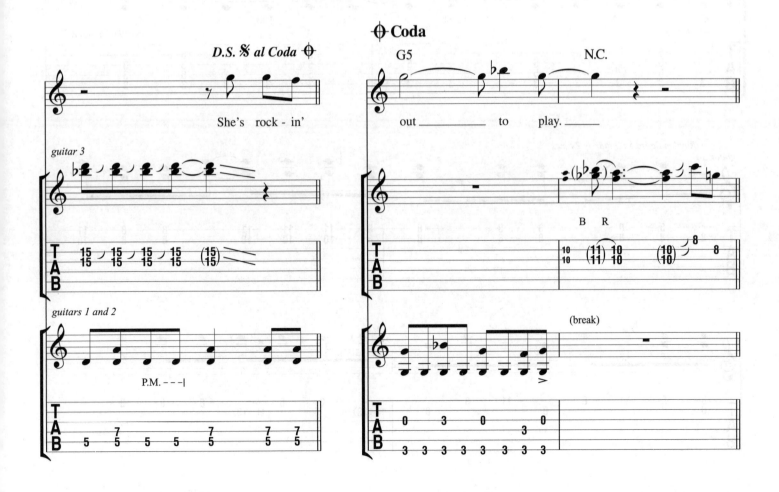

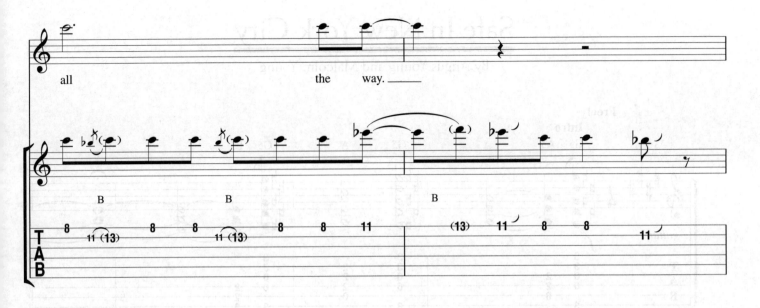

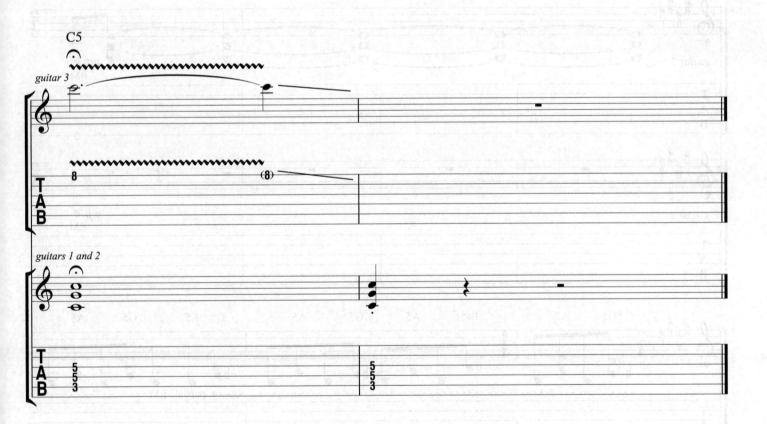

Additional lyrics

3rd Verse:
She's sexy in her boots, yeah
Tear up all the news
Shoot you in the back
Drivin' you mad
Come on, hear me out
And take my advice
She won't stop until you're in her sights

Safe In New York City

By Angus Young and Malcolm Young

*Bass plays E through all verses and choruses.

Verse

E5   E

1. Hel - lo ba - by, give_ me your hand._
2. *See additional lyrics*

guitar 1 & 2

Rhythm figure 1   end Rhythm figure 1

guitars 1 & 2 with Rhythm figure 1 (two times)

E5   E

Check out the high spots, the lay of the land._

E5   E

You don't need a rock - et or a big lim - ou - sine._   Ooh,

Chorus
E5

come on o - ver, ba - by, and I'll make you ob - scene._   I feel

guitar 1

Rhythm figure 2

guitar 2

Rhythm figure 2A

Verse
guitars 1 & 2 with Rhythm figure 1 (three times)

guitar 3 tacet

3. Mov - in' all o - ver like a jump - in'— bean,—

guitar 3

take a look at that thing— in the tight— ass jeans.

Com - in' your way,— now, you

may be— in luck;

608

Outro

guitar 2 with Rhythm figure 4A (three times)

610

*Strike only the bottom note.

*guitars 1 & 2

*two guitars arranged for one

612

*Flick pickup switch back & forth as quickly as possible, gradually slowing
down as bent note is released.*

Additional lyrics

2. All over the city and down to the dives,
   Don't mess with this place, it'll eat you alive, yeah:
   Got a lip smackin' honey to soak up the jam;
   On top of the world ma ready to slam.
   (to Chorus)

Satellite Blues

By Angus Young and Malcolm Young

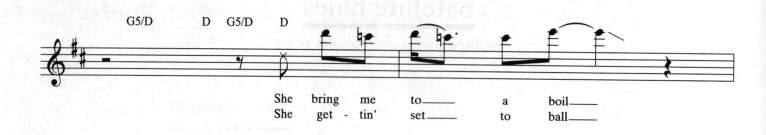

She bring me to_____ a boil_____
She get - tin' set_____ to ball_____

She like to give_____ it out some
I like to chew_____ it up some

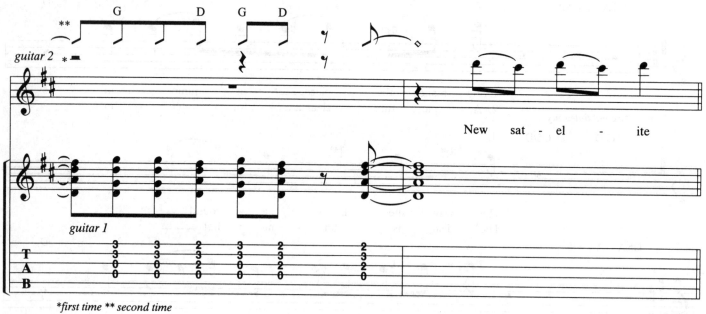

guitar 2

New sat - el - ite

guitar 1

*first time ** second time

Chorus

Rhythm figure 2A

blues_____

New sat - el - lite

Rhythm figure 2

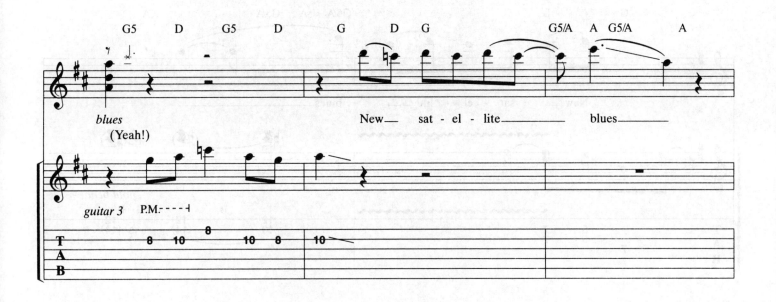

Shake A Leg

By Angus Young, Malcolm Young and Brian Johnson

Fight - in' on the wrong side of the law,__ of the law,__ yeah.__

end Rhythm figure 2   with Rhythm figure 2

__ Don't kick,__ don't fight, don't sleep at night and shake__

a tempo

__ a leg, shake__ a leg, shake__ a leg. Shake__ it a -

gain.

Rhythm figure 3

end Rhythm figure 3   with Rhythm figure 3

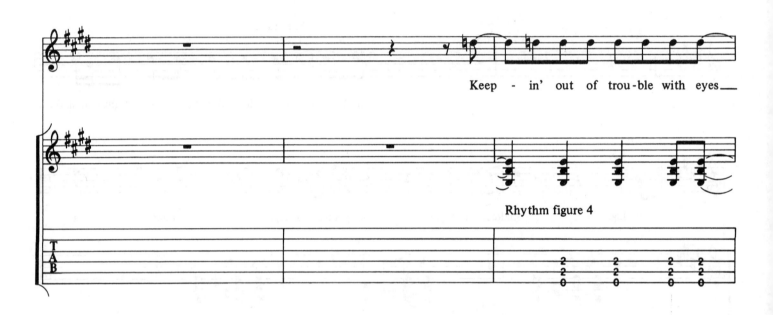

Keep - in' out of trou-ble with eyes____

Rhythm figure 4

____ in the back of my   face.   Kick - in' ass____

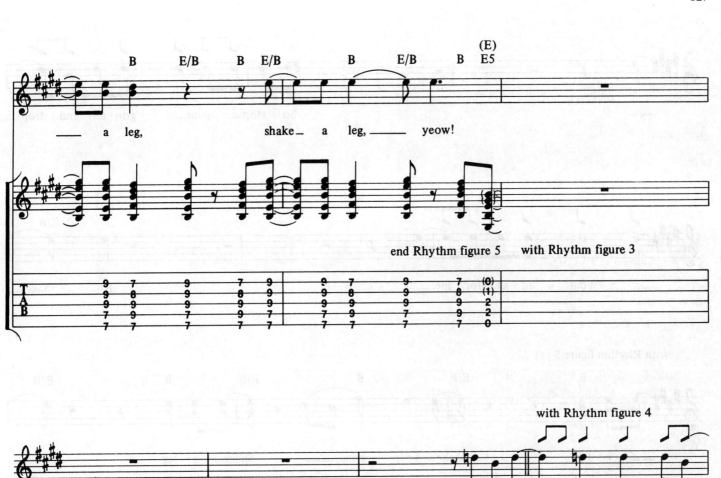

_____ a leg,   shake _ a leg, _____ yeow!

end Rhythm figure 5   with Rhythm figure 3

with Rhythm figure 4

Mag-a-zines, _ wet dreams, dirt-y

wom-en on ma-chines for me. _____   Uh, big _

licks, skin flicks, trick-y dicks are my chem-is-try. _

Goin' a-gainst _ the grain, _ tryin' to keep a me sane, _ with you. _

628

So stop— your— grin-nin' and drop—

— your lin-en for me.— Ah, shake—

with Rhythm figure 5

— a leg, shake— your head,— Shake— a leg, wake—

— the dead,— Shake— a leg, get— stuck in, — Shake—

— a leg, shake— a leg.— Yeah!——— Shake it!

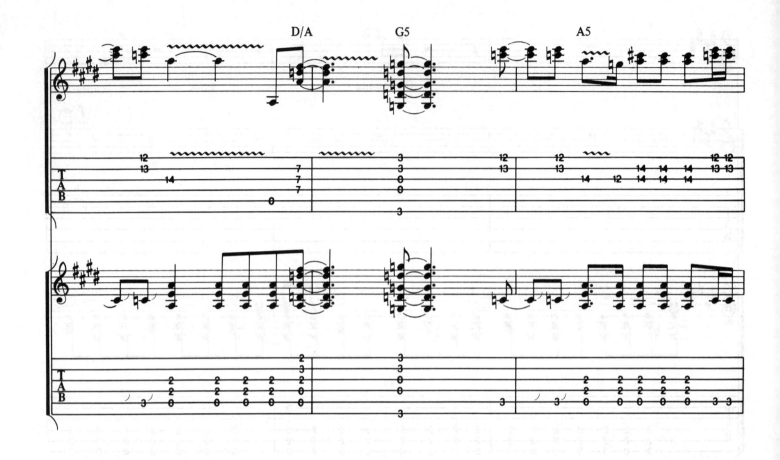

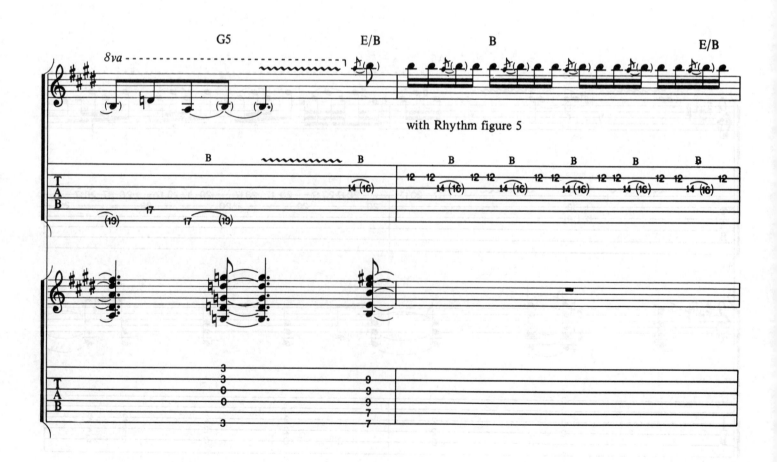

633

634

She Likes Rock N Roll

By Angus Young & Malcolm Young

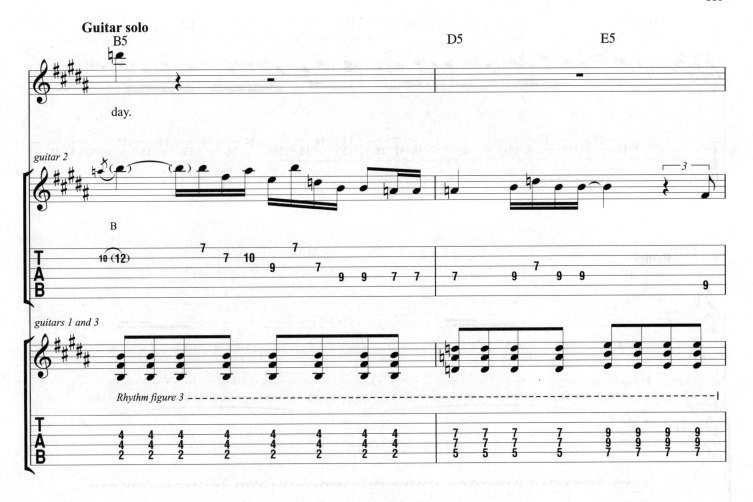

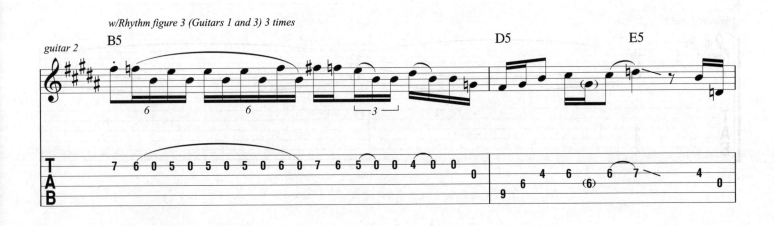

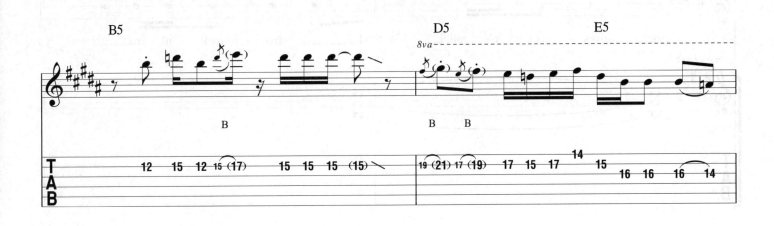

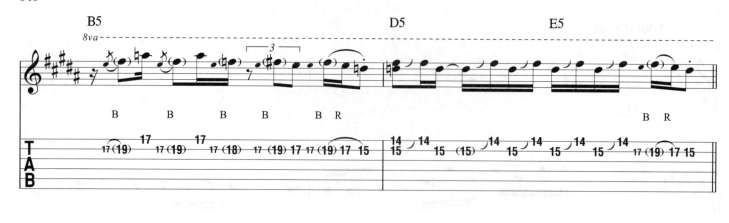

Bridge

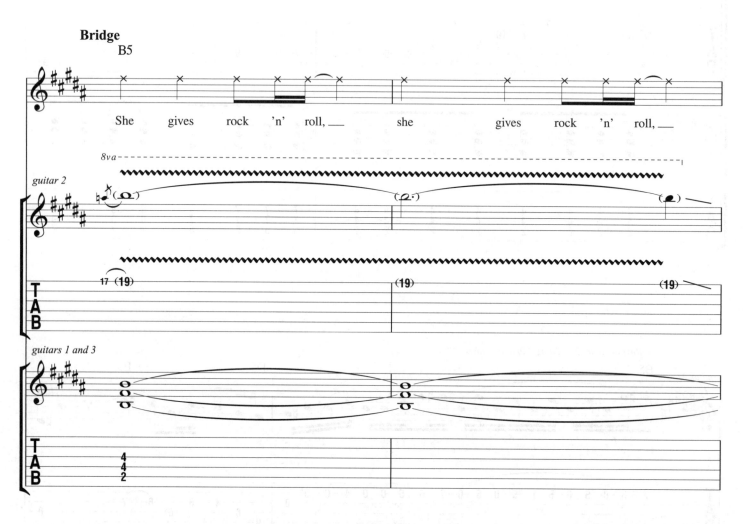

She gives rock 'n' roll, ___ she gives rock 'n' roll, ___

guitar 2

guitars 1 and 3

D.S. 𝄉 al Coda ⊕

she gives rock 'n' roll, ___ I ___ like rock 'n' roll. ___

guitars 1 and 3

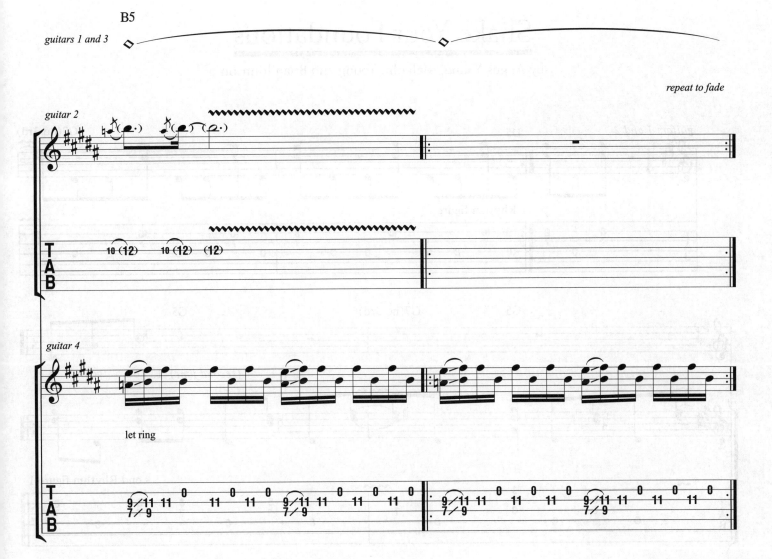

Additional lyrics

2nd Verse:
You're gonna rock, you'll rock the night away
You're gonna roll, baby, and I'll make the grade
We're gonna rock now, rock 'n' rollin' all in the town
You're gonna make it right, we're gonna need to rock all night

3rd Verse:
We are a gang coming down
We're gonna rock all night, rock 'n' rollin' all the time
She may be home, rollin' out the groove
You know that rock 'n' roll's squeezin' out the tube

4th Verse:
I'm gonna dance all night long
And rock into the room, yeah
She likes sugar and I like honey, too
We're gonna rock it, I ain't gonna mess around with you

Shake Your Foundations

By Angus Young, Malcolm Young and Brian Johnson

646

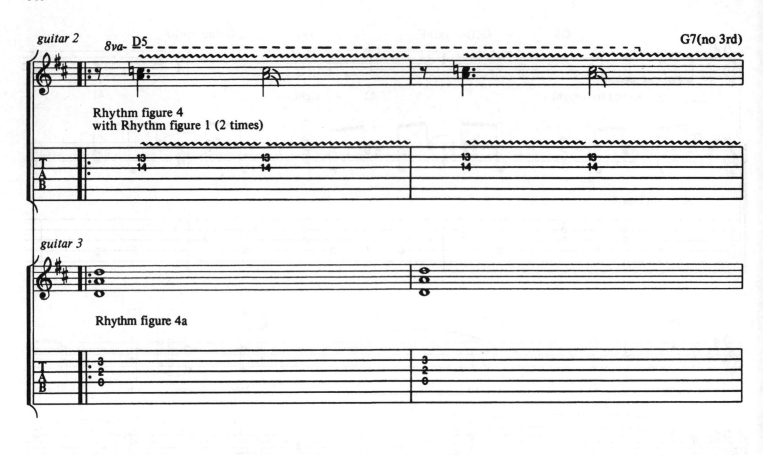

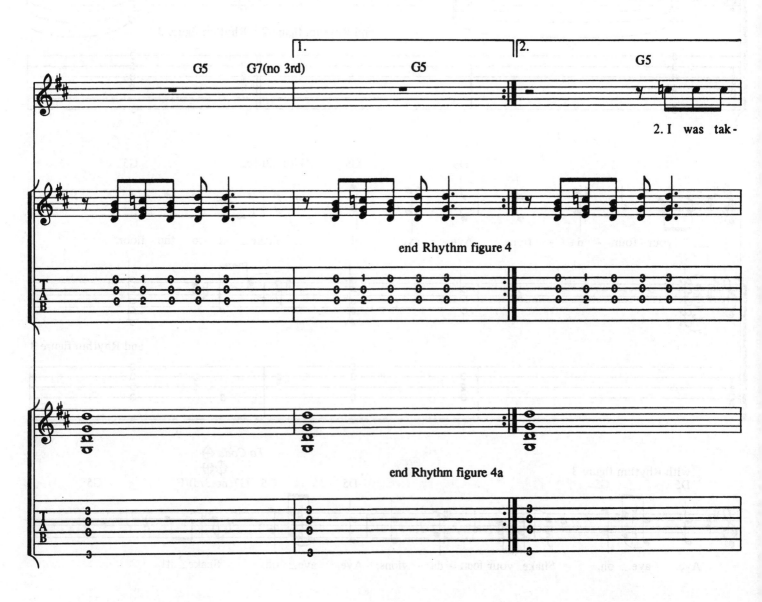

648

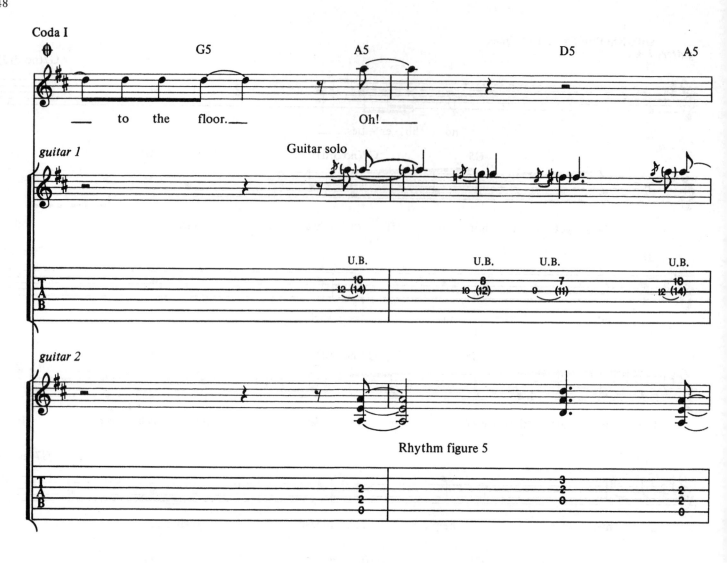

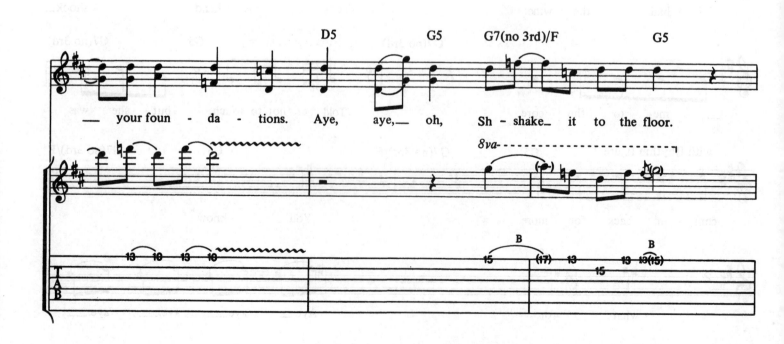

She's Got Balls

By Angus Young, Malcolm Young and Bon Scott

1. She's got

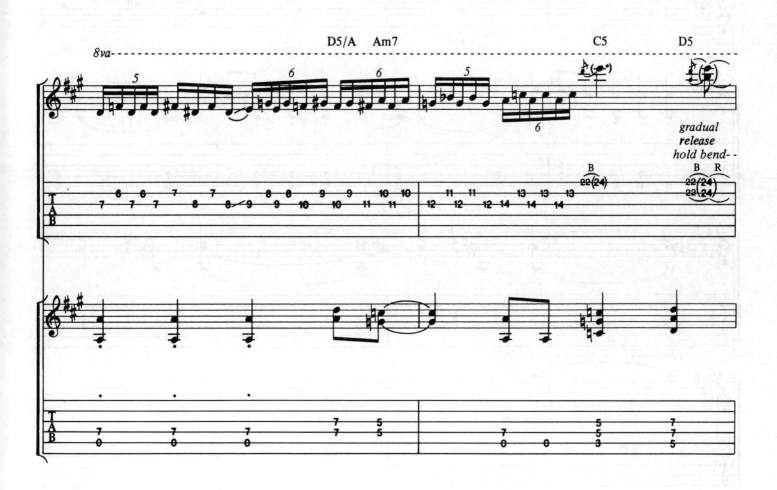

3. And she's got

659

taste, my la - dy,___ Pace, my la - dy.___

Makes my___ heart race___ with

662

Additional Lyrics

2. She's got soul, my lady,
   Likes to crawl, my lady,
   All around the floor,
   On her hands and knees,
   Ooh, because she likes to please me.

Shoot To Thrill

By Angus Young, Malcolm Young and Brian Johnson

%Chorus

Coda

shoot   to   thrill, ___   play ___ to   kill. _____

Interlude

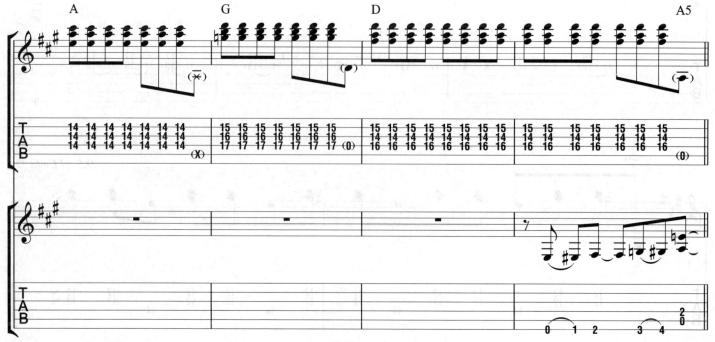

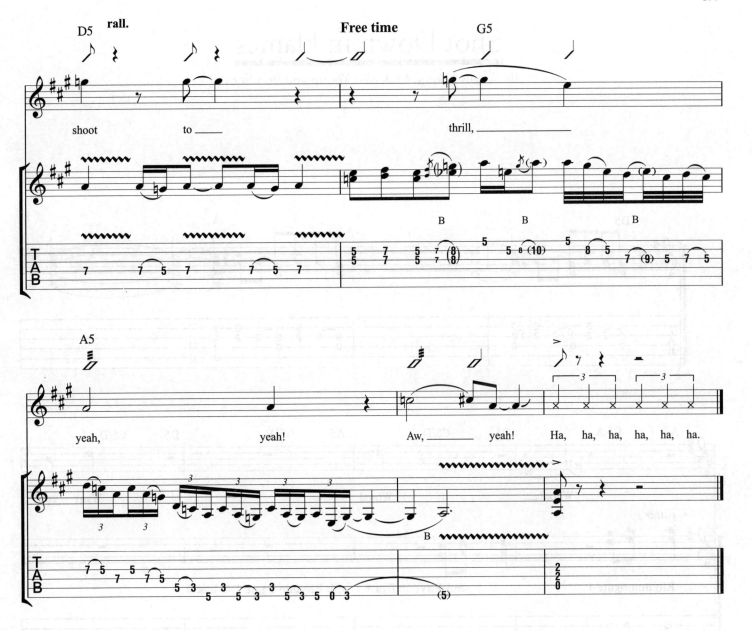

Additional lyrics

2. I'm like evil; I get under your skin,
   Just like a bomb that's ready to blow.
   'Cause I'm illegal; I got everything
   That all you women might need to know.

Shot Down In Flames

By Angus Young, Malcolm Young and Bon Scott

I said "Ba - by what's the go - ing price?" She told me to go to hell.

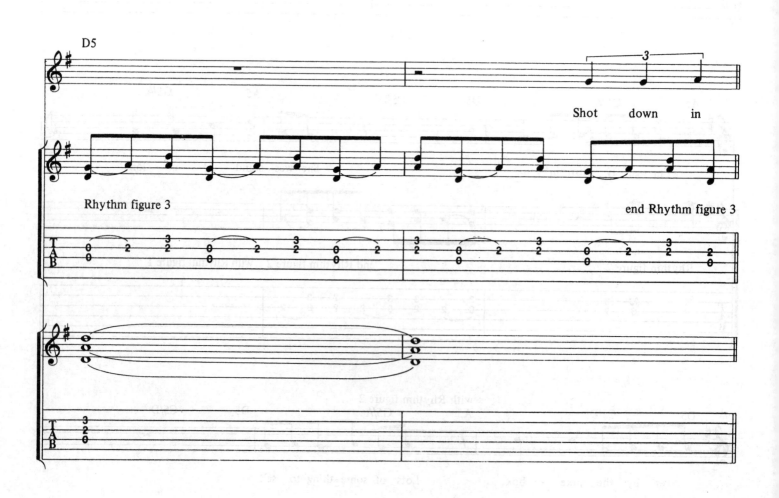

Shot down in

Rhythm figure 3

end Rhythm figure 3

682

684

flames.

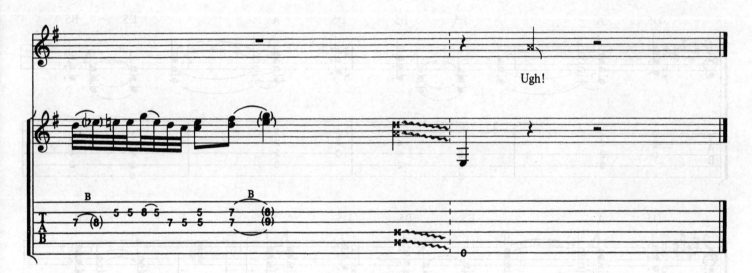

Ugh!

Additional Lyrics

2. Singles bar,
   Got my eye on a honey,
   Hangin' out everywhere.
   She might be straight
   She might want my money,
   I really don't care, no!
   Said, "Baby, you're driving me crazy."
   Laying it out on the line.
   When a guy with a chip on his shoulder says,
   "Toss off buddy, she's mine."

Sin City

By Angus Young, Malcolm Young and Bon Scott

Sink The Pink

By Angus Young, Malcolm Young and Brian Johnson

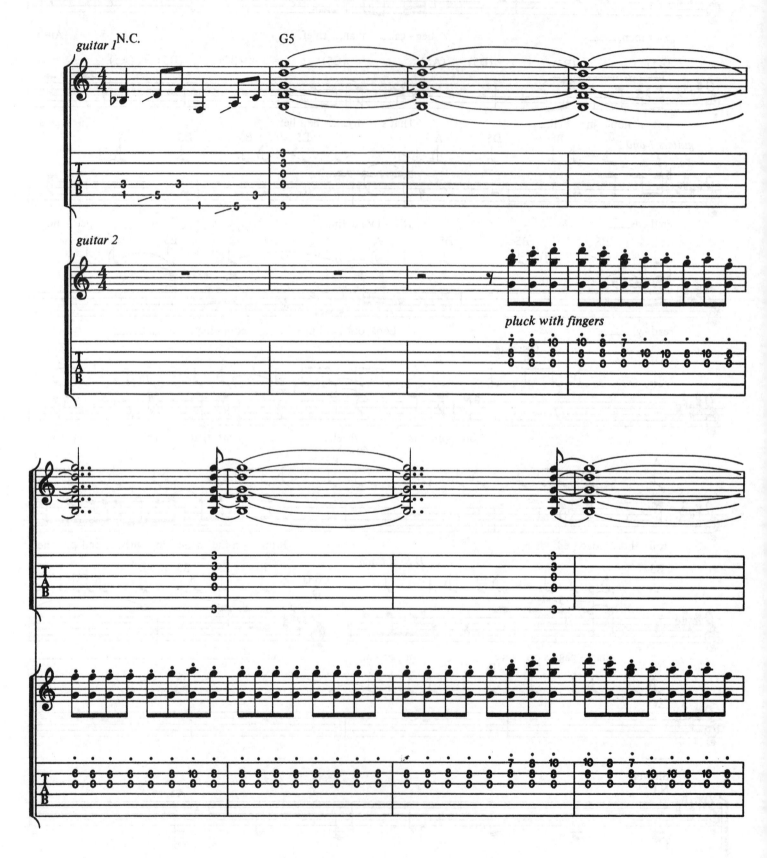

pluck with fingers

G5 Csus4 C G5 Csus4 C G5 Csus4 C G5
ter, gim - me wine.__ Gon - na show__ you a good
Rhythm figure 6
end Rhythm figure 6 with Rhythm figure 6
with Rhythm figures 1 and 1a
Csus4 C G5 Csus4 C Csus4 C G5
time. Sink the pink.__ Sink the pink.__
To Coda
Csus4 C N.C.
guitar 1
guitar 2

698

Coda

To the cit - y of Bom- bay._

guitar 2

pluck with fingers

guitar 1

F5

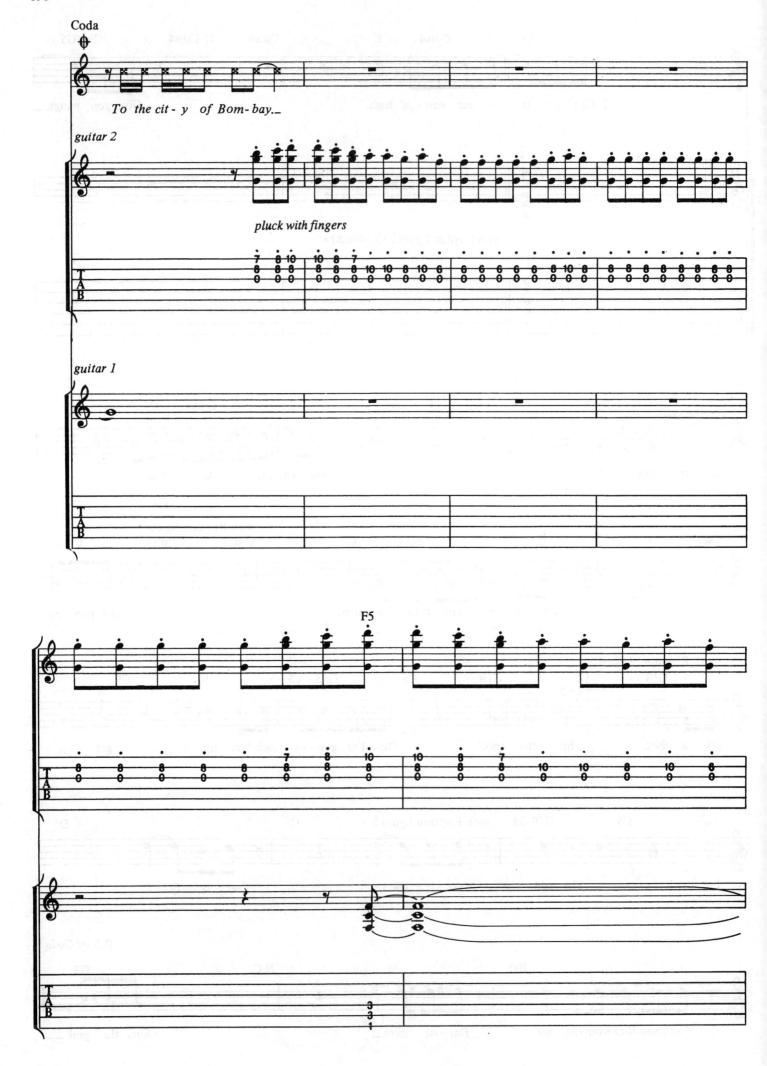

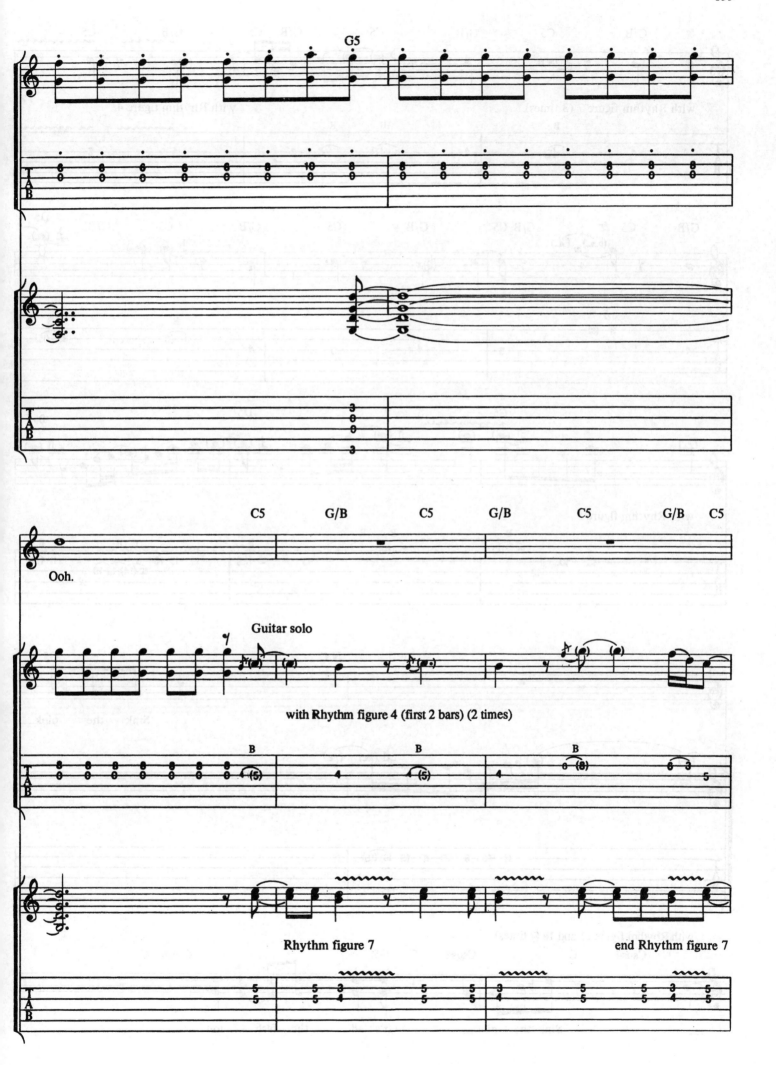

700

Squealer

By Angus Young, Malcolm Young and Bon Scott

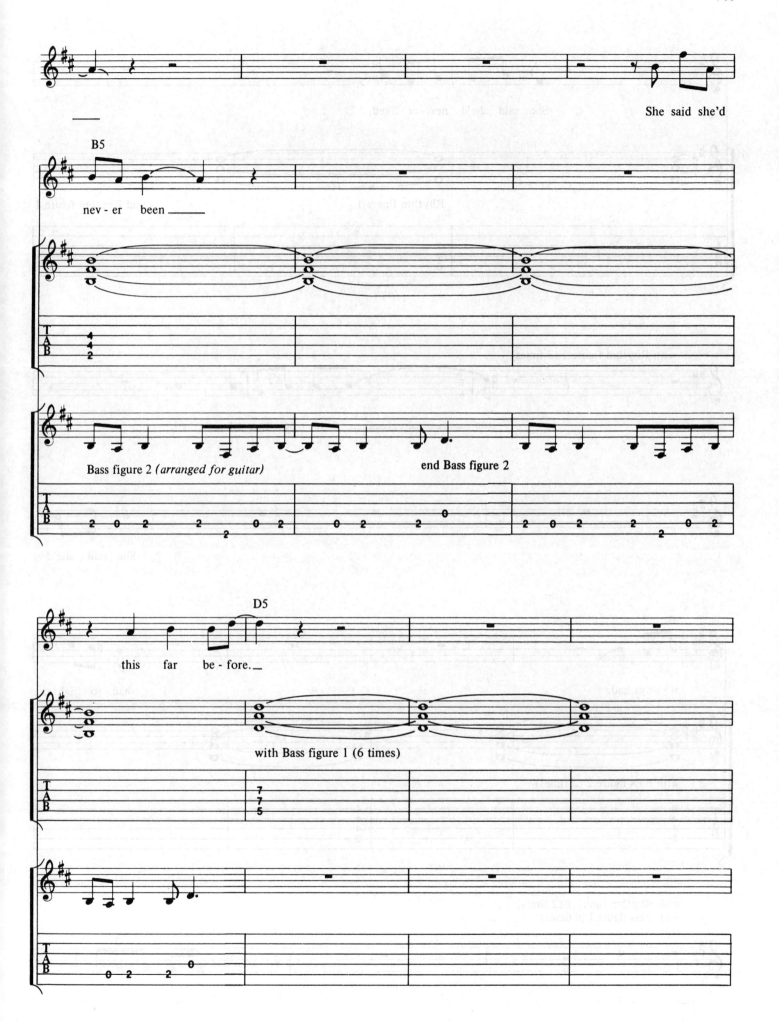

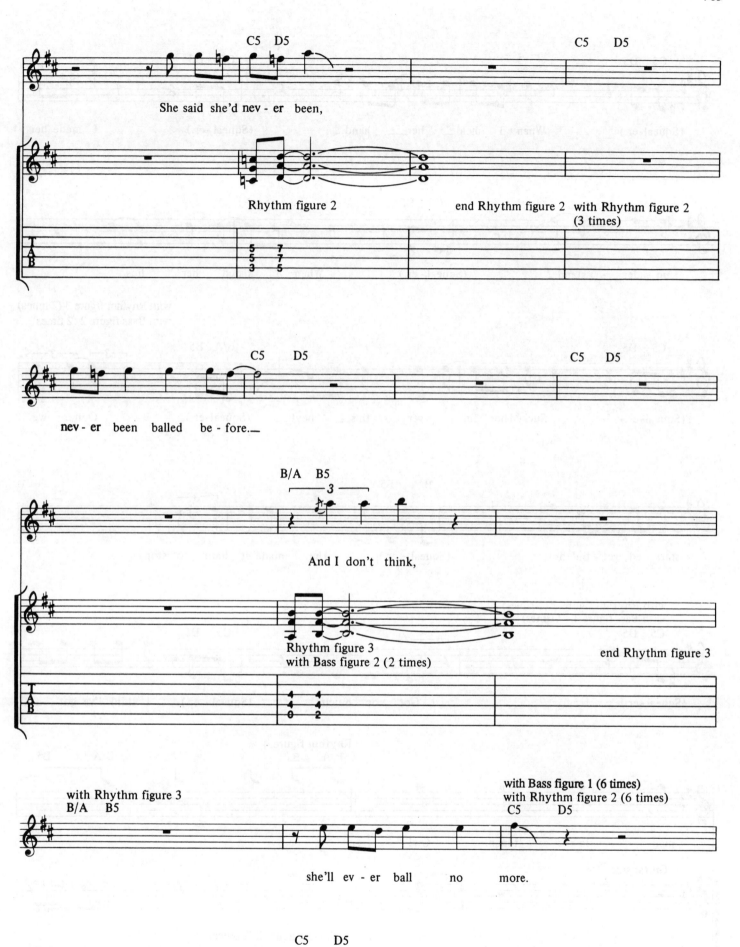

She said she'd nev - er been,

nev - er been balled be - fore.—

And I don't think,

she'll ev - er ball no more.

Fixed her good.

Hey!

712

with vocal ad lib throughout

Stiff Upper Lip

By Angus Young and Malcolm Young

718

Guitar solo

guitars 1 & 2 with Rhythm fills 1 & 1A   *guitar 1 with Rhythm figure 1 (three and a half times)*
guitar 2 with Rhythm figure 2

yeah,   shoot from the   hip._____   Yeah, yeah.

guitar 2 with Rhythm figure 3 (two and a half times)

Yeah._____

Rhythm fill 1   **Rhythm fill 1A**

guitar 1   *guitar 2   let ring ------|*

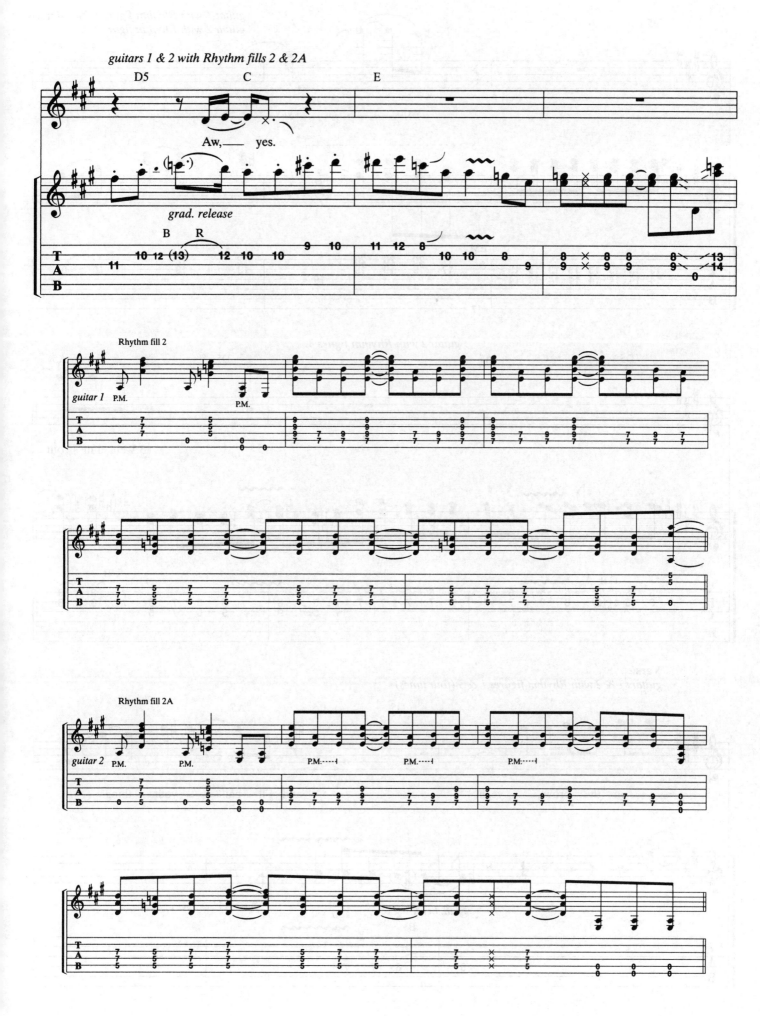

I got the teeth that - 'll bite you;——— can you feel———

——— my sting? Babe,— I keep a

Chorus
guitars 1 & 2 with Rhythm figures 1 & 3 (two and a half times)
guitar 3 tacet

stiff up - per lip,——— and I shoot— from the hip.—

I keep a stiff up - per lip,———

724

shoot from the hip.—

*Rapidly flick pickup switch
back and forth.*

Additional lyrics

2. Well, I'm workin' it out
And I've done everything.
And I can't reform, no;
Can you fell my sting?
Man, I keep a...
(to Chorus)

T.N.T.

By Angus Young, Malcolm Young and Bon Scott

730

732

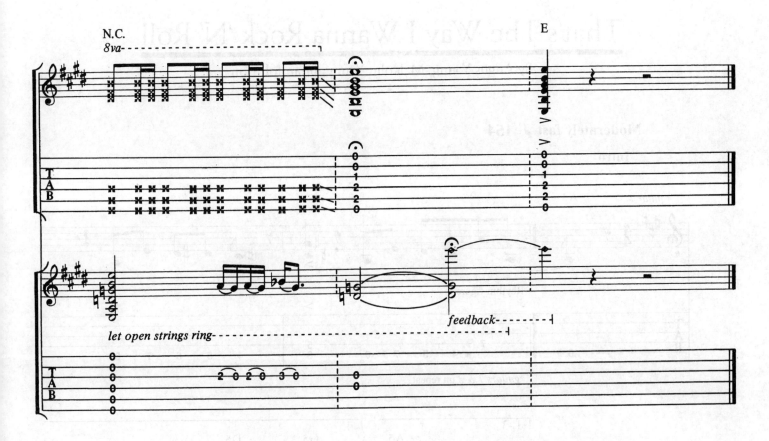

Additional Lyrics

2. I'm dirty, mean, and mighty unclean.
   I'm a wanted man,
   Public enemy number one,
   Understand?
   So lock up your daughter,
   Lock up your wife,
   Lock up your back door,
   Run for your life.
   The man is back in town,
   So don't you mess around.

That's The Way I Wanna Rock 'N' Roll

By Angus Young, Malcolm Young, Brian Johnson

Moderately fast ♩ = 154

Intro

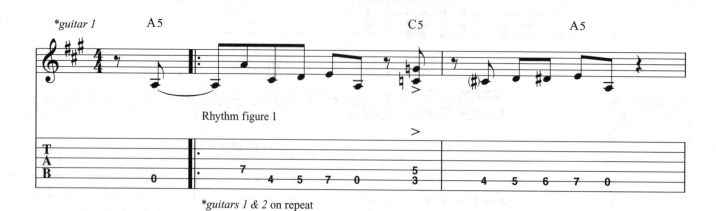

*guitars 1 & 2 on repeat

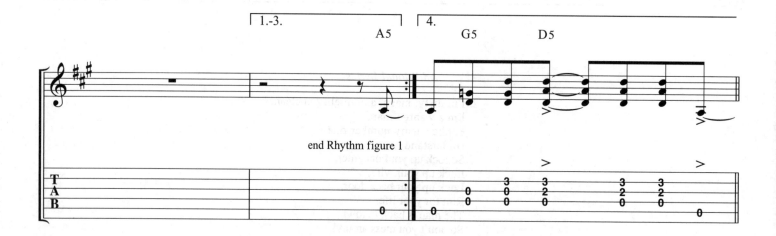

Verse

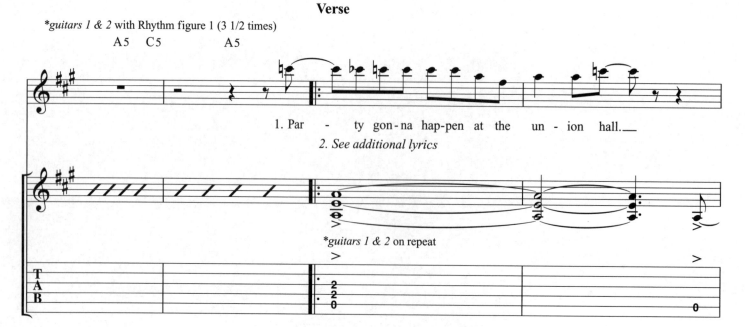

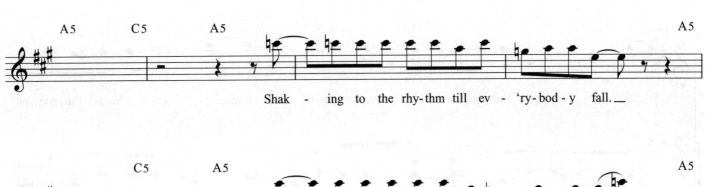

Shak - ing to the rhy-thm till ev - 'ry-bod-y fall.___

Pick - ing up my wom-an in my Chev-ro-let.___

Glo - ry hal - le - lu - jah, gon - na

Chorus

rock the night a-way. I'm gon-na roll,___ roll, roll.___ I'm gon-na roll, roll, roll.

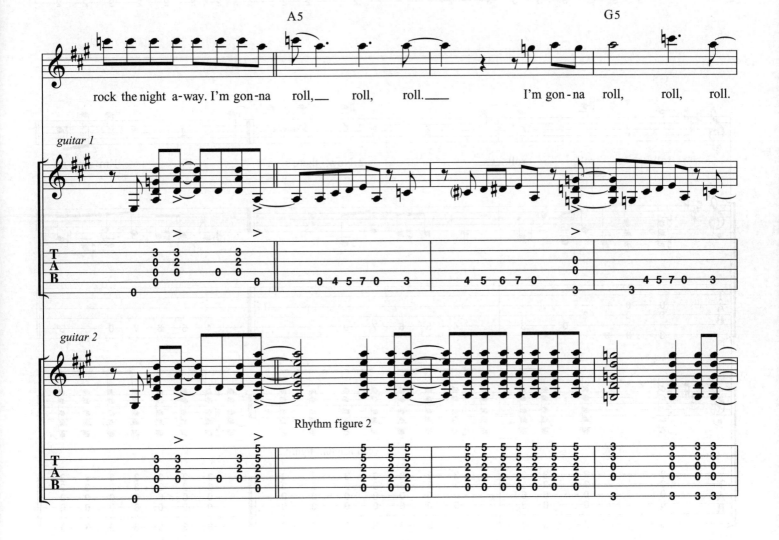

rock 'n' roll,___ that's the way___ I want my rock 'n' roll.___

Guitar Solo

guitars 1 & 2 with Rhythm figure 1 (2 times)

C5   A5

That's the way! ____

guitar 3

A5   C5   A5

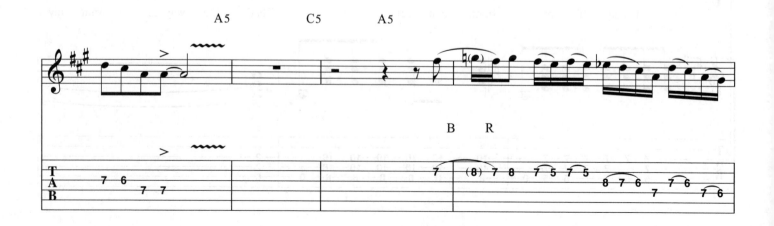

That's the way__ I want my rock 'n' roll,__ that's the way I want my rock 'n' roll.__

Interlude

That's the way,__ that's the way, __ that's the way__ I want my rock 'n' roll.__

guitar 3 (ad lib. on repeat)

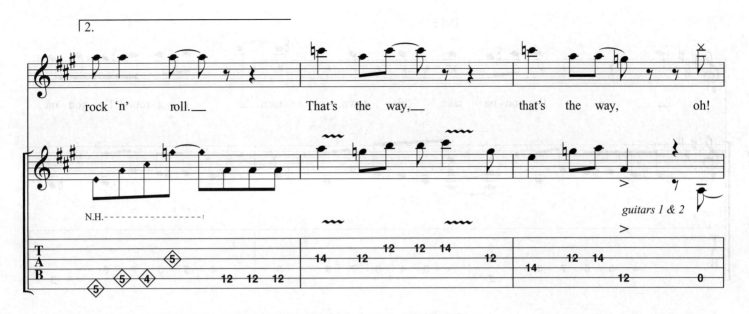

rock 'n' roll.___ That's the way,___ that's the way, oh!

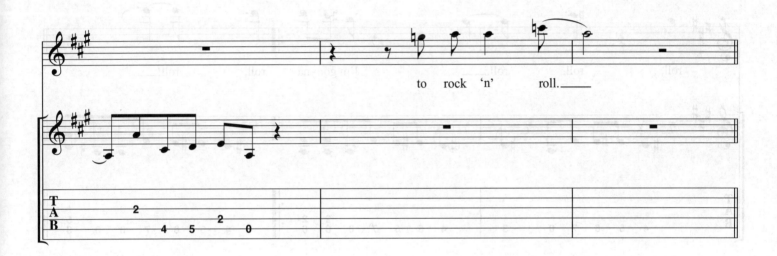

to rock 'n' roll.____

Chorus

guitar 2 with Rhythm figure 2
vocal ad lib. on repeat

Roll,___ roll, roll,___ I'm gon-na roll, roll, roll.

Additional Lyrics:

2. Now there's a blue suede bopping on a high-heeled shoe.
   Ballin' 'round together like a wrecking crew.
   Oh, be-bop-a-lula, baby, what I say,
   You gotta get a dose of rock 'n' roll on each and every day.

War Machine

By Angus Young & Malcolm Young

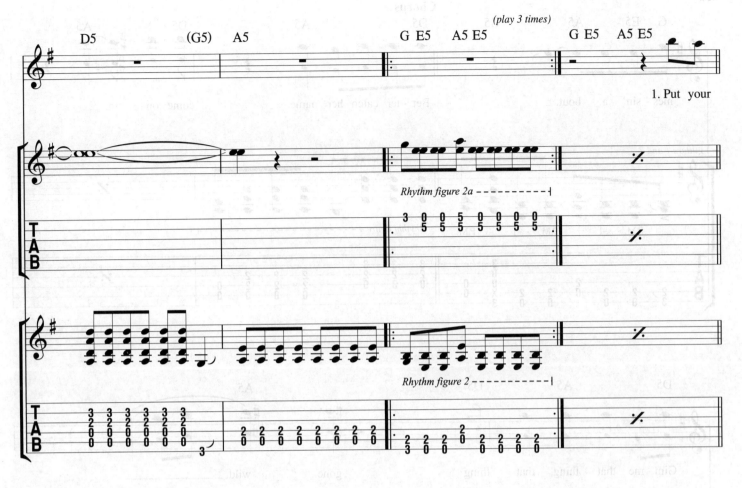

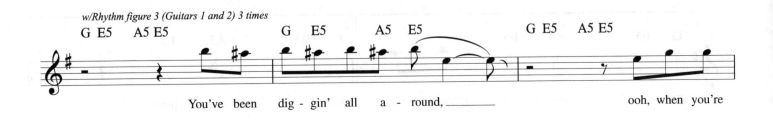

Chorus

mes - sin' a - bout. __ Bet - ter catch her name, come on in. __

Gim - me that thing, that thing gone wild. _____

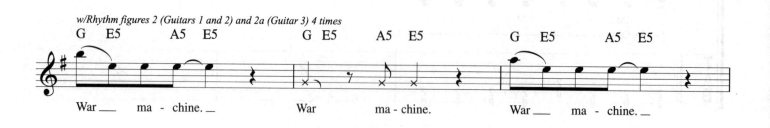

War __ ma - chine. __ War ma - chine. War __ ma - chine. __

War ma - chine. 2. Make a War ma - chine.

Breakdown

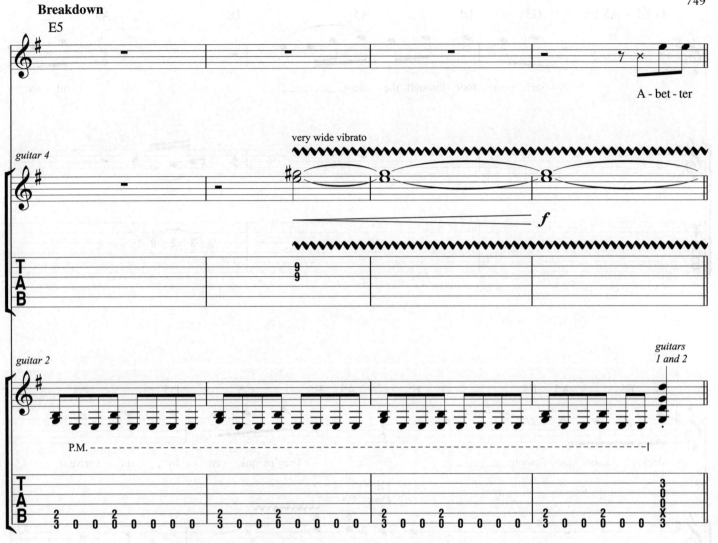

A - bet - ter

Bridge

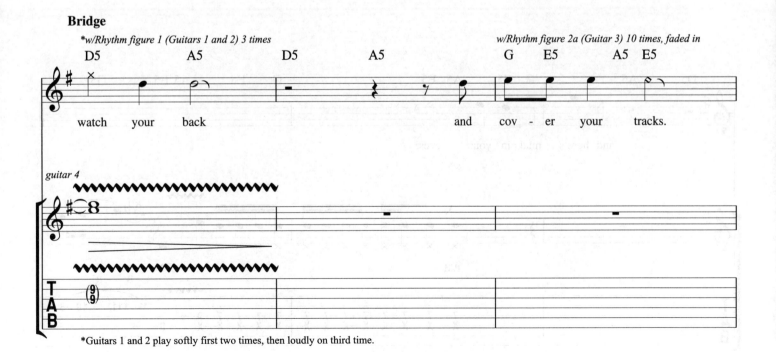

watch your back   and cov - er your tracks.

*Guitars 1 and 2 play softly first two times, then loudly on third time.

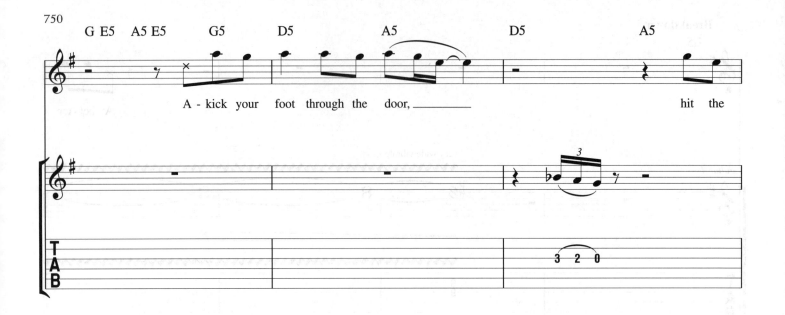

A - kick your foot through the door, _____ hit the

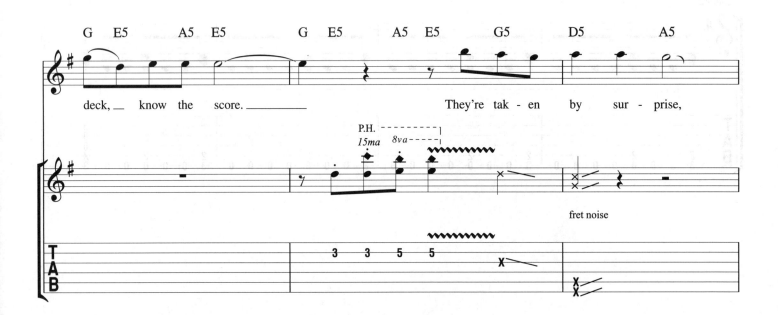

deck, _ know the score. _____ They're tak - en by sur - prise,

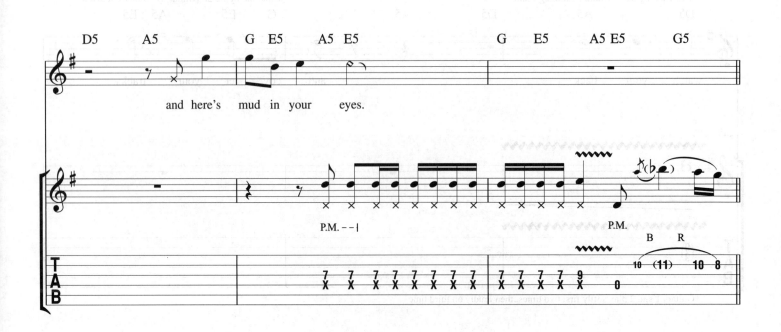

and here's mud in your eyes.

Chorus

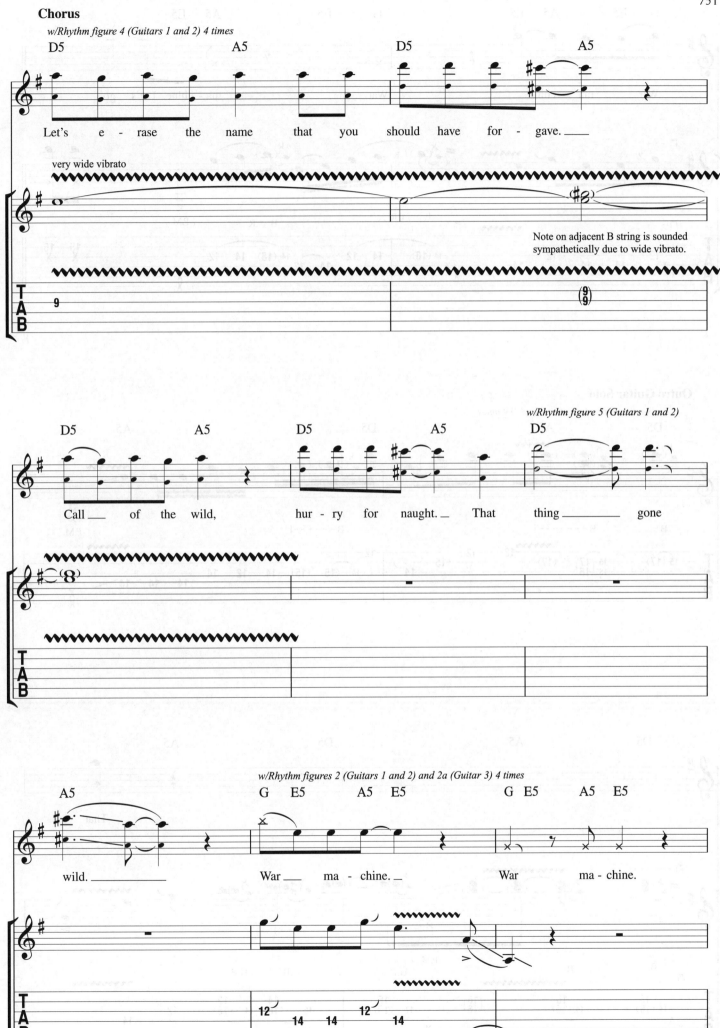

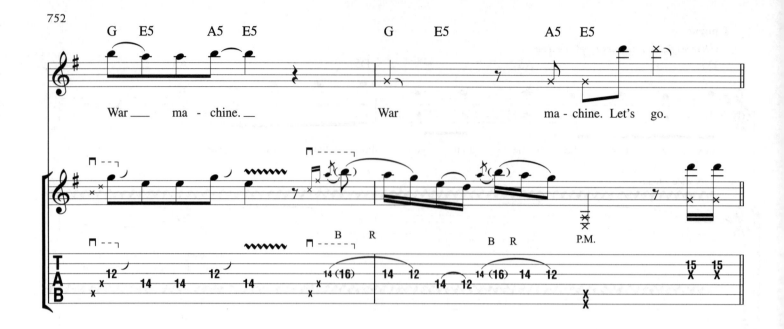

War __ ma - chine. __   War   ma - chine. Let's   go.

Outro Guitar Solo

w/Rhythm figure 4 (Guitars 1 and 2) 4 times

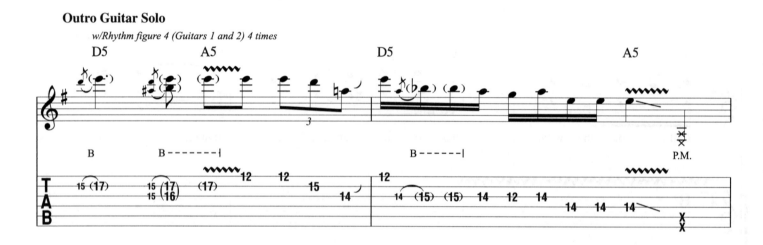

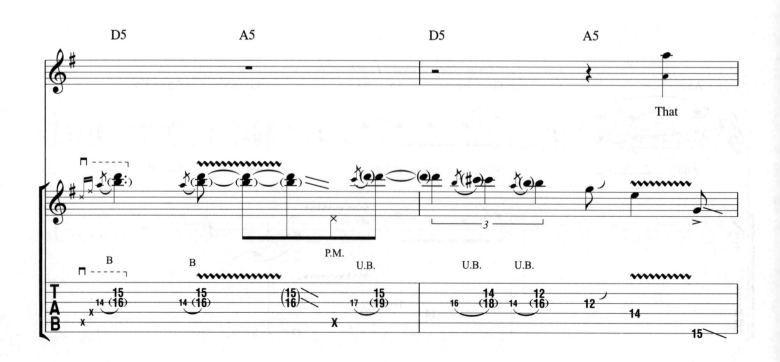

That

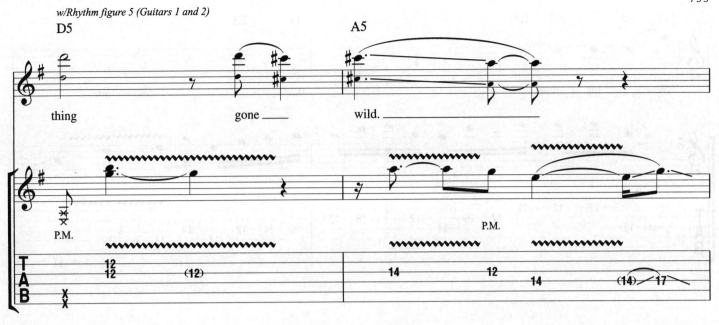

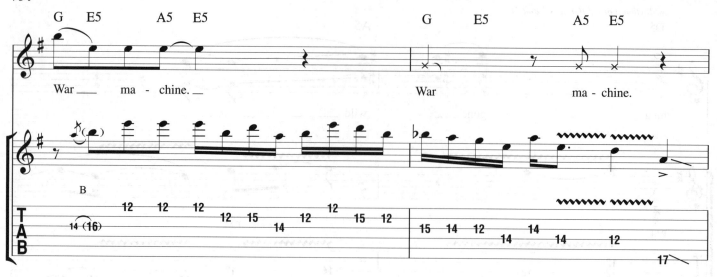

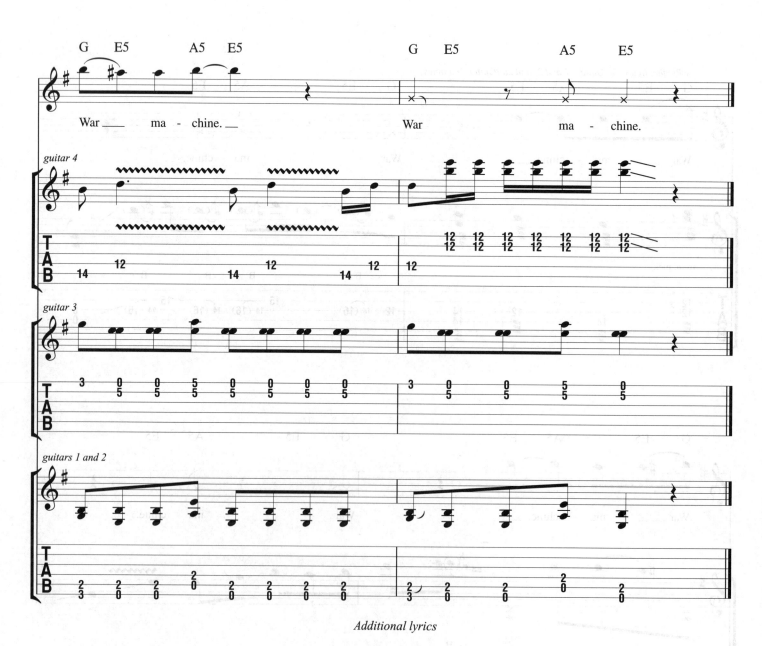

Additional lyrics

2nd Verse:
Make a stand, show your hand
Call in the high command
Don't think, just obey
I'm like a bird of prey

This House Is On Fire

By Angus Young, Malcolm Young and Brian Johnson

756

This house___ is on fire and the flame_

___ is gon - na burn you, you,_____ oh.

P.M.

guitar 1 Rhythm figure 4   end Rhythm figure 4

guitar 2 Rhythm figure 4a   end Rhythm figure 4a

2. She got me run - nin' for shel - you.

You got me burn - in' and burn - in'.

You got me toss - in' and turn - in'.

Guitar solo

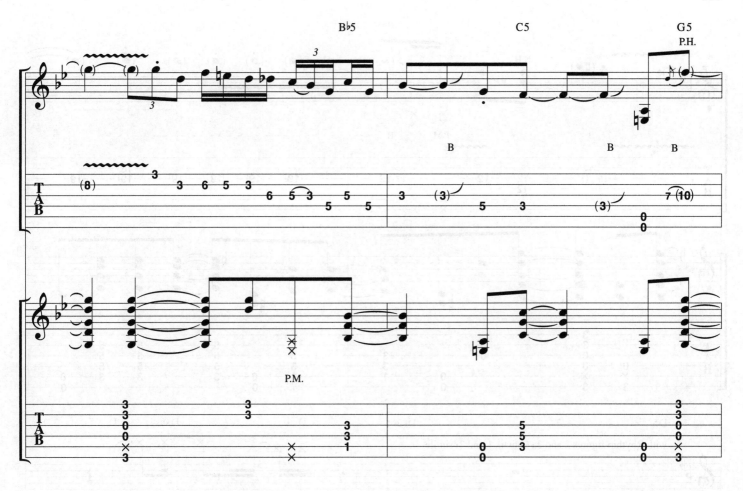

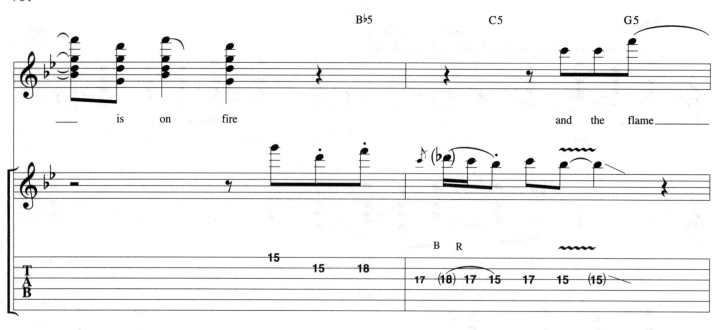

is on fire   and the flame

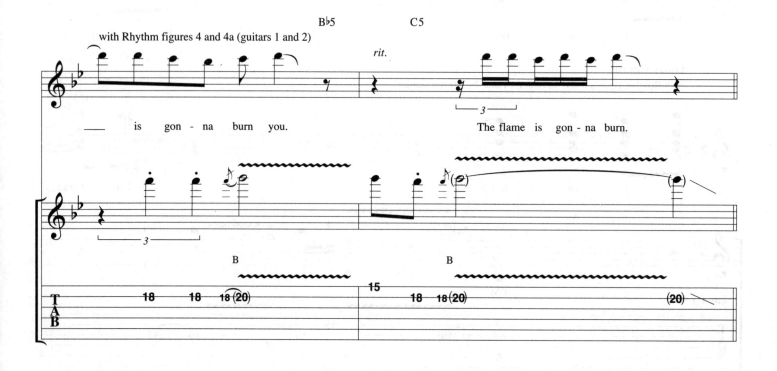

with Rhythm figures 4 and 4a (guitars 1 and 2)

is gon - na burn you.   The flame is gon - na burn.

Freely

You're   gon - na   burn,   you.

guitar 1

guitar 2

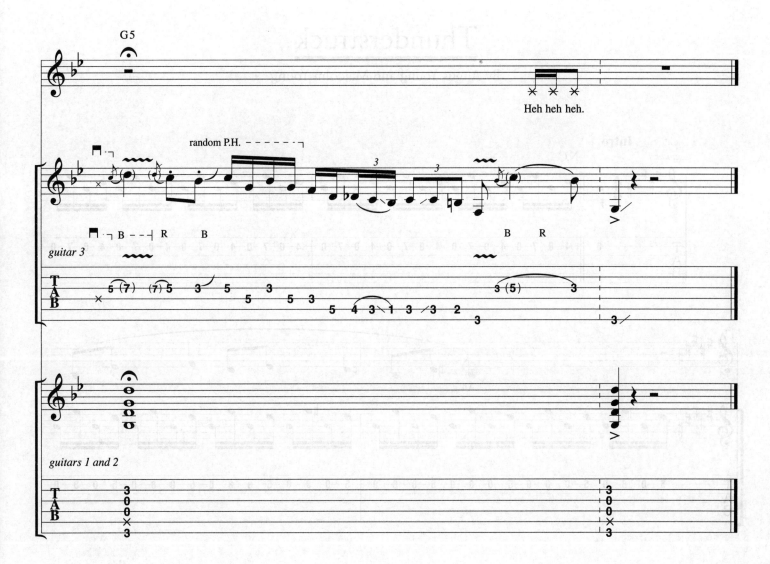

Heh heh heh.

random P.H.

guitar 3

guitars 1 and 2

Additional Lyrics

2. She got me running for shelter,
   Needin' quarantine.
   She got me red-hot and wired.
   Call an emergency.

Thunderstruck

By Angus Young and Malcolm Young

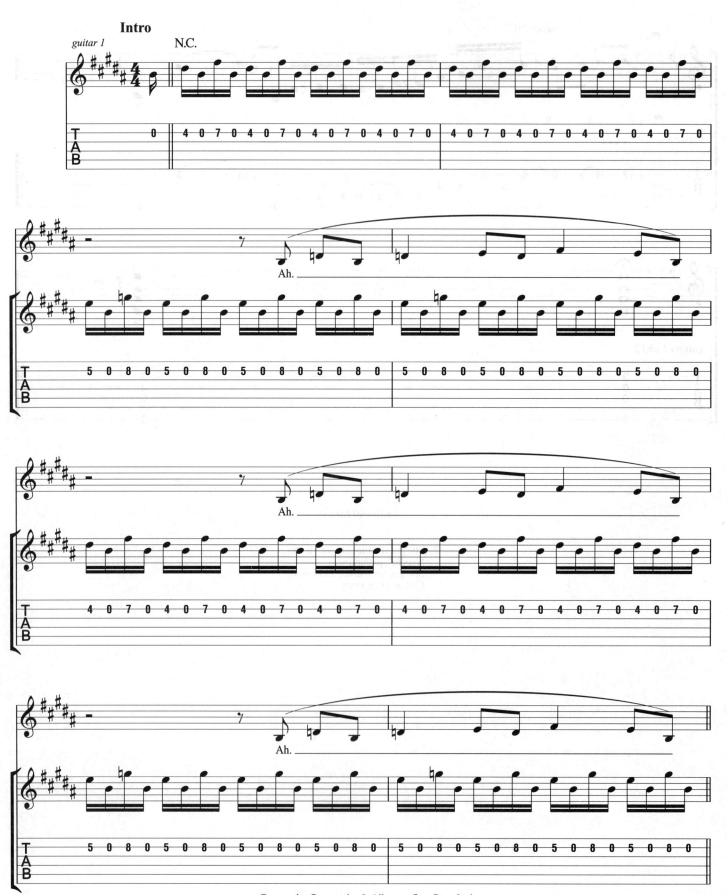

770

Chorus
w/Rhythm figure 1 (Guitar 1) 4 times
w/Rhythm figure 3 (Guitars 2 and 3)

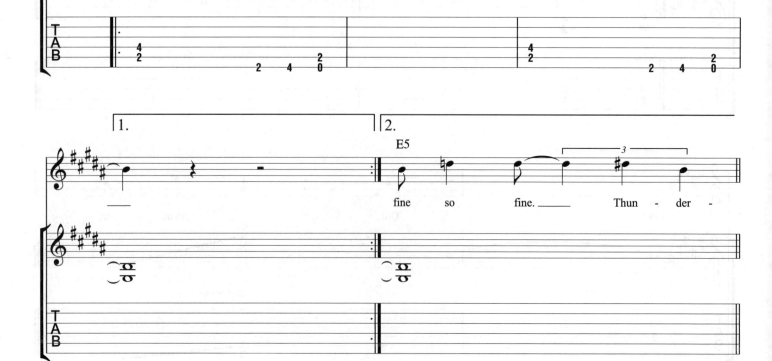

Outro

w/Rhythm figure 1 (Guitar 1) 8 times
w/ Rhythm figure 3 (Guitars 2 and 3) 2 times

Touch Too Much

By Angus Young, Malcolm Young and Bon Scott

Walk All Over You

By Angus Young, Malcolm Young and Bon Scott

with Rhythm figures 3 and 3a (2 times)

1. Out of my way I'm a - run - nin' high, ___
2., 3. *See additional lyrics*

Rhythm figure 4

Rhythm figure 4a

Take a

end Rhythm figure 4

end Rhythm figure 4a

with Rhythm figures 4 and 4a (2 times)

chance with me and we'll give it a try. ___

*Trap the 2nd and 3rd strings with the 3rd finger.

Tempo I
with Rhythm figure 6 (3 times)
ad lib solo (5 bars)

you. —
(Walk all o - ver you. —)

I'm gon - na walk all o - ver you —
(Walk all o - ver you. —)

Do a - ny-thing you want me to —
(Walk all o - ver you. —)

I'm gon na walk all o - ver

you. Ow!

I'm gon-na walk all — o - ver you.

Additional Lyrics

2. Whoa, baby I ain't got much
   Resistance to your touch.
   Take off your high heels, let down your hair,
   Paradise ain't far from there.

3. Reflections on the bedroom wall,
   I know you thought you'd seen it all.
   We're risin', fallin' like the sea,
   You're looking so good under me.

4. Moanin' and groanin' in stereo,
   So gimme the stage, I'm gonna steal the show.
   Leave on the lace and turn off the light,
   Tonight is gonna be the night.

What Do You Do For Money Honey

By Angus Young, Malcolm Young and Brian Johnson

Verse

Guitar solo

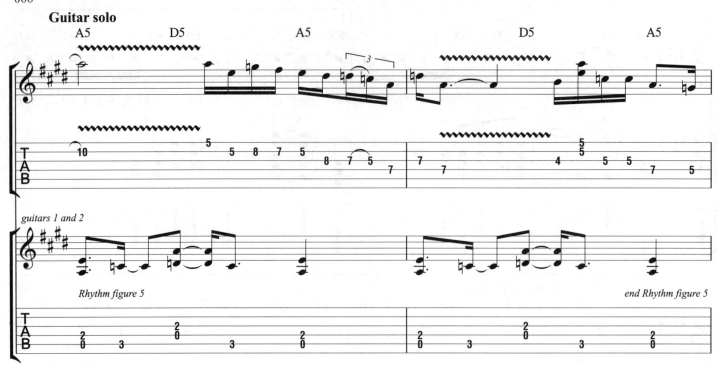

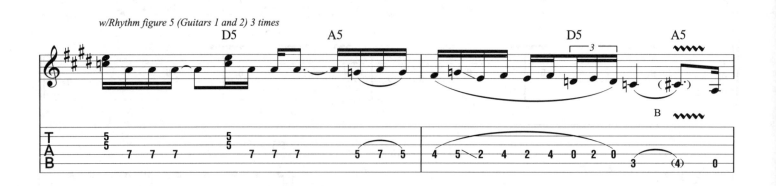

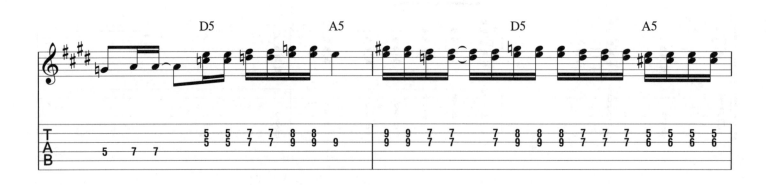

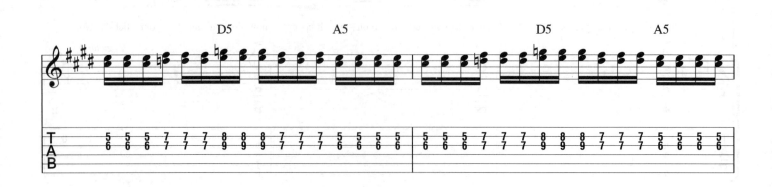

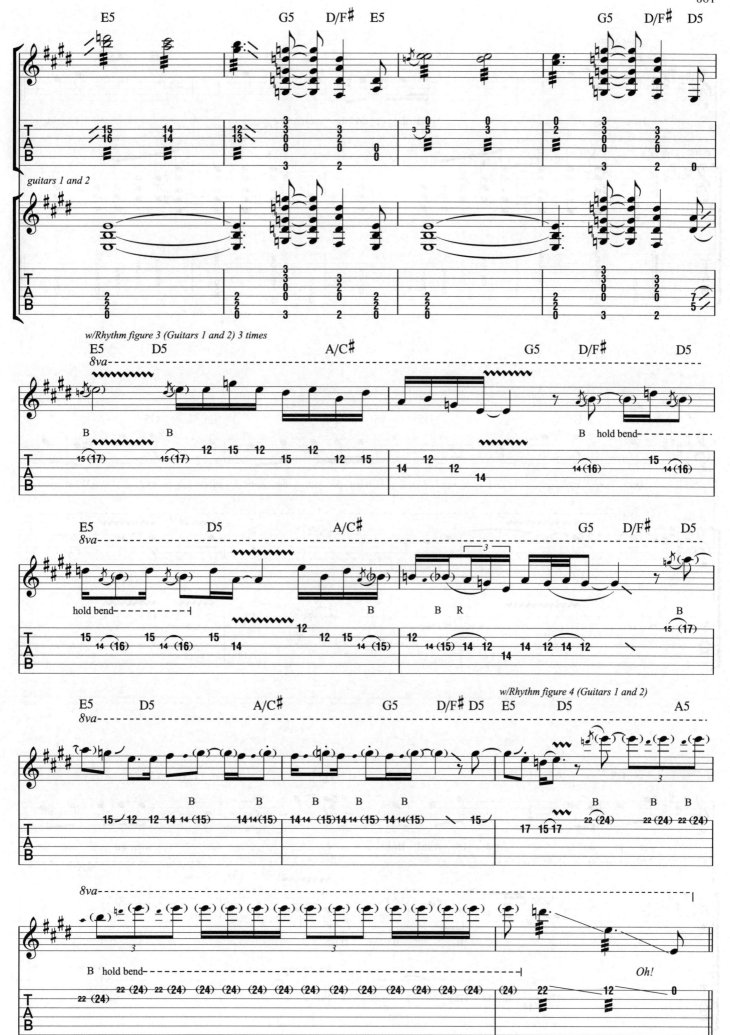

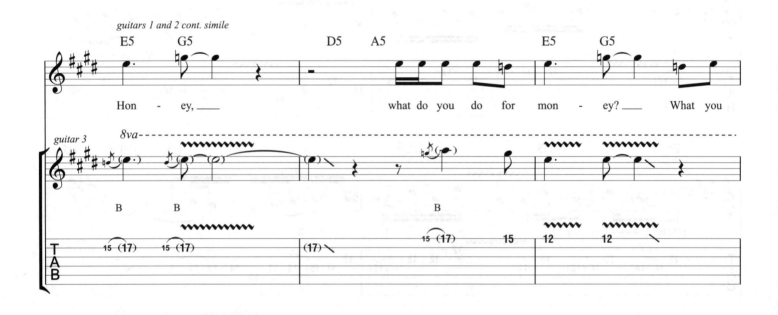

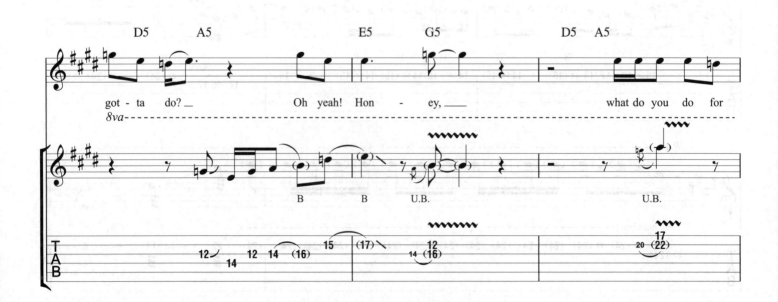

Additional lyrics

2. You're lovin' on the take and you're always on the make,
   Squeezin' all the blood outta men.
   They're all standin' in a queue just to spend a night with you;
   It's business as usual again.
   You're always grabbin', stabbin', trying get it back in
   But girl you must be gettin' slow.
   So stop your life on the road,
   All your diggin' for gold.
   You make me wonder!
   Yes I wonder, yes I wonder!

Who Made Who

By Angus Young and Malcolm Young and Brian Johnson

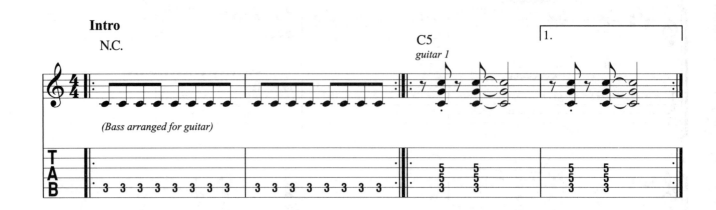

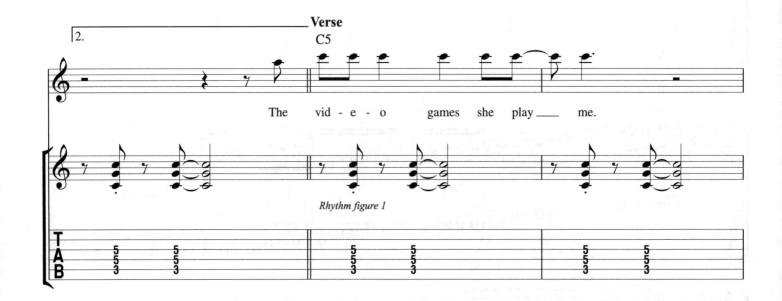

The vid - e - o games she play ___ me.

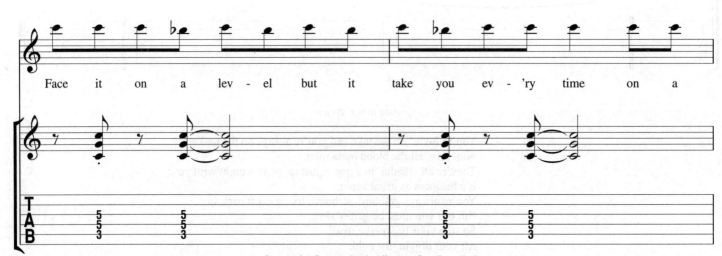

Face it on a lev - el but it take you ev - 'ry time on a

% Chorus

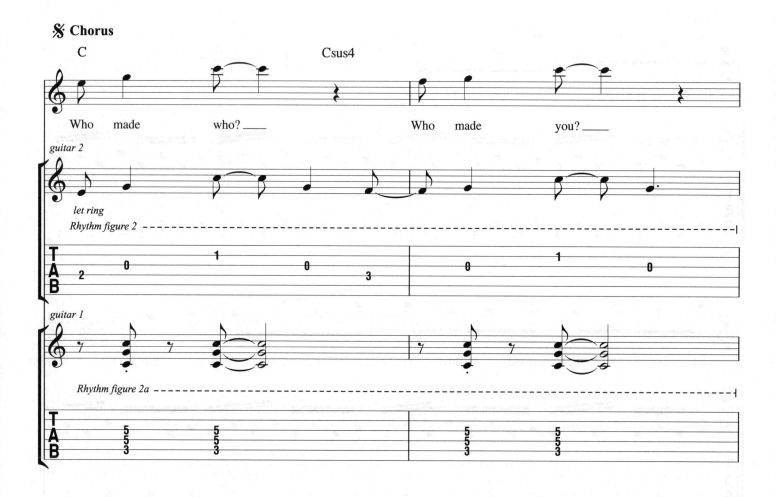

Who made who? ___ Who made you? ___

guitar 2

let ring

Rhythm figure 2 -

guitar 1

Rhythm figure 2a -

w/Rhythm figures 2 and 2a (Guitars 1 and 2) 3 times

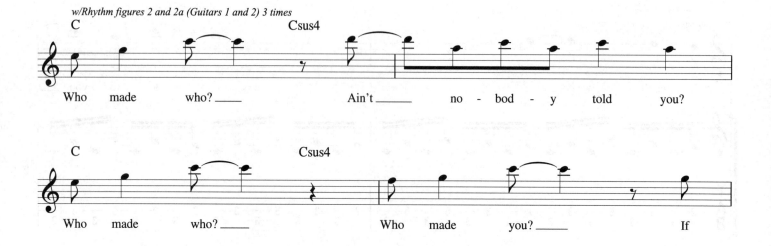

Who made who? ___ Ain't ___ no - bod - y told you?

Who made who? ___ Who made you? ___ If

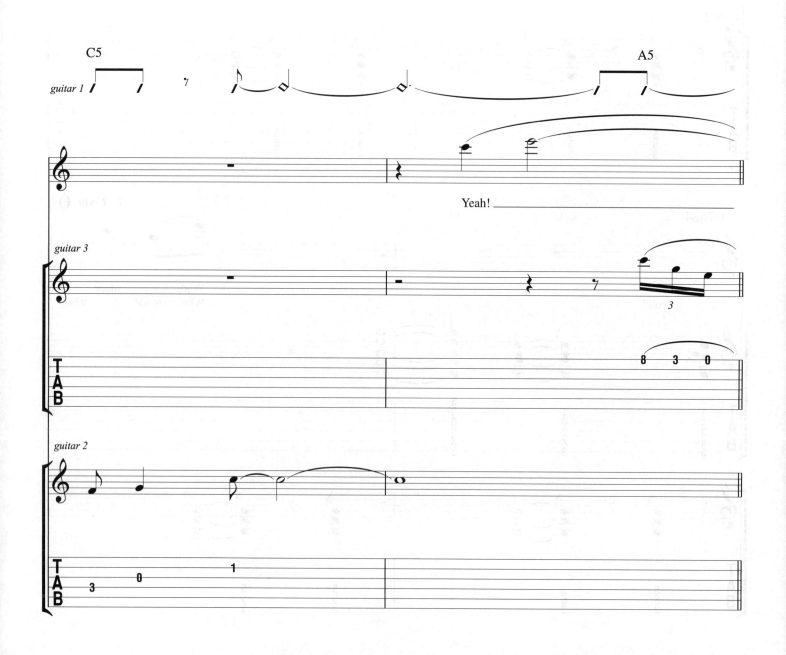

(+ = tap)

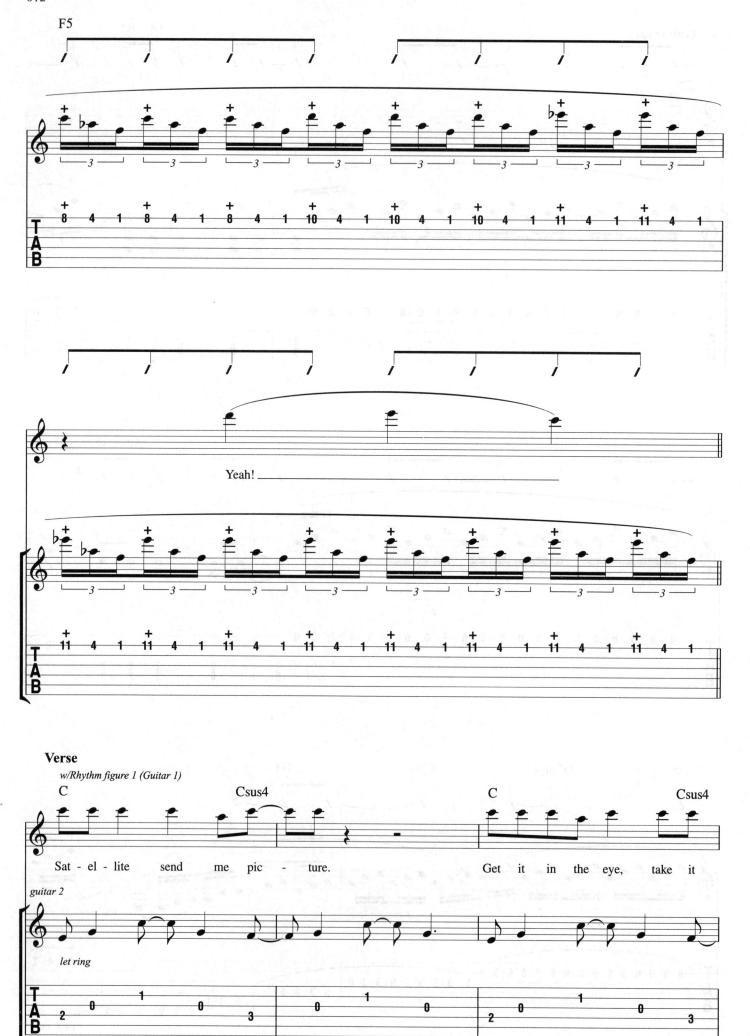

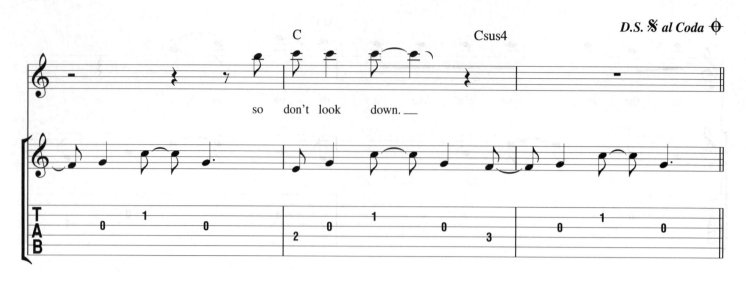

(Who made you? who?)

Yeah!

Outro

No - bod - y told you.

rit.

(repeat to fade)

Whole Lotta Rosie

By Angus Young, Malcolm Young and Bon Scott

Intro

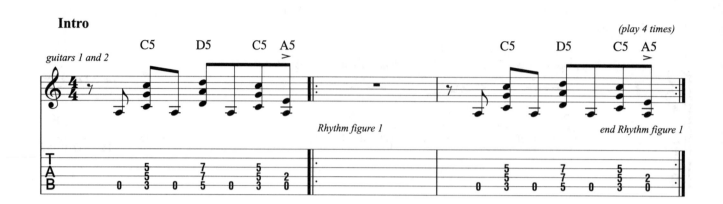

Verse

Chorus

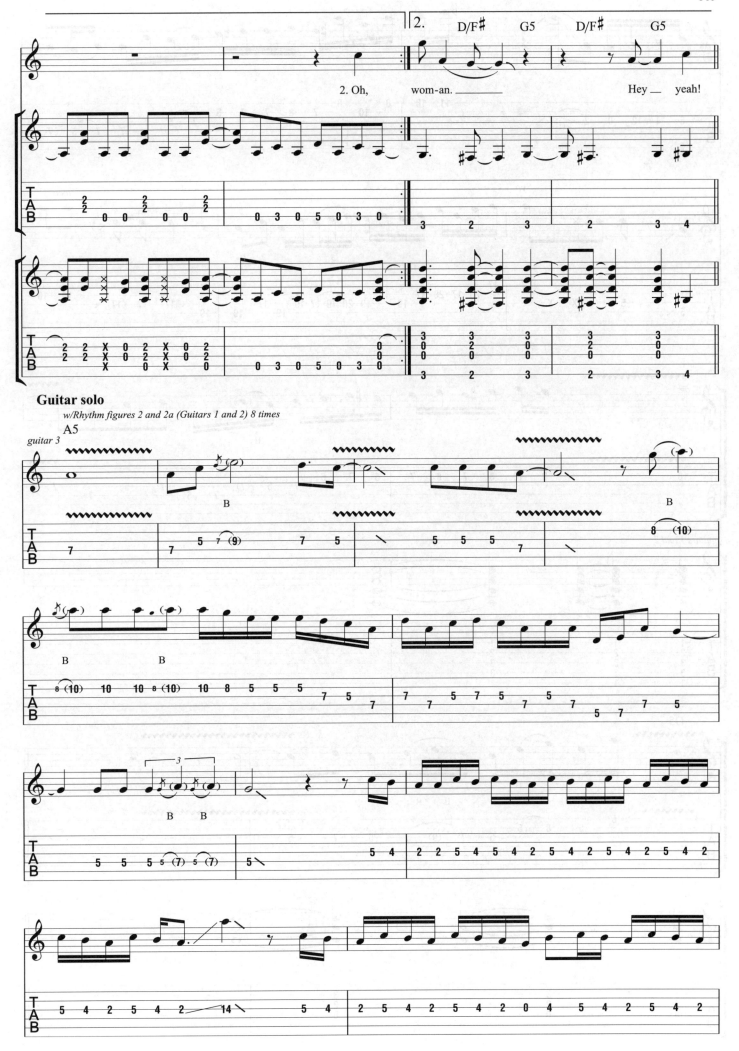

Interlude

Guitar solo

w/Rhythm figures 2 and 2a (Guitars 1 and 2) 8 times

whole lot - ta Ros - ie. _____ *(cont. vocal ad lib.)*

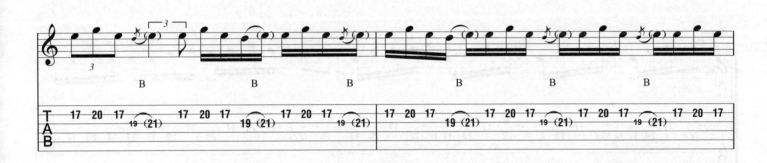

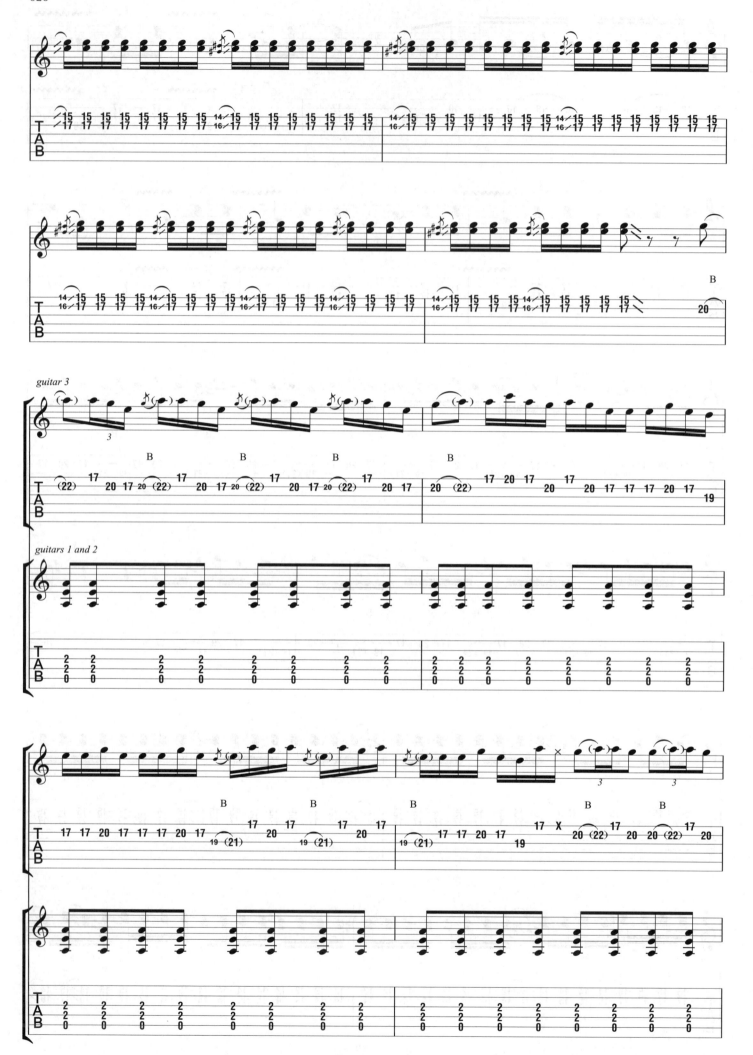

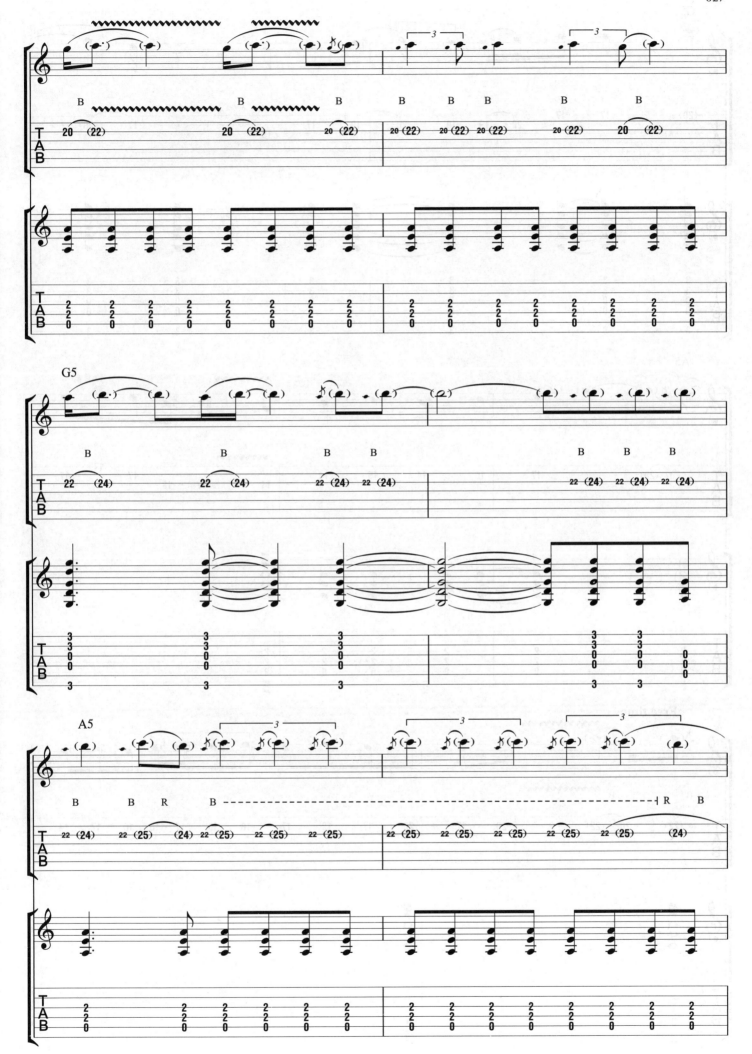

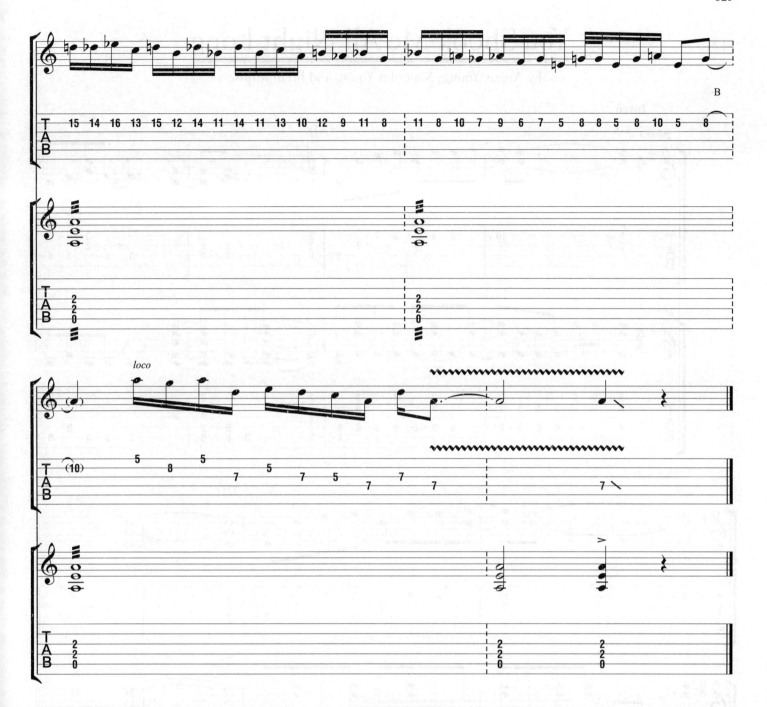

Additional lyrics

2. Honey you can do it
   Do it to me all night long
   Only one who turn me
   Only one who turn me on
   All through the night time
   Right around the clock
   To my surprise
   Rosie never stops

   She was a whole lotta woman
   Whole lotta woman
   Whole lotta Rosie....

You Shook Me All Night Long

By Angus Young, Malcolm Young and Brian Johnson

Intro

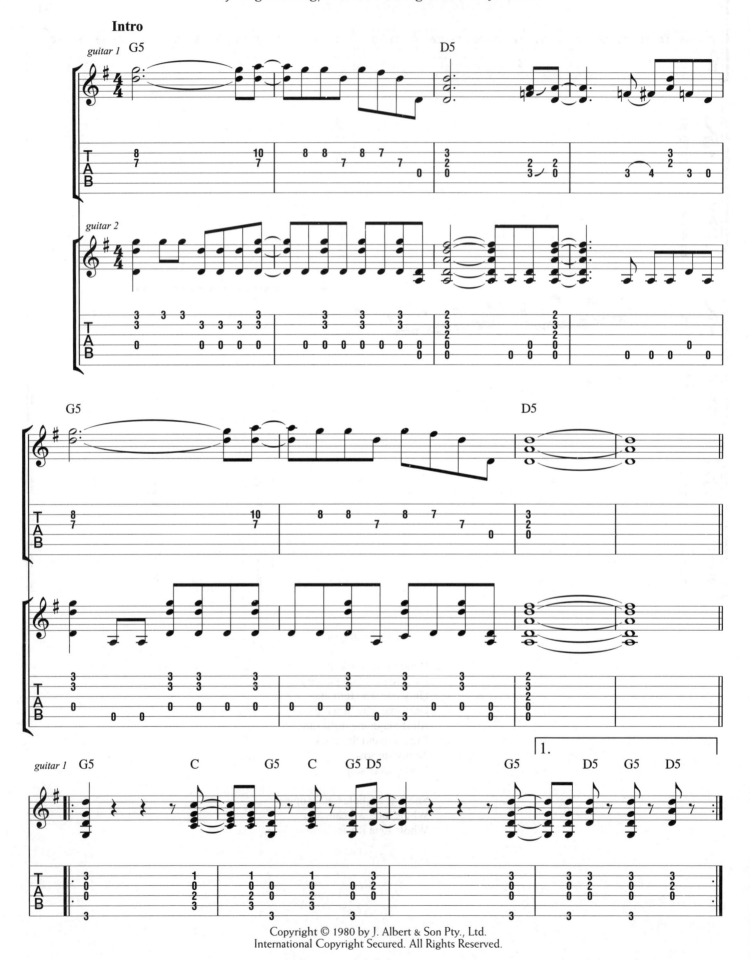

Verse

1. She was a fast ma - chine, __ she kept her mo - tor clean, __ she was the
(2.) dou - ble time __ on the se - duc - tion line, __ she was one

(2nd time with guitar 2)

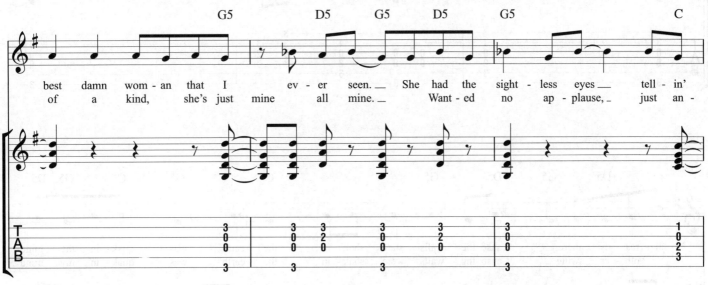

best damn wom - an that I ev - er seen. __ She had the sight - less eyes __ tell - in'
of a kind, she's just mine all mine. __ Want - ed no ap - plause, __ just an -

me no lies, __ knock - in' me out __ with those A - mer - i - can thighs. Tak - ing
oth - er course. __ Made a meal __ out - ta me, and come back for more. Had to

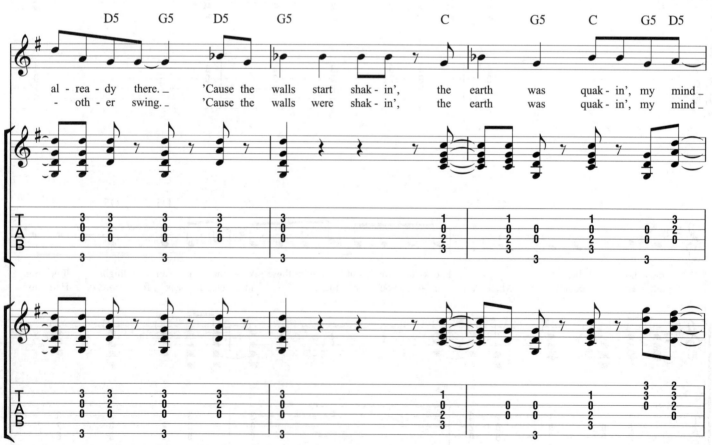

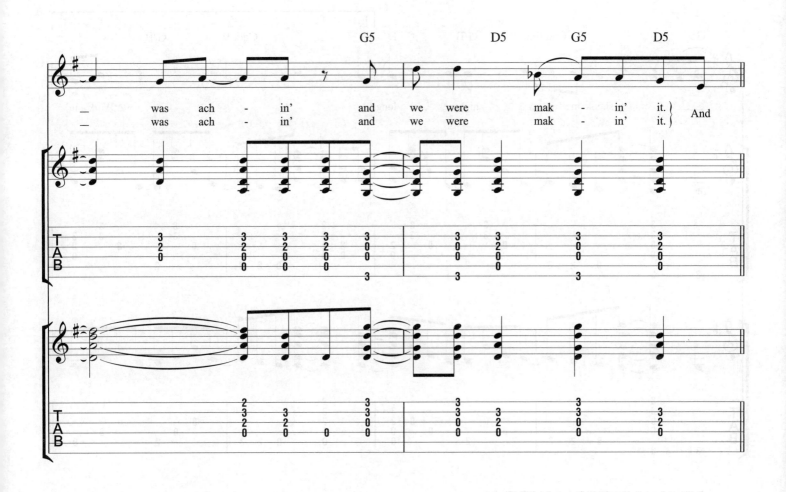

Chorus

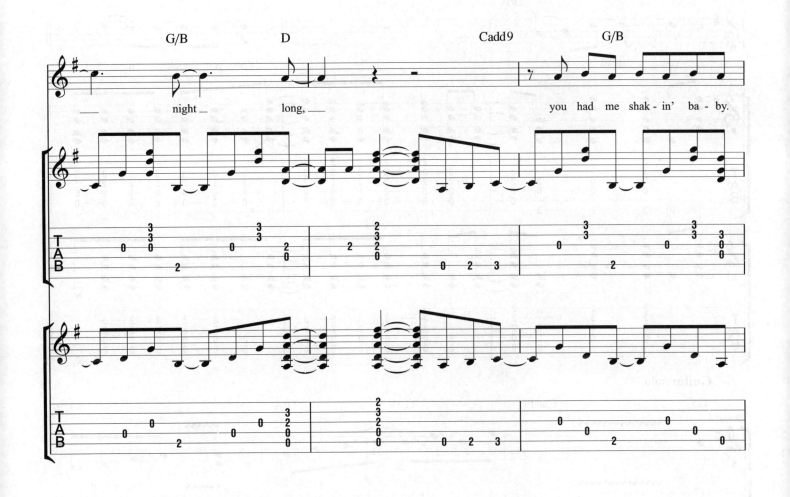

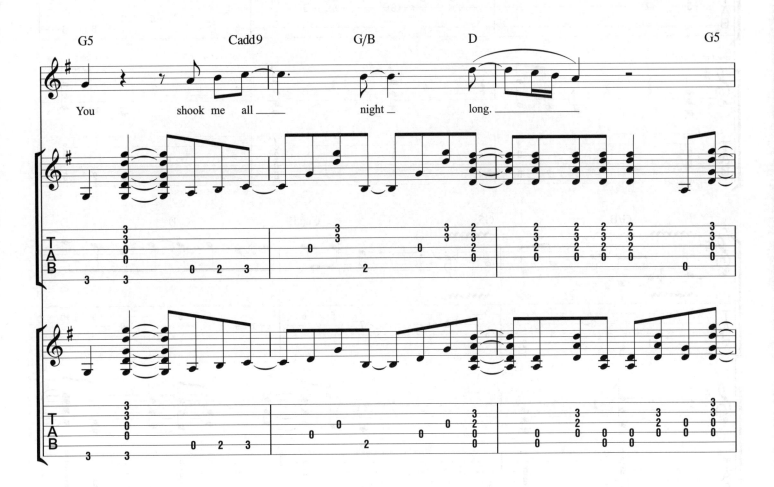

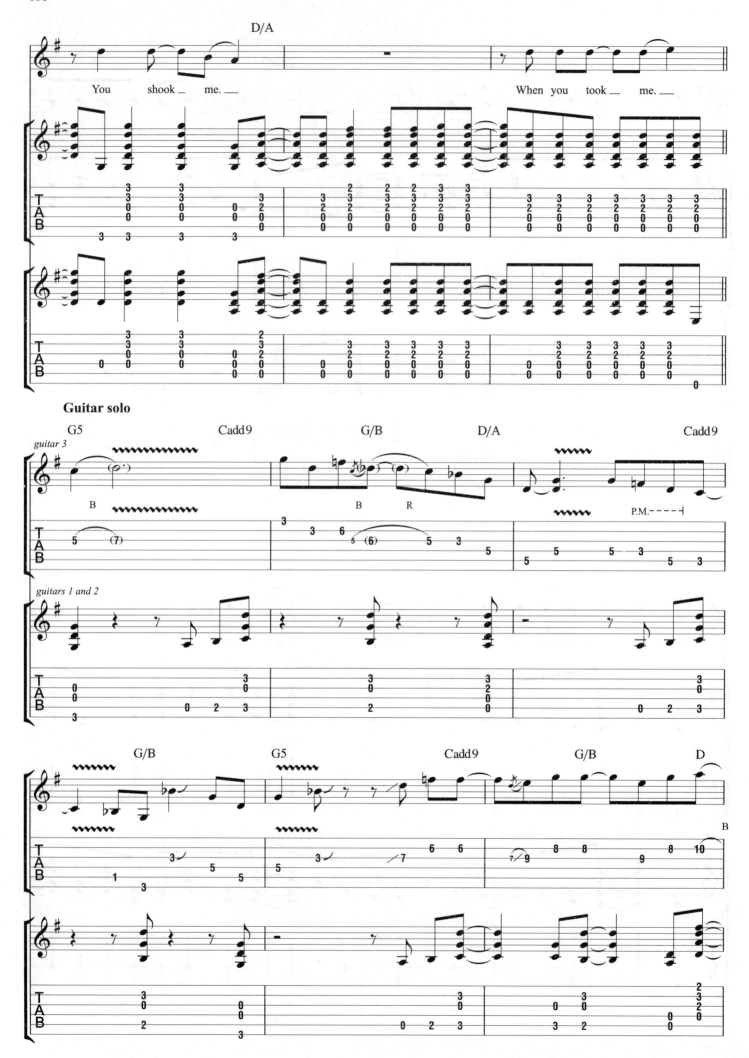

Guitar solo

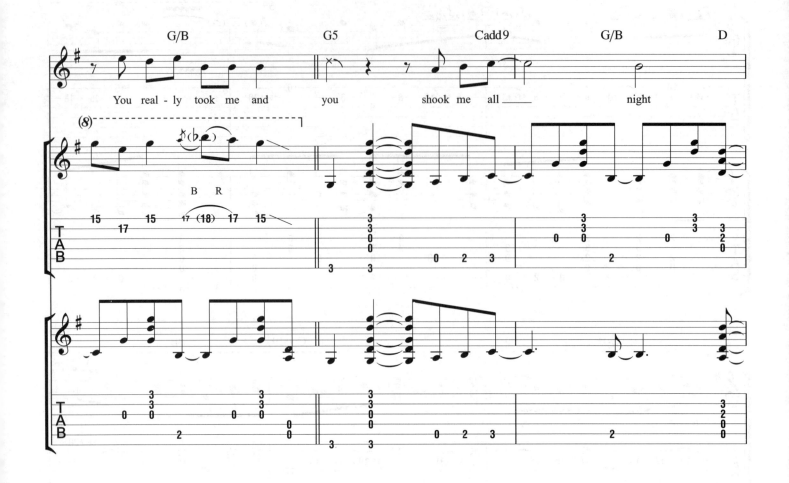

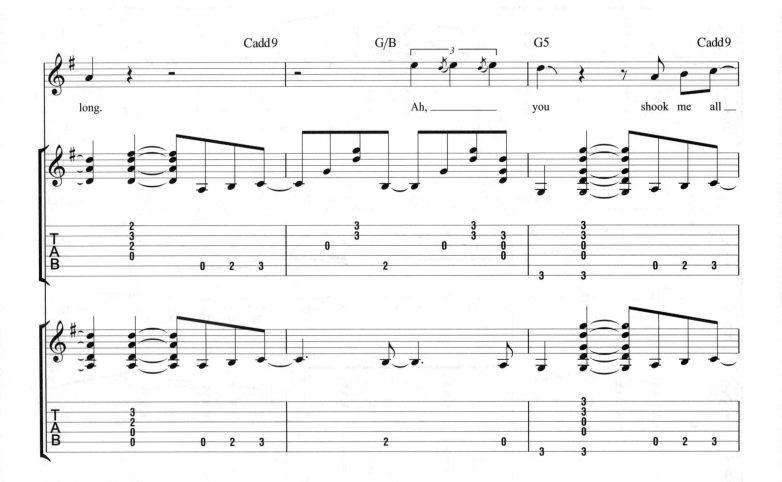

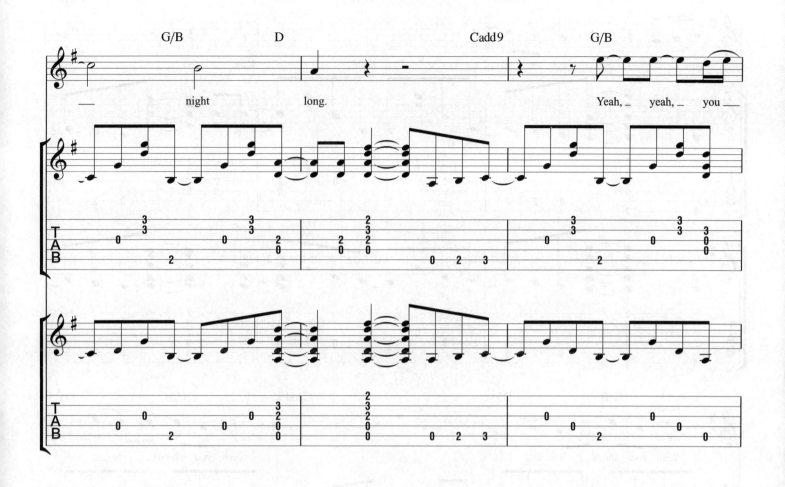

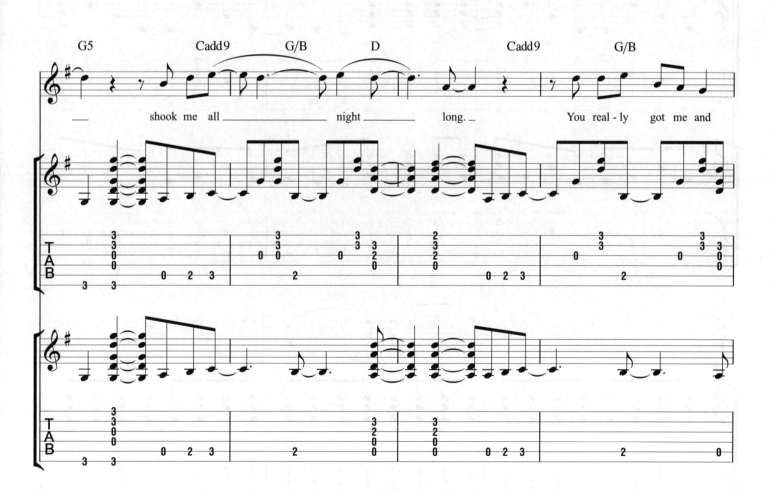

Printed in Croatia - 12/15(196012)